ORIGIN
IN A
BRAVE NEW WORLD

THE PARADOX OF EUROPE

An account of the negotiation
of the Treaty of Amsterdam

BOBBY McDONAGH

Foreword by Jacques Santer
President of the European Commission

INSTITUTE OF EUROPEAN AFFAIRS

Published by the
Institute of European Affairs
Europe House
8 North Great George's Street
Dublin 1, Ireland
Tel: (01) 874 6756 Fax: (01) 878 6880
e-mail: publicat@iea.iol.ie

ISBN 1-874109-40-0

Cover design by Victor McBrien

Printed by
Brunswick Press Limited
Dublin, Ireland

Contents

JACQUES SANTER
President of the European Commission

FOREWORD BY PRESIDENT J. SANTER

Bobby Mc Donagh's fine book on the inner workings of this strange animal called an Intergovernmental Conference provides the interested citizen with a fascinating insight into the workings of the EU. As President of a Commission which has right from its coming into office tried to promote greater transparency in European matters, I warmly welcome this book written by one of the architects of the new treaty.

Mr Mc Donagh explains in clear and straightforward terms how 15 different member States plus the European institutions grapple with an apparently thankless task : the task of rewriting and improving the treaty which is our common bible and the constitutional basis for European cooperation. Contrary to the impression which is sometimes conveyed, this is not about running rough-shod over national interests nor about pursuing lofty ideals unconnected to everyday reality.

It is about the constant, difficult search for the common good, an intelligent and mature way for States to further their legitimate interests by working together in a Union characterised by strong common institutions and the rule of law. I am grateful to the author for showing that the EU is a "truly Brave New World, the most exciting experiment in the relationship between free democratic countries in history but[it is] no Utopia". I share his view that the best service to render Europe is "to explain rather than preach, to provide information rather than justification, to address its weaknesses rather than to pretend that they do not exist or to wish them away".
I would add that what has been achieved over the last 40 odd years is something we as Europeans can all be proud of. The successful completion of a true Monetary and Economic Union which will now enter into force on 1st January 99 illustrates the continuing success of a venture based on painstaking negotiations where the interests of all, small and big, are taken care of. The growing line of European States wanting to join the family of the Union bears testimony to the attractiveness of this kind of European unification. Amsterdam is yet another milestone on the way to the ever closer union of peoples which the Paris Treaty of 1952 already referred to. Bobby Mc Donagh's account of the negotiation of the Treaty of Amsterdam should be read by all Europeans interested in their own destiny.

Preface

The development of the European Union moves forward in small steps, and these movements are usually formalised by changes to the basic Treaties. After Ireland's entry to the European Community in 1973, the next major change came after fourteen years, but the pace has quickened since then and change now takes place much more regularly. For Ireland, this means regular referenda to approve the changes, and in this process, the claim is often made that there is a lack of information available to the general public. This is very understandable, because at the end of the day, changes to treaties must be made in a legal form acceptable to all the partners to them.

In the case of the Amsterdam Treaty, considerable efforts were made to bring the deliberations closer to the citizen, including the Reflection Group which involved the European Parliament, and also considered submissions from governments, public organisations and numerous NGOs across the Union. The Institute also played its part.

In the draft treaty prepared by the Irish Presidency in December 1996, an explanation was inserted before each chapter, but this perforce disappeared in the final text of the treaty. In Ireland, the Government produced a lengthy White Paper on the Treaty and also published a more condensed version for a wider audience both of which were widely hailed as examples of clarity and precision. Indeed, this might be seen as a model for future explanations of the outcome of what are, necessarily, complex negotiations. This clearly establishes a role for the Council of Ministers in bridging the comprehension gap with the electorate. Furthermore, a clear summary of proposed new treaty amendments should be attached to any enabling Bill going through each parliament.

Bobby McDonagh in this book has gone a stage further in explaining, as an active participant, the process of the negotiations during the IGC leading up to the Amsterdam Treaty. He gives a unique insight into the inner workings of the negotiations process. The IEA is proud to be associated with the publication of this book, which I am sure will be of interest not only to all those involved in "European affairs" but to a much wider interested public.

Terry Stewart
Director General
Institute of European Affairs

Author

Bobby McDonagh is an Irish diplomat. He was educated at Gonzaga College, Dublin, and at Balliol College, Oxford. Since he joined the Department of Foreign of Affairs in 1977 he has worked extensively on European Union matters, both in Dublin and at Ireland's Permanent Representation to the EU in Brussels. He has also worked for two years with the European Parliament and for four years with the European Commission (first in the cabinet of Commissioner Ray MacSharry and later as deputy *chef de cabinet* of Commissioner Padraig Flynn). Most recently, he was closely involved, as deputy to Ireland's IGC Representative, in the negotiations leading to the Treaty of Amsterdam, a key phase of which fell during Ireland's Presidency of the European Union in 1996.

Acknowledgements

I am indebted to the many people from whom I have received help and encouragement in writing this book

I am grateful first of all to the Department of Foreign Affairs for its ready willingness to allow me to publish it. The views expressed are, of course, my own and entirely personal.

The Institute of European Affairs plays an important role in stimulating thinking about the European Union in Ireland and much further afield. I wish to thank the Institute, particularly its Director General, Terry Stewart, and that rare thing – a thinker who makes things happen – Brendan Halligan, for deciding to publish this book. I am also deeply indebted to Iain MacAulay and Margaret Ahearne for their professionalism and patience. I am delighted that this personal contribution to explaining how the European Union works will now be added to the outstanding efforts of the Institute to that end.

I am grateful for the encouragement and perceptive advice of Professor Brigid Laffan of UCD, especially for prefacing her remarks when I first mentioned my project to her with two simple words of advice: "Do it!".

The help, patience and drafting advice of my wife Mary made this book possible. Special thanks are due also to my daughters – Róisin, Caitríona, Gráinne and Sorcha – for letting me hog the computer.

In the course of writing this book, as I meandered down the memory lane of the two years of negotiations which led to the Treaty of Amsterdam, I was constantly reminded of the qualities, commitment and kindness of those involved at both official and political level – my Irish colleagues as well as those from every other Member State, the European Commission, the European Parliament and the Council Secretariat (the last named always remembered with particular fondness by those, like Ireland, who have been through a Presidency of the European Union). In effect this book is about those friends and colleagues and my deep appreciation extends to them all.

Finally, the only constraint on the tribute which should be paid to Noel Dorr, the Irish Member of the IGC Representatives Group who chaired the Group during Ireland's Presidency of the European Union in 1996, is that he would not wish his name to be mentioned at all. It was an honour and a pleasure to serve as his deputy in the negotiations. Noel said (frequently) that I should write this book and commented helpfully on the draft. Whatever insights this book may be able to bring stem from the long months we spent together during the negotiations – teasing out the complexities, understanding the personalities and sizing up the options. Whatever errors of fact or judgement it may contain would be rectified if it prompts him to write a book of his own.

Bobby McDonagh

Introduction

Amsterdam, 18 June 1997. It is after three o'clock in the morning. A large floorspace outside the Holy of Holies in which 15 Heads of State or Government, with their Foreign Ministers, have spent the best part of 48 hours putting the final touches to their revision of the constitution of the European Union. The only furniture in the outer sanctum a sprinkling of small rib-high occasional tables, each large enough to allow up to four or five *proches collaborateurs* to measure out their life in coffee spoons. A short interruption in proceedings. One last piece of the jigsaw puzzle to put in place. Make or break. Huddled around one of the tables three Heads of Government and perhaps 20 officials (with varying degrees of justification for being there or none) – a throng, several civil servants deep, like the crowd which gathers around the three-card trick man at a racecourse.

The Intergovernmental Conference (IGC) between the Member States of the European Union which culminated in the small hours of the morning on 18 June 1997 with agreement on the Treaty of Amsterdam represented, in both its decisions and its indecisions, an important step in the development of the European Union.

This book attempts to make sense of the negotiations leading to the final trade-offs at Amsterdam, a process which had lasted more than two years.

During those two years, I had the good fortune to have a ringside view of the bout, which went the full fifteen rounds – one round, one might say, for each Member State. From the first bell, namely the opening of the Reflection Group in Taormina in June 1995, to the split decision at Amsterdam two years later I was the second, as it were, in the Irish corner; first as deputy to the Irish member of the Reflection Group and then as deputy to Ireland's IGC Representative. The Irish Presidency of the European Union in the second half of 1996 offered us an exceptional insight into the workings of the Conference, as well as an opportunity to land a few punches ourselves (on behalf of Europe).

The boxing metaphor as applied to the IGC is, of course, in many respects misleading. The negotiations were based more on cooperation than on confrontation. There were heavyweights and lightweights in the same ring. There were no winners and losers. And, of course, Queensbury Rules have not yet been adopted as part of the secondary legislation of the European Union.

In writing the book I have set out to do three things.

First, I decided to try to write a book about the IGC which could be understood by any interested citizen rather than a book designed for initiates or academics. Europe belongs to its citizens and I hope that this book can be of some small service in explaining to those who may be interested how one set of important European decisions was taken on their behalf. I hope that the book may be of some use also to those who follow European developments in a more professional way, some of whom may be involved in similar negotiations in the future. Reading a book which at least tries to cut through some of our usual jargon may give my fellow Euro-Groupies a little of the pleasure that I had in writing it.

Second, I have set out to write not an analysis of the Treaty of Amsterdam but an account of how it was negotiated. My focus is on the means rather than the end. Any added value of understanding which I may be able to bring, as one who participated in the negotiations, relates to the process rather than to the end product, although inevitably the two are intertwined.

Third, because the book is more about process than product, I have allowed myself a certain licence in its structure. I contemplated first a sequential account of the negotiations from beginning to end, almost in diary form. However, that would tend to convey a mass of undigested and incomprehensible information with no coherent sense of substance or strategy. I then considered carving up the material by subject area, but that would have lost any sense of the dynamic of the overall negotiation.

I have therefore opted for a more instinctive mixture of the sequence and substance which together make up the dynamic of a negotiation. The chapters of this book alternate between, on the one hand, a sequential account of the negotiations and, on the other hand, reflections on the underlying issues and process. I hope to have thus gone some way towards capturing the essence of what it was all about. In a few instances, I have described individual meetings in some detail to add a pinch of flavour to my account.

Part I (Taking Off) deals with the preparations for and background to the Intergovernmental Conference. It sets out the challenges, explains the decision-making processes involved and summarizes the work of the preparatory Reflection Group. *Part II* (Taking Shape) concerns the initial stages of the Conference leading to the acceptance in December 1996 of the Irish Presidency's Outline Draft Treaty as the basis for work in the final phase of the negotiations. *Part III* (Taking Decisions) deals with the final shaping of the package during the Netherlands Presidency and the ultimate trade-offs at the Amsterdam European Council in June 1997. *Part IV* (Taking Stock) assesses briefly the outcome of the Conference and makes some modest proposals for the future.

The substance of the work of the Conference fell into five main areas. Reflecting the blending of sequence and substance which I have chosen, two of these areas (*The Union and the Citizen* and *An Effective and Coherent Foreign Policy*) are dealt with as they presented themselves during the Irish Presidency (in Part II). The other three areas (*Institutions*, *Flexibility*, and *Freedom, Security and Justice*) are dealt with in the context of the Netherlands Presidency (in Part III).

It has been necessary to try to strike a certain balance in the book as regards the level of detail. On the one hand, no real understanding of the complex subject matter is possible without a significant amount of detail. Anyone who would like the negotiations boiled down to uncomplicated sound bites or simple platitudes should read a different account. On the other hand, detailed though my account inevitably is, it has been necessary to summarize and be selective about a process which lasted two years. Important issues have been reduced to their essence. Some less important issues have been left aside.

The nature of an Intergovernmental Conference, the system of negotiation, is far from perfect. If it is easy to criticize, however, it is more difficult to identify how the system might be improved. A bit like democracy. In the final chapter, I make a few suggestions.

At the outset, I should also lay my credentials on the table. I am a committed European and I am a pragmatist. Europe needs vision, but a vision firmly rooted in the realities and constraints of the world in which we live. My firm conviction, which I have tried to reflect in a practical way in writing this book, is that the best service one can render to Europe is to explain rather than preach, to provide information rather than justification, to address its weaknesses rather than to pretend that they do not exist or to wish them away.

The European Union is truly a Brave New World. It is the most exciting experiment in the relationship between free democratic countries in history. It carries much of the responsibility for the future of prosperity and stability on the wider European continent. But it is no Utopia – far from it. For all the importance of its shared objectives and for all its achievements, the European Union self-evidently cannot change human nature. It remains, like democracy, an interplay of sometimes ferociously competing interests. Original Sin in a Brave New World – that is the paradox of Europe.

The portrait in this book is of the European Union, warts and all. Even with its blemishes, the European Union is without question still the best option for its peoples.

PART I

TAKING OFF

Chapter 1

The Tangle of Our Minds

**God made angels to show
him splendour – as he made animals for innocence
and plants for their simplicity. But Man he made to
serve him wittily, in the tangle of his mind!**
(Robert Bolt, *A Man for all Seasons*)

What on earth is an Intergovernmental Conference (IGC)?

The question which I try to answer in the first part of this chapter, and ultimately in this book, is not the academic question of a student of European law. It is rather the somewhat bored and sceptical question of the average citizen. What on earth is an Intergovernmental Conference?

The reader should be under no illusion. The workings of an Intergovernmental Conference are painstaking, complex and intricate. There is no easy short cut to understanding the workings of the European Union. No important aspect of the Union can be understood on the basis of an occasional skim through a newspaper article.

However, although the devil may be in the detail, the complexity can be explained in plain English. It is possible, with a little effort, to discern the wood and not only to look at the individual trees. The European Union and the direction of its further development are of the greatest importance to its citizens. It is imperative that every effort be made to bridge the gap between the Union and the citizens to whom it belongs.

An Intergovernmental Conference of the European Union is usually referred to as an IGC. The purpose of an IGC is to amend the Treaties on which the European Union is founded. The Treaties are in a sense the constitution of the European Union. Not only must all European legislation and every action of the European Union's institutions be in conformity with the Treaties,

3

but each piece of European legislation must be based on a specific provision in the Treaties.

The European Union's Treaties are, at this stage, a complex patchwork of provisions, a sprawling higgledy-piggledy construction. The Union of today does not represent the coherent conception of a master architect invited to design an elegant structure on a green-field site. It is a rambling set of buildings designed by their own strong-willed and sometimes squabbling inhabitants. The European construction does not have the symmetry of a new housing estate and may at times appear somewhat ramshackle. It is nevertheless the envy of its neighbours and admired by architects of regional integration throughout the world.

The buildings which constitute the European Union, originally designed for a family of six, must accommodate an ever-growing number of residents. It is not surprising that the buildings are regularly redesigned, extended and redecorated as the growing number of inhabitants demand new amenities, better security and improved decision-making in the residents' association.

When the Treaties fall for revision an IGC is convened to provide, as it were, the planning permission for further extensions. An IGC is quite distinct from the meetings of the Council of Ministers which take place week-in, week-out in Brussels and Luxembourg. The Council of Ministers *is an institution of the European Union.* In the Council of Ministers the representatives of each of the 15 Member States (e.g. the Foreign Ministers, the Finance Ministers or the Agriculture Ministers, depending on the subject matter) meet to adopt legislation or to take other measures. Many of its decisions are directly binding on the Member States, even if detailed implementing decisions often remain to be taken at national level.

An IGC, on the other hand, is outside the structures for conducting the ongoing business of the European Union. It is not an institution of the European Union. It is, as its name proclaims, *intergovernmental.* It is a conference of the *governments* of the Member States of the European Union. An IGC is the procedure according to which the Member States which constitute the European Union can decide to alter the nature, scope and decision-making processes of the Union.

The European Union was established by the Treaty on European Union signed in 1992 (popularly known as "the Maastricht Treaty"). It consists of three "pillars".

The "first pillar" comprises three Communities: the European [Economic] Community, the European Coal and Steel Community, and the European Atomic Energy Community. *Each of those Communities was established by its own treaty in the 1950s.*

The "second pillar" consists of the Common Foreign and Security Policy *(provided for in the Maastricht Treaty).*

The "third pillar" consists of cooperation in the area of Justice and Home Affairs *(also provided for in the Maastricht Treaty).*

The "first pillar", most particularly the European Community, constitutes the original foundation of the overall construction and its most supranational element. The other "pillars", added later, are more intergovernmental in nature.

Apart from the main Treaties establishing the Union and the individual Communities, the existing patchwork of Treaties consists also of a range of amending Treaties. *The Single European Act signed in 1986, for example, amended the European Community Treaty in a number of significant ways, notably to make possible the completion of the internal market and the development of the policy of cohesion. The 1992 Maastricht Treaty, in addition to establishing the European Union, amended the already existing Treaties in several respects, most importantly by incorporating in the European Community Treaty the basis for achieving Economic and Monetary Union. The Treaties are also adjusted on the occasion of each enlargement of the Union.*

For the sake of readability, this book generally refers to the existing construction simply as "the Union" or "the European Union", and to the existing patchwork of treaties on which it is based as "the Treaties". On occasion, however, where the sense requires it, reference is to made to the European Community or its mechanisms (i.e. the supranational mechanisms associated with the first pillar), or to a particular Treaty.

The intergovernmental nature of an IGC has two important consequences:

- every detail of the outcome of an IGC must be agreed unanimously by the Governments of the Member States of the European Union

- the outcome – which takes the form of a treaty between the Member States – must then be ratified by each Member State in accordance with its constitutional requirements. In every case this involves approval by national parliaments. In some Member States a referendum may also be required.

This double-lock – unanimity and national ratification – has very important consequences. It means that in the negotiations *each Government* must accept every last comma of the new treaty provisions and at the same time be satisfied that the overall package will obtain sufficient *popular approval* at home, at least at the level of its national parliament.

A major IGC, such as that which negotiated the Treaty of Amsterdam, is not a "conference" in the most commonly used sense of that word – a single continuous event over a number of days or weeks. Rather it is an ongoing process of negotiation over many months, or even a few years, involving meetings at the level of officials, of Foreign Ministers and of Heads of State or Government. (For very minor Treaty changes, a much more limited IGC may be convened.)

An IGC cannot, of course, be boiled down to a legal definition of its role or to its method of functioning. Seen from the inside, an IGC is about people – their abilities and weaknesses, their personalities, their humour and their foibles. The Treaty of Amsterdam is as much the result of myriad snap personal judgements and instinctive interventions as a coherent coming together of best-laid plans. National points of view and the effectiveness with which they are conveyed are inextricably bound up with the individuals who express them. Chapter 4 explores the IGC's "human factor".

The Treaty of Amsterdam reflects a balance between the interests of the Member States, but it is not the product of a mathematical formula. Europe, thank God, will never be designed by a computer.

The challenges facing the European Union and the Intergovernmental Conference

No two IGCs are the same. As the European Union evolves, each IGC faces new challenges to be addressed in new circumstances. The Treaty of Amsterdam can be properly understood and evaluated only against the background of the nature and the scale of the challenges facing the European Union as the IGC set about its work. The remainder of this chapter sketches my perception of those challenges.

It will be apparent from what I have to say that there are no simple solutions to the challenges facing the European Union. I emphasize this, although it should perhaps be obvious, because there are some who contest this view. On the one hand, there are those who hanker after what they see as the simple solution of rolling back the European Union or even withdrawing from it. On the other hand, there are those who would have us believe that the solution to Europe's problems is a simple and courageous leap into the Euro-dark. Both of those perceptions, representing opposite ends of the tabloid-defined spectrum from Euro-scepticism to Euro-enthusiasm, are erroneous. Both are based on an outdated view of Europe. Both carry dangers for the European Union's further development.

Personally, I am firmly convinced that the continued process of European integration is profoundly in the interests of ordinary people in every Member State and on the wider European continent. But just as the challenges facing Europe are complex, so too are the solutions. To borrow the words of Robert Bolt, it is not through innocence or simplicity but only wittily in the tangle of our minds that we will be able to construct a Europe for the future which can meet the concerns of its citizens, which can play a role on the international stage commensurate with its capacity, and which can shoulder its responsibilities on the wider European continent.

The European Union, in my view, faces four major interrelated challenges. These are what I would call:

* the challenge of direction

* the challenge of enlargement

* the challenge of public support

* the challenge of identity.

These challenges were, and of course remain, much wider and more enduring than the IGC alone. The task of the IGC was to contribute a partial response rather than to find definitive all-embracing solutions. The four challenges continue in effect to constitute the work programme of the European Union as a whole. The future success of the Union depends on addressing them effectively.

The challenge of direction

The first challenge faced by the European Union is to identify the direction for its future development.

When the original European Communities were established in the 1950s there were only six Member States. The institutional structure was much simpler. The fields covered by their cooperation were relatively limited. (Occasional whiffs of nostalgia could be detected in the comments of some old Brussels hands during the IGC. Things ain't as simple as they used to be.)

Over the next three decades, up to the 1980s, as the Union enlarged to nine, ten and then twelve Member States, the process of closer European integration was not always smooth, coherent and logical. As the camel is said to be a horse designed by a committee, so too the strange European beast could be said, almost literally, to have been designed by a committee. A key point, however, with regard to those three decades is that the development of Europe never lost its sense of direction.

Progress may at times have been in fits and starts. The highest of ideals may sometimes have got lost among the lowest of common denominators. But all the mishmash of developments over those decades – from the introduction of cooperation on foreign policy to the first directly-elected multinational parliament in the world – took place broadly in the comfortable aura of cosy consensus and shared purpose. Europe knew where it was going, even if it was not always getting there very quickly.

The major Intergovernmental Conference convened in 1985, which led to the adoption of the Single European Act, faced little problem of direction. Its principal purpose had been clear from the outset. Inspired by the European Commission under its then President, Jacques Delors, the aim of the IGC was to make it possible to create a genuine single market, the largest in the world. This was to be achieved principally by changing the Treaties to allow most of the necessary decisions to that end to be taken by majority decision in the Council (by a so-called qualified majority) rather than, as had been the case until then, requiring the unanimity of all Member States. The completion of the single market was to be accompanied notably by a new Treaty chapter on cohesion to ensure, by strengthening the Union's regional policy and its policy of social cohesion, that the benefits of the single market could flow equitably to all parts of the Union and to all sections of society. Although the stakes were high, the IGC effectively lasted less than four months. This reflected the fact that – although there had been some dispute as to whether the IGC should be convened in the first place – the Member States were agreed, with varying degrees of enthusiasm, on the *direction* it should take.

Incidentally, it is sometimes forgotten that in June 1985 Margaret Thatcher's Conservative Government, which later trumpeted the single market as one of its great achievements in Europe, voted against convening the IGC that made the single market possible. (The element of knee-jerk scepticism in the approach of John Major's Government to Europe was later to be a significant factor at the 1996/1997 IGC right up to its departure from office in May 1997, six weeks before agreement on the Treaty of Amsterdam.)

After the Single European Act, the next great challenge for Europe's sense of direction was the negotiation of the Maastricht Treaty. Again the detailed negotiation was inevitably difficult but the general sense of *direction* was clear. The main thrust was to agree Treaty provisions to provide for the achievement of Economic and Monetary Union and to make possible the establishment of a Common Foreign and Security Policy. The negotiations lasted less than one year. Moreover, by formally establishing the "European Union" (subsuming the earlier "European Communities"), the Maastricht Treaty gave the impression of a firm sense of where Europe was heading.

However, Maastricht also saw the emergence of the first serious problems of direction. If the Maastricht Treaty was a map for Europe's future, it involved significant topographical experimentation. Some Member States had created their own "no go" areas on the map of Europe's future. Some, for example, explicitly retained their right not to participate in a single currency. "Here be dragons", they pencilled onto their copies of the map. At the last moment in the negotiations, at the Maastricht European Council itself, the UK also secured an opt-out from the development of aspects of the Union's social policy. "Beware the wicked witch."

The Maastricht negotiations had also seen controversy about whether the word "federal" (popularly known as the "F word") should appear in the Treaty. Although for some, on either side of the argument, it became the litmus test of orthodoxy or heresy, it was in a sense a false problem. The word "federal", after all, has quite different meanings in different Member States. However, the fact that so much negotiating energy could be devoted to a theological irrelevance was a further indication of hesitation at the crossroads.

The sense of Europe's purpose and direction was given a further jolt by the public reaction to the Maastricht Treaty in several Member States. The Danish people initially rejected the Treaty in a referendum, although in a second referendum they endorsed it on the basis of a range of opt-outs for Denmark. In France, more surprisingly, the referendum called by President Mitterand turned out to be a very close-run thing. The parliamentary ratification process in the UK revealed deep divisions, notably within the Conservative Party, and went to the wire. While the Maastricht Treaty was ultimately ratified through the democratic process in every Member State, a widespread sense lingered that it had been negotiated out of public view, that it was difficult to understand and that it was not relevant to the most pressing concerns of citizens.

The criticisms were to an extent misplaced. It was not so much that the Maastricht Treaty lacked relevance as that its relevance had not been not clearly demonstrated. But the Maastricht experience added to a sense of insecurity about where Europe was heading.

Shortly afterwards, the European Union, which had just assimilated the accession of Spain and Portugal, enlarged yet again with the accession of Sweden, Austria and Finland. It now consisted of 15 Member States. While the incorporation of those countries into the Union has been smooth and its effect positive, the growing number of Member States has inevitably made the

Union more heterogeneous, its decision-making more cumbersome and its ultimate destination more difficult to define.

It is worth observing that, since the mid-1980s, the language in general use relating to the process of European integration has changed significantly, even if at first almost imperceptibly. Over those years, language expressing the aspiration to political union and the "ever-closer process of integration" has gradually been dropped in favour of language about effectiveness, openness and, above all, relevance to citizens. This shift has occurred in the vocabulary of speechmaking throughout the European Union, in varying degrees in every Member State without exception.

The challenge of enlargement

I need to recall only briefly the challenge of enlargement which, although in its way the most important one, is well-known and straightforward. The European Union must incorporate the ten democracies that have recently emerged in Central and Eastern Europe. It has no moral or political alternative. Indeed, it should do so with open arms. Yet the Union cannot enlarge significantly without changing its own nature. The challenge is to find a way for the Union to enlarge while at the same time continuing not only to function effectively but also to develop further in the pursuit of its objectives. The Union must solve the riddle of widening and deepening at the same time.

Some, of course, would like nothing more than to see a further widening of the European Union precisely because they hope that it will have the effect of putting a stop to the deepening of the Union. Some have always wished the Union to develop into little more than a free trade area (or actually believe the myth that the Union was once nothing more than a "common market"). It would, however, be a fatal mistake for Europe to fall into that trap. It would serve the interests of no one, least of all the applicant countries from Central and Eastern Europe, if the Union were to dilute its purpose or abandon the very features that make it so attractive to those who wish to join.

Equally, however, it would be a mistake to try to prevent the effective widening of the Union. Blocking enlargement is simply not an option. A more subtle danger to be avoided would be to accept the appearance of enlargement while at the same time creating a solid impermeable core group of Member States – a Union within the Union.

An effective response to the challenge of enlargement requires that the widening and deepening go hand in hand. One at the expense of the other would derail the entire European project.

The challenge of public support

The third and perhaps greatest challenge facing the European Union is that of maintaining and, if possible, developing public support.

The problem, of course, should not be exaggerated. Put in the simplest terms, "Europe" has a great deal more support than "non-Europe". Each Member State's membership of the European Union and participation in its further development have the assent of its people expressed through a democratically elected government and parliament and, in some cases, also directly through referenda. Moreover, the European Union itself is, of its nature, deeply embedded in the democratic process. It has a directly elected Parliament. Each Member State is represented in the Council of Ministers by its elected Government. Each national parliament contributes to the establishment of its Government's policy in Europe.

However, there is undoubtedly a sense, to one degree or another in every Member State, that Europe is something apart, something that happens elsewhere – in Brussels or Strasbourg or Luxembourg. In some Member States at least, this sense has grown in recent years. It is not that Europe is not relevant to public concerns (although it can always be made more relevant), but rather that its relevance is often not explained or understood.

There are people in every Member State who firmly oppose the concept of European integration. In most cases they are a relatively small minority. Part of the challenge of public support is to win over such people, although there is no doubt that some of them will hold on to their quite legitimate point of view. There is, however, a different, wider and in some senses more important challenge of public support. It is the challenge not of selling Europe to the hostile few, but of explaining Europe to the indifferent many.

The level of media coverage of the European Union is not remotely commensurate with Europe's importance to people's lives. Take my own country, for example. In Ireland the quality and extent of media coverage of Europe is impressive in comparison with many Member States. (One anecdote will illustrate this. I was informed, when I spent some days in the House of Lords several years ago, that the section of its library dealing with European issues took two daily newspapers – the *Financial Times* and the *Irish Times*! It takes some quality for an Irish newspaper to find itself a preferred choice in that bastion of British tradition.) Irish people, moreover, are relatively interested in public and international affairs. However, even in a country like Ireland, the European Union accounts for only a very small proportion of media coverage. This relative sparsity of coverage bears no relation to the significance for the Irish economy and for Irish society more generally of the decisions taken in Europe.

Of course the relatively limited media coverage of Europe, in most if not all Member States, should not be seen as the "fault" of the media. The quality of the coverage, if not its quantity or its reach, is often very impressive. (Still less is it my intention to criticize the media in Ireland. The fact that a problem of public comprehension exists even in a Member State with relatively good media coverage of Europe merely serves to underline the extent of the problem.)

Moreover, politicians, civil servants, interest groups, the education system at all levels, and the European institutions must also play their part in explaining Europe. Indeed, people themselves have to make a significant effort if they wish to understand the workings of the Union.

There appears to be a vicious circle. Many people are bored by Europe because they do not understand it. They do not understand Europe because of the limited coverage which it receives. It receives limited coverage because people are bored by it.

Perhaps the main reason for this phenomenon is that people everywhere in the Union still identify with the local – the local face, the local issue, the local scandal. To an extent, at least, national politics are also seen as local. The European Union, by contrast, is still perceived as something a little distant, a little incomprehensible. It is seen as a fact of life which affects us rather than a process which we can help to shape. Europe is seen as something we participate in rather than part of what we are. The challenge is to overcome the boredom, to unshroud the mystery, to show that Europe too is local in its relevance. Much has already been done to address this challenge, to make Europe more transparent and comprehensible and alert to the concerns of citizens. However, a great deal remains to be done.

During the Intergovernmental Conference leading to the Treaty of Amsterdam, each delegation attached central importance to its public opinion, to ensuring that the Treaty emerging from the negotiations would have sufficient popular support at home. One of the five main themes of the IGC was "Europe and the Citizen". Another of the themes, "Freedom, Security and Justice", also grew directly from the desire to address the concerns of citizens, notably as regards the fight against crime. Perhaps the most fundamental shift in the Union's priorities represented by the Treaty of Amsterdam was that the concerns of citizens were moved centre-stage. The conduct of the IGC was also much more open than had been the case with previous IGCs.

But addressing the concerns of citizens at the IGC, and being seen to address those concerns, was much easier said than done for several reasons, of which I will mention three.

First, the levers for addressing such concerns – such as unemployment or the fight against crime – are often in the hands of national governments. One of the concerns of many citizens is precisely *that such issues should remain in the hands of national governments.* It is not that people do not want action at European level on these issues – on the contrary. The paradox is that people often *do* want more action at European level but *not at the expense of national prerogatives.*

Second, an IGC concerns solely the negotiation of changes to the European Union's Treaties, not the subsequent development of concrete policies on the basis of the Treaty provisions agreed. An IGC therefore strengthens the basis for future action but does not itself implement the action provided for. The language in the Treaty of Amsterdam on Justice and Home Affairs, for example, is inevitably couched in legal terms and may appear a far cry from the practical police cooperation which will flow from it.

Third, and perhaps most importantly, public concerns differ very significantly from one Member State to another. Some delegations may therefore press for more action at European level on, say, the environment or employment. Others may press for more action on fraud or for improved decision-making or for a greater role for national parliaments. Furthermore, public concerns are sometimes even directly contradictory from one Member State to another. Most obviously, the Governments of larger Member States would like to be able tell their electorates that they have won more influence in the Union at the expense of the smaller Member States. The Governments of the smaller Member States would like to be able to tell their electorates that no such shift has taken place. For some Governments, to cite another example, a further step towards a common defence policy would represent a strong selling point at home. For others the opposite is the case.

The challenge of identity

Finally, Europe faces what I call the challenge of identity. The fact is that decisions are taken at European level and in the European interest by people who continue to think largely in national terms.

The simple fact is that the pursuit of national interests remains at the heart of the European Union. In my view that is not something to be deplored, although the lowest national common denominator can end up serving the interests of no one. Nor, on the other hand, is it a badge of honour to be trumpeted under the banner of sovereignty, although it does reflect the workings of democracy at the present stage of the Union's development. The continued pursuit of national interests should be seen simply for the *fact* that it is. If the fact is ignored it will not go away; rather it risks becoming a festering sore. If, on the other hand, the reality of national interest is recognized, it can be transformed slowly so that it is seen increasingly as embracing the wider European interest.

When Member States act, as they often do, in what is perceived as a "European" way, they do so not because they have ceased to be Belgians or Finns nor out of a sense of altruism. They act thus because they have identified their own interests as being best addressed at the European level by a European Union which functions effectively. Trampling on national interests or concerns would offer no basis for progress. Pretending that they are a thing of the past is the simple self-delusion of the ostrich. The challenge is to be aware of national interests and sensitivities, to accommodate them and to encourage their gradual "sea-change/into something rich and strange".

Conclusion

These are, in my view, the four main challenges facing the European Union. I have set them out at some length because they are the key to understanding and evaluating the Inter-governmental Conference. They served at once as both the motivation for and the constraints on the negotiations.

Each of the four challenges was complex. Each contained its own internal tensions: differences of preferred direction, widening versus deepening, different popular priorities to satisfy, conflicting national interests.

It was essential for the IGC to address *each and every one* of those challenges with a degree of success. Picking and choosing between the challenges was not an option. The IGC had to sketch out a direction for the future. It had to make possible the next step in the process of further enlargement while permitting at the same time the further deepening of the Union. It had to win sufficient public support throughout the Union. It had to accommodate the concerns of every Member State.

In the final chapter of this book I have set out some reflections on how the conduct of IGCs might be improved for the future. I would like to think that there may be more effective ways of handling some aspects of such negotiations. What is certain, however, is that the inescapable starting point will always be the real challenges and the real constraints which those challenges impose. The solution will always lie somewhere in the tangle of our minds.

Chapter 2

The Decision-making Mechanisms

A mighty maze! but not without a plan.
(Alexander Pope, *An Essay on Man*)

The decision-making mechanisms in the European Union are vastly complex. It is inevitable that this should be so. No doubt management consultants would arrange things differently.

The decision-making mechanisms are necessarily complex because the European Union is an extraordinarily delicate, sensitive and indeed unprecedented experiment in relations between free democratic countries. The institutional arrangements are the most innovative and important legacy left by the founding fathers of the European Communities. The arrangements may be cumbersome and complex. They may at times be slow or opaque. But they are the foundations on which the peace and prosperity of the European Union have been constructed. They are the fulcrum which must now carry the weight of responsibility for the stability and development of the wider European continent. The decision-making mechanisms of the European Union are, of course, quite hilarious, but not quite as funny as the centuries of war which preceded them.

The institutional arrangements and decision-making mechanisms of the European Union are not set in stone. Indeed, one of the principal challenges of the IGC was to examine how they might be improved (see in particular Chapter 14). One thing is, however, certain. There are no simple alternatives to the present arrangements. There are no quick institutional fixes.

This chapter outlines the complex decision-making machinery of an Intergovernmental Conference.

Levels of decision-making

There are essentially *four levels* involved in the decision-making process of an IGC.

First, at the apex of the system, is *the European Council* – in practice the supreme decision-making body of the European

Union. This consists of the "Heads of State or Government". This formula reflects the fact that, while 13 Member States are represented by their Prime Ministers at such meetings, two Member States – France and Finland – are represented by their Heads of State. The President of the European Commission is also a member of the European Council. The principals are assisted by their Ministers for Foreign Affairs and by a Member of the Commission. European Council meetings are often referred to as "Summits".

The European Council has a formal meeting towards the end of each six-monthly Presidency of the European Union. The work of the European Union as a whole revolves around those end-of-Presidency meetings. Of course, by far the greater part of ongoing Union business does not need to be referred to such a high level. However, much of the political energy during each Presidency is channelled into the preparation of the European Council which crowns it. The European Council strikes the key deals where necessary. It effectively establishes the agenda and priorities for the Union for the following six months.

The practice has developed in recent years that the Heads of State or Government, in addition to their regular end-of-Presidency European Council meeting, have a second meeting in the course of each Presidency. These additional meetings, however, tend to be relatively informal, without conclusions and therefore less important. Alternatively, they may be devoted to one specific issue.

It is worth recalling a few of the key features of European Councils:

- Prime Ministers (or Heads of State) are accompanied in the meeting room only by their Foreign Ministers (and for some items now also by their Finance Ministers). No national officials are present (other than from the country which holds the six-month Presidency). This distinguishes European Councils from meetings at ordinary Ministerial level. (I recall Genscher once comparing the throng at a Foreign Ministers' meeting in Luxembourg to a plenary session of the Chinese Communist Party.) It is not just a question of numbers. It is a question of atmosphere, of moving from the details to the essentials. It is a question of cutting deals.

- The personalities of individual Prime Ministers or Heads of State matter very significantly at European Council level – more significantly than at Ministerial level. The performance of individual members of the European Council impacts directly on the outcome. The relationship between individual members of the European Council – reflecting sympathy or irritation or friendship – can be crucial.

- The meetings generally last two days. The first day is devoted to general discussion and the second day to a drafting session to finalize agreed "conclusions". Those "conclusions" are distributed for the first time, in draft form, to each national delegation by the Presidency at dawn on the second day of the meeting. After a flurry of activity of bleary-eyed officials, an identification of problems in the draft, a networking with other delegations and a hasty briefing of Prime Ministers, discussion on the second day is devoted to a page-by-page examination of the draft conclusions.

- The European Council, as the level which cuts the final deals, often becomes a "negotiation" in the traditional sense. Depending on the agenda, some European Councils are low-key and uncontroversial. At others, wheeler-dealers are in their element.

The second level is the *Ministerial level.* The Madrid European Council, in December 1995, decided that the IGC would "meet regularly, in principle once a month, at the level of Foreign Ministers, who will have responsibility for all proceedings".

Throughout the Conference, there was a monthly Ministerial level IGC meeting on the occasion of each regular General Affairs Council. (The Council of Ministers meets in several compositions – e.g. Finance or Agriculture or Fisheries Ministers – to deal with the ongoing business of the European Union. Foreign Ministers meet as the "General Affairs Council", so called because it has not only responsibility for Europe's foreign relations but also a general coordinating function).

The decision that Foreign Ministers should have responsibility for all the proceedings of the IGC was important. It was designed to ensure the coherence of the negotiations. The IGC would be dealing with numerous areas which, if they were to be dealt with as part of ongoing Community business, would be dealt with by specialized compositions of the Council (e.g. environment, crime, employment). It was recognized as essential by all delegations that the IGC negotiations should not be allowed to spill over into disparate fora and that the coherence and "unicity" (or unity) of the negotiations should be preserved.

While informal discussion of IGC matters occasionally took place in formations of the Council other than Foreign Ministers, those discussions had virtually no impact on the negotiations. It was repeatedly emphasized, and for the most part understood, that what was relevant was not what, say, the 15 environment ministers might discuss informally among themselves, but rather the extent to which individual environment ministers could influence the position taken by their IGC delegation within the actual IGC negotiations.

The Ministerial level was sandwiched somewhat between the European Council level above it and the level of the Ministers' IGC Representatives below it. The key deals were to be struck at the highest level. The vast bulk of the detailed examination of issues and texts inevitably took place below Ministerial level. Discussion at Ministerial level, therefore, in a sense fell between two stools.

Against this background, there was at times criticism of discussion at Ministerial level, including by some Ministers themselves who felt they were not getting their teeth into the substance of the negotiations. A degree of uncertainty, and indeed on occasion disappointment, about the precise role of Ministerial discussions was understandable. However, criticism cannot validly be directed at the Ministers themselves. It was right on the one hand that the necessary detailed work be done below their level. Equally it was inevitable that fundamental positions would not be conceded by delegations at Ministerial level as long as the European Council remained available as a higher "court of appeal". This growing dilemma for Foreign Ministers, notably in the General Affairs Council, is of considerably wider relevance than the IGC alone.

Nevertheless, within its unavoidable constraints, the Ministerial level performed its function effectively in the IGC under the chairmanship successively of Lamberto Dini, Dick Spring and Hans van Mierlo. Each Ministerial meeting represented incremental progress in establishing the priorities of delegations and in identifying trends in discussion. Even in cases where Ministers to a considerable extent repeated discussions which had taken place at a lower level, that in itself represented a further necessary phase in the evolutionary process.

The third level was that of *IGC Representatives*. The Madrid European Council had specified that "preparations will be conducted by a working party made up of a representative of each Member State's Minister for Foreign Affairs and of the President of the Commission". It was principally at the level of IGC Representatives that the hard graft was done and that the Treaty of Amsterdam took shape.

The IGC Representatives, one nominated by each delegation, consisted of a mixture of Ministers of State (5), Permanent Representatives to the EU (6) and others (4), plus a Member of the European Commission. These met for two days more or less every week over a 15-month period.

A potential fourth level of negotiation was the *working group level,* in so far as the IGC Representatives could appoint one or more working groups under their authority to assist them in their work. While the possibility of farming out some work to a subsidiary level was considered by IGC Representatives on a number of occasions, in practice this device was used very sparingly. Virtually all the work of the Conference was seen as "political". It was generally considered impractical to try to draw a distinction between political aspects and more technical aspects which might be considered in the first instance at working group level. Keeping discussions at IGC Representative level also helped to ensure the coherence and unity of the negotiations.

In practice, one (essentially legal) working group was set up for a period to consider the largely technical issue of simplifying and consolidating the existing treaties (apart from whatever changes of substance might be agreed by the IGC). Also, a so-called "Friends of the Presidency" working group was set up in the very final weeks of the negotiation before Amsterdam to refine some of the less controversial issues (see Chapter 16). That group also carried out the necessary tidying-up work on the Treaty texts after Amsterdam.

Types of meeting

Apart from the various *levels* at which the negotiations took place, a Presidency also has at its disposal various *types* of meeting.

The most obvious and frequent type of meeting was the routine formal meeting at Representative level (every week) and Ministerial level (every month). Typically these formal meetings – especially at Ministerial level – took the form largely of a series of *tours de table* (or "table rounds") in the course of which each delegation put forward its views on the range of issues which had been identified for discussion. Formal meetings could on occasion take place in "restricted session" (i.e. with the number of members of each delegation restricted to maybe only one or two).

On the occasion of most of these formal meetings, more informal discussions (one person per delegation) usually also took place over dinner or lunch. These informal discussions offered an opportunity for a less structured and often more revealing exchange of views. Procedural questions relating to the conduct of the Conference, for example, were frequently handled in the context of such informal discussions.

Apart from the routine formal meetings and the informal dinner/lunch discussions which accompanied them, full informal meetings were convened from time to time at every level: European Council, Ministerial and Representative level. Informal European Councils were convened during both the Irish and Dutch Presidencies. These differed significantly from the normal European Councils, notably in that no formal conclusions were adopted. Informal meetings at Foreign Minister and IGC Representative level were also convened at various stages.

Presidencies also had the option of convening "confessionals", i.e. short bilateral meetings with each of the Member States in turn. The Irish Presidency, in the second half of 1996, did so twice.

"Confessionals" are a recognized instrument in European Union negotiations which offer a Presidency the possibility of obtaining an insight into the neuralgic concerns and real bottom line of individual delegations.

Role of the Presidency

The Presidency of the European Union rotates every six months. It is a system which generally functions effectively. It brings a new impetus and energy to the work of the Union twice every year. Moreover, it gives a particular opportunity to each Member State in turn, and to its people, to identify with the Union.

The role of the Presidency is to preside over the work of the Council at every level over a period of six months. This involves, most obviously, the chairing of meetings. It also involves the preparation of and follow-up to meetings and, more generally, the shaping and managing of the Union's agenda. The conduct of a Presidency represents a large responsibility for the Government and administration of the Member State in question. The principal burden of a Presidency falls on its Permanent Representation in Brussels.

A Presidency is of particular importance in the case of an IGC because, in addition to what would be considered normal Presidency functions, the Presidency of an IGC is also responsible almost single-handed, with the help of the Council Secretariat, for preparing and tabling the papers and proposals for discussion. This distinguishes an IGC from normal Council business, in relation to which the European Commission has the sole right of initiative for tabling legislative proposals.

Many individual delegations tabled papers or proposals in the course of the IGC, but these were very rarely treated as the basis for discussion. The significance of such national proposals lay principally in the extent to which they influenced papers tabled by the Presidency of the time. It is important for a Presidency to maintain tight control over agendas, papers for discussion and the conduct of business.

A Presidency is, of course, greatly helped by the Council Secretariat. I will return to this aspect in the later chapters on the Irish Presidency.

Organization and conduct of meetings

A Presidency is in the first instance responsible for drawing up, and subsequently adapting as necessary, its *calendar of meetings*. This involves issues of significant strategic importance and sometimes issues of great sensitivity for individual Member States.

The Presidency is also responsible for establishing the *agenda for individual meetings*. The shape of agendas for individual meetings is best signalled – at least tentatively – in the Presidency's advance calendar of meetings. Agendas must be confirmed three to five working days before a given meeting is to take place. Again, many practical and tactical questions arise.

Most importantly the Presidency must, where necessary, as indicated above, table *papers for discussion*. Ideally such papers should be circulated during the meeting prior to the meeting at which they are to be discussed. If not they are e-mailed or faxed directly to capitals by the Council Secretariat. A Presidency's thought process always has to be at least one step ahead of the posse. In the course of meeting X during the Irish Presidency, we were usually finalizing papers for meeting $X + 1$, discussing among ourselves an outline approach to the issues for discussion at meeting $X + 2$, and even shaping the agenda for meeting $X + 3$.

The *conduct of meetings*, of course, involves an array of questions concerning objectives, tactics, tone, timing and conclusions.

The most striking thing about the *follow-up to meetings* is that there is essentially no official record, public or private, of the detail of what has transpired. Each delegation keeps its own records, detailed or otherwise, as it sees fit. Of course, an enormous effort and a great deal of time would be required to get an *agreed* account of any meeting (sometimes even within a delegation). Report writing is not an exact science.

The conclusions of a European Council constitute a statement of what has been agreed at the meeting in question, but do not record what was said. Council Secretariat press releases after each Ministerial IGC meeting also summarize in a very anodyne way what has transpired, but again there is no official record of the various interventions. At IGC Representative level also, it was for each delegation to keep whatever records it considered necessary.

Other dimensions of the negotiations

The present chapter summarizes the decision-making mechanisms of the IGC. The picture would not be complete, however, without brief reference to the fact that the negotiations have many other dimensions.

There are, for example, frequent *bilateral contacts and meetings at political and official level* at every stage of the process. These range from brief casual chats in the Council building in Brussels to fully-fledged summits between Prime Ministers. A shared espresso at the bar in the Justus Lipsius building – accompanied by the inevitable unsolicited chocolate – is the oil which helps to make the European machinery turn. Full bilateral meetings offer an opportunity to explain and to understand concerns. Such meetings usually start and finish with reference to how much the two Member States "have in common". Although a degree of diplomatic nicety may be involved, I find striking the extent to which the opportunity for a mutual exchange of views throws up shared concerns and perceptions which are less obvious at more formal meetings involving many delegations. Bilateral contacts are also maintained through Member States' embassies in other Member States.

There are also meetings between groups of like-minded countries – either established groups (notably Benelux: Belgium, Netherlands and Luxembourg) or *ad hoc* groups on certain issues.

A further dimension to EU negotiations that merits books of its own is, of course, the role of the media which, beyond its reporting function, can influence significantly the negotiations themselves.

Two years, two days: two negotiations

The first part of this chapter sets out the negotiating *mechanisms and procedures* of an Intergovernmental Conference. It is also essential to understand the *nature* of the negotiation.

Between the opening in Taormina on 3 June 1995 of the Reflection Group (described in Chapter 3), which helped to prepare the work of the IGC, and the agreement on the Treaty of Amsterdam on 18 June 1997 (described in Chapter 16) there were in effect two negotiations. The first negotiation lasted two years. The second negotiation lasted two days.

The *first negotiation* was the essential but painstaking process of giving shape to a package, a draft treaty, which could be submitted for consideration at Amsterdam. The *second negotiation* was the endgame at Amsterdam itself. These two negotiations – the gradual shaping of the package and the final deals and adjustments – produced as their common fruit the complex Treaty of Amsterdam agreed by all Member States in the early hours of 18 June 1997.

The first negotiation, over two years, saw the introduction, demise, merging or survival of conflicting and converging ideas. The Reflection Group in the latter half of 1995 effectively launched the process. This was followed by the opening of the IGC itself as well as its initial stages under the Italian Presidency in the first half of 1996. An intensification of the negotiations took place from the beginning of the Irish Presidency in the second half of 1996. In effect the stage of statements of position had ended. The phase of real negotiation had begun. Discussions increasingly were based not on free-floating ideas but on specific draft treaty texts leading to an Outline Draft Treaty in December of that year. The Netherlands Presidency, in the first half of 1997, had the decisive task of developing and adapting the package which was emerging until it was ready for submission at Amsterdam in June.

In my view, this two-year process can usefully be understood as a single negotiation. At no definable moment during that process was any issue definitively agreed. At no single meeting was it possible to conclude that an issue or a text had been put to bed. Explicit conclusions at the end of each meeting would have been counterproductive. It was generally more effective for a Presidency to leave unsaid at the end of each meeting, for fear of contradiction, the fact that certain ideas were gaining ground or that others were slipping into the quicksand. It was prudent to let the ideas live or die without providing a running commentary.

Every single meeting, however, made its contribution to the evolutionary process – to shaping the final package in a way which could ultimately meet the concerns of all. The elements of eventual compromise emerged not from the click of a magician's fingers but with the patience of a sculptor's art.

The media were sometimes frustrated during the two years because they had little sense of deals being struck, of negotiations in the traditional sense ("You give me this; I'll give you that"). Even those most closely involved in the negotiations, especially Ministers used to striking political bargains at home, often asked themselves when the "real" negotiations would start. But that was to misunderstand the process, to miss the point. The painstaking and at times repetitive process of refining the overall package, meeting by meeting, was *itself* the negotiation. The progress of the negotiations was often no more amenable to sound bites than the patient work of a sculptor chiselling meaning from a lump of granite, but the progress was every bit as certain and irreversible.

The media would have liked to have been in a position to announce agreement on parts of the package at various stages of the IGC. In the absence of such agreement, some reported "lack of progress". Some Ministers also, reflecting their natural symbiotic love–hate relationship with the media, would, in the course of the negotiations, like to have announced definitive progress in the form of "agreement" to parts of the Treaty – fine in theory, but impossible in practice because each delegation would have its own firm view on which parts of the Treaty should be subject to such pre-agreement.

The need to give shape to an overall package was at the heart of everything. Even in a bilateral negotiation, involving only two countries, it is often the case – if the issues are sensitive – that "nothing is agreed until everything is agreed". That is all the more true in a negotiation between 15 Member States.

At every stage of the Conference each delegation did what it could to influence the shape of the package: what should be in and what should be out; the level of ambition in relation to each element; how each provision should be phrased. Each delegation had subjects to which it was devoted or allergic or indifferent. Each delegation had its preferred phrasing for virtually every provision. It would have been futile to ask individual delegations to drop their wish-lists, to embrace their pet hates or to change their preferences. The aim of the negotiation was not to convert each delegation on every detail, although each delegation would in the end have to accept every last comma in the Treaty. The aim was to bring each delegation to a position where it could accept the overall package, the rough as well as the smooth.

Each meeting had its own significance. Each meeting had its own undercurrents of views, its own trends in discussion, its own personality clashes, its own influence on the Treaty of Amsterdam. However, to describe the meetings one by one rather than the process of which each was part would not only require a book of much greater length but also tend to miss the essence of the negotiation.

The *second negotiation*, the two-day negotiation at Amsterdam itself (described in detail in Chapter 16) was the endgame. There the nature of the negotiation, as with every major negotiation, changed fundamentally. The issue for each Member State at Amsterdam was no longer its preference on each point of detail. The question at that point became whether each Member State would, at the end of the two-day meeting, be able to accept the overall package; whether it would be able to sign up to the Treaty of Amsterdam.

In so far as any negotiation involving 15 countries as well as the European Commission can be said to conform to any known pattern of problem-solving, the Amsterdam meeting was a "negotiation" in the more usual sense of the term. Amendments proposed and accepted at Amsterdam would become part of European law. Rejected suggestions or wording would be lost and gone forever.

Major negotiations in the European Union necessarily follow the two-stage pattern described in this chapter. First shape the package. Then strike the deals. It can be no other way.

Chapter 3

The Reflection Group:
Survival of the Fittest Ideas

If superior creatures from space ever visit earth, the first question they will ask, in order to assess the level of our civilisation, is "Have they discovered evolution yet?"
(Richard Dawkins, _The Selfish Gene_)

A Reflection Group was established to prepare the work of the IGC. It held its first meeting in June 1995 and met regularly over a period of six months. The present chapter falls into two parts: first, it describes in some detail the inaugural meeting of the Reflection Group with a view to conveying an impression of the flavour of such a meeting; second, it assesses briefly the role and work of the Reflection Group. The Reflection Group was the first phase in the evolutionary negotiating process during which only the fittest ideas would survive.

The Maastricht Treaty in 1992 had provided that a further IGC should take place in 1996. The timing of the impending IGC was therefore predetermined and somewhat artificial. While an IGC would have been necessary at some point before the further enlargement of the European Union, the precise timing of what came to be known as the "1996 IGC" (until it drifted into 1997!) stemmed not from the natural flow of events but from the specific provision in the Maastricht Treaty that there should be such an IGC in 1996.

The forced nature of the timing of the IGC conferred a particular importance on its preparation. With that in view, a Reflection Group was set up by decision of the Heads of State or Government at the Corfu European Council in June 1994. When the Reflection Group opened in June 1995, it had six months to prepare its report for the European Council in Madrid on 15/16 December.

The inaugural meeting of the Reflection Group

The Reflection Group opened in Taormina, near Messina, in Sicily on Saturday 3 June 1995. The location had been chosen because of its historical significance. It was at the Messina Conference 40 years earlier that the original six Member States of the European Union had succeeded, in the words of the then Belgian Foreign Minister, Paul-Henri Spaak, in "relaunching Europe". It was at the Messina Conference in 1955 that the decisions had been taken that led to the setting-up of the European Economic Community.

Europe has changed almost beyond recognition since the original Messina Conference. Two incidental features of that Conference are, however, perhaps worth recalling since they illustrate that some things nevertheless have a reluctance to change.

First, it is said that Messina was chosen as the location for the Conference in 1955 to assist the Italian Foreign Minister, Gaetano Martino, who was facing an election in Sicily. Even on occasions of the most lofty vision, the politics of Europe retain a significant local dimension.

Second, the UK did not participate at the 1955 Messina Conference. The UK observer dispatched by London is reported to have said "I leave Messina happy because even if you continue meeting you will not agree; even if you agree nothing will result; and even if something results it will be a disaster". For much of the 1996/1997 IGC the UK, while offering its views in a constructive spirit, was to continue its efforts to lead Europe from the sidelines.

Gay Mitchell, Ireland's Minister of State for European Affairs and member of the Reflection Group, suggested at the opening meeting of the Reflection Group that the historical relevance of Messina might stretch back 400 rather than 40 years. Recalling that Shakespeare had set *Much Ado About Nothing* in Messina, he suggested that Shakespeare's description of "strange disguises" was indeed prescient:

> "as, to be a Dutchman to-day; a Frenchman to-morrow; or in the shape of two countries at once; as, a German from the waist downward..., and a Spaniard from the hip upward..."

(Perhaps *Measure for Measure* might in retrospect constitute a more balanced judgement on the Reflection Group and the IGC than *Much Ado About Nothing.*)

Foreign Ministers and their delegations arrived at Messina on Friday 2 June for a day devoted to ceremonies to mark the fortieth anniversary of the Messina Conference. A bland Solemn Declaration to mark the occasion was adopted. A series of stolid and worthy speeches by the Presidents of each of the Union's Institutions allowed for a gentle siesta at the Palazzo Comunale. The only striking speech was a trenchant appeal for vision by Klaus Hänsch, the President of the European Parliament. He was to make a very constructive contribution to the IGC process. Later that evening Italian hospitality included the ballet *A la Memoire* by Micha Van Hoeke at the outdoor Teatro Greco in Taormina.

The Reflection Group met for the first time at a rectangular table formation in a small conference room at the Hotel San Domenico in Taormina at 9.30 a.m. on the following day, Saturday 3 June. Two people per delegation. Like Noah's ark. Members of the Reflection Group and their deputies. No seats at the back. Cramped.

More like 9.45 before the meeting would start. A regulation 15 minutes' grace is allowed at the outset of European Union meetings – in some ways the most important 15 minutes of any meeting: last-minute ferreting out of how like-minded Member States intend to play things; contact work on issues for next week's meeting; material maybe for a short report ("I understand informally from the Spanish delegation..."); procedural requests to the Presidency – a request perhaps to take the floor early or to raise a point under Any Other Business.

On the occasion of the first meeting of the Reflection Group, an opportunity to get to know your neighbours. The seating arrangement at European Union meetings follows the sequence of six-monthly Presidencies. So, on Ireland's left, the Italians who would in due course precede Ireland as Presidency. Their Representative on the Reflection Group was Silvio Fagiolo, an old European hand and a charming diplomat. No one in the course of the Reflection Group and the IGC would take a more systematically pro-integrationist line. On our right, the Dutch who would follow us as Presidency and bring the IGC to its conclusion at Amsterdam. Michiel Patijn, the Netherlands Minister of State for Foreign Affairs would, I imagine, be happy to be described as the effective, straight-talking, no-nonsense man that he is. A man to get the business done. Beside him his talented and witty deputy Tom de Bruijn.

Around the table there were many familiar faces. There always are at European Union meetings. For individuals closely involved in European negotiations, the process gets into the bloodstream like malaria. Once it's in the system, you never quite get rid of it. Figures from your past keep cropping up, often in new incarnations: in a new job, promoted or even serving a new master. Many of the usual suspects had been rounded up.

Eighteen members of the Reflection Group – one from each of the 15 Member States (personal representatives of their Foreign Ministers), one from the Commission and two from the European Parliament. A mixture of Ministers, officials and more independent spirits. (The full list of Members of the IGC Reflection Group is given in Annex 1.)

The Ministers included the European Ministers of France and Germany, Michel Barnier and Werner Hoyer, on close personal terms with each other and both later reappointed for the IGC negotiations themselves.

Spain was also represented by its European Affairs Minister, Carlos Westendorp (subsequently Foreign Minister and the European Union's Representative in former Yugoslavia). He was the chairman of the Group. At European Union meetings the country exercising the "Presidency" (or chairmanship) normally also has a national delegation to represent its national view, thus increasing the freedom of the Presidency as such to think and act in a neutral impartial way. In view of the "reflective" nature of the Reflection Group, the Spanish Presidency chose not to have a separate national delegation.

The European Commission – initiator of legislation, manager of business, guardian of the Treaties – was represented by Commissioner Marcellino Oreja. His deputy was the quiet, effective and experienced Michel Petit, head of the Commission Task Force on the IGC, who had served in former Commission President Delors' cabinet. (Michel once represented France in fencing at the Olympic Games. At an IGC, one cannot be quite so sure from which direction the thrusts will come!)

The two representatives of the European Parliament, Elisabeth Guigou (later a senior Minister in the French Government) and Elmar Brok, were a finely balanced team – Socialist and Christian

Democrat Members of Parliament respectively; one French and one German.

The participation for the first time of the European Parliament in such an "intergovernmental" group, albeit one established for the purposes of reflection, was a recognition of its increasingly important role in the European Union. The two MEPs, working in close collaboration with the then President of the Parliament, Klaus Hänsch, made an important contribution to the work of the Reflection Group and later to the IGC itself. They acted, to an extent, as the European "conscience" of the negotiations. Importantly, they did so in a focused and realistic way. It would be all too easy for the Parliament's approach to become a compendium of single issues, an amalgam of good causes. What was more difficult and at the same time more important for the Parliament was to be relevant and to have a real impact. That the Parliament had such an impact is due to the coherence imposed by the individuals involved on the generally positive but potentially diffuse instincts of the Parliament.

Eighteen deputies were also around the table, in the case of the Member States essentially Foreign Ministry officials.

Flanking the Spanish Presidency and completing the dramatis personae were officials of the Council Secretariat, the experienced Brussels-based European civil servants who support each succeeding six-monthly Presidency. They are sometimes affectionately known as "the permanent Presidency".

Inevitably there were some national sensitivities in the air. In the usual European manner a way was found to accommodate those sensitivities. The Reflection Group, whose work would coincide largely with the Spanish Presidency of the European Union in the second half of 1995, was starting on 3 June at the tail-end of the *French* Presidency but already with a *Spanish* Chairman. Moreover, because of the historical Messina commemoration ceremony, the first meeting of the Group was in *Italy*. The matter was handled delicately by Carlos Westendorp. He arranged that the Italian Foreign Minister would address the opening meeting of the Reflection Group and that the meetings of the Group prior to the European Council in Cannes later in June (the culmination of the French Presidency) would be on what he called a "provisional" basis. The Cannes European Council would "launch" the Reflection Group.

A bell calls the meeting to order. *Les jeux sont faits.* A silence of expectancy on centre court. Spain to serve. The Italian Foreign Minister, Susanna Agnelli, speaks briefly about the work of the Conference (lamenting the almost complete absence of women around the table). She greets warmly the Parliament's appointment of Elisabeth Guigou to the Group.

Before moving to a first discussion of the substance, certain procedural aspects of the work of the Reflection Group had to be addressed. Westendorp emphasized that the members of the Group were "personal" representatives of Foreign Ministers. They should, therefore, be as free as possible to speak on a "personal" basis. The purpose at this stage, he stressed, was reflection rather than negotiation.

From the point of view of the Presidency, the chairman was sending the right message. However, the message was easier stated than acted on. The European Union is still, as I argue in this book, made up of competing and overlapping interests, principally national interests. It would not be realistic to believe that those interests can be ignored by those who represent the Member States, even if they are designated as *personal* representatives.

A work programme was agreed. There would be about three meetings a month – mostly in Brussels. Each meeting would involve a combination of formal sessions and informal working dinners. A first synthesis report would be prepared by the Presidency during the summer.

Two further important procedural considerations emerged clearly at that first meeting of the Reflection Group.

First, it was evident that each meeting of the Group would inevitably take a long time. A relatively short, straightforward *tour de table* (or table-round), allowing each of the 17 delegations to intervene for three minutes, would take almost an hour. A *tour de table*, as would often be the case, on a complex range of issues would take two to three hours. There would, therefore, be no alternative to frequent and relatively lengthy meetings.

Second, the importance of keeping the public informed was recognized by delegations from the outset. The press would be briefed by the chairman after every meeting (a practice which was carried through at the IGC by all subsequent Presidencies). Individual members of the Reflection Group would also be free to brief the media. A degree of confidentiality, appropriate to an intergovernmental negotiation, about the positions taken by individual delegations should be maintained. But there was a determination that the mistakes of the Maastricht Treaty, which had been seen by the public in some Member States as the result of a secret negotiation by experts behind closed doors, would not be repeated.

The chairman then moved discussion on to the substance. Very tentative. Very preliminary.

Each of the areas identified by the Presidency for consideration by the Reflection Group was to be examined in some detail at later meetings of the Group. At the first meeting of the Group, each Personal Representative made an initial statement on points of particular concern against the background of the areas identified. Each emphasized some points as important and other points which in their view should not be pursued. It was very much a first discussion. No formal or specific conclusions could be drawn. However, already a number of points were becoming clear.

First, the priorities of Representatives were quite different and sometimes contradictory.

Second, there was already an emphasis on a number of issues of direct concern to citizens. Employment, in particular, was emphasized by a number of Representatives as an area in which the treaty provisions should be strengthened.

Third, the institutional area was clearly from the outset one of the most sensitive ones.

The Presidency had identified in advance eight broad topics for consideration by the Reflection Group:

(1) Challenges and Objectives

The challenges facing the Union; the fundamental principles and objectives of the Union; the nature and scope of the Conference.

(2) The Institutional System I: Institutional Balance

This covered the adaptation of the institutional balance to the new context and in particular to the requirements of further enlargement of the Union. The Presidency suggested a reform directed at strengthening democracy, efficiency and transparency in the decision-making process.

(3) The Institutional System II: The Institutions

The modifications considered necessary in respect of each institution.

(4) The Citizen and the Union I: European Citizenship

The definition, content and development of "European citizenship"; fundamental rights; the need for a treaty comprehensible to the citizen.

(5) The Citizen and the Union II: An Area of Freedom and Security

The development of cooperation in the area of Justice and Home Affairs.

(6) The Union's External and Security Policy I: External Action by the Union

Improving the coherence of the Union's external policy; strengthening the Common Foreign and Security Policy.

(7) The Union's External and Security Policy II: Security and Defence

This covered an examination of existing concepts in the light of changes in the general context of European security and defence; links between EU/WEU/(NATO).

(8) Instruments at the Union's Disposal

- Community law: including subsidiarity ("Who does what?")

- Resources: the system of the Union's budgetary resources (so-called "own resources"), budgetary powers, the adequacy of resources

- Policies: deepening common policies; new fields of actions.

Fourth, the issue of introducing new "flexibility" mechanisms into the Treaties – to increase the scope for action within the Union's institutions by a number of Member States less than the full membership – was signalled as a significant issue. It was seen as important both by some delegations who favoured it and, perhaps even more, by a few that appeared already quite defensive about it.

Fifth, to the surprise of nobody, the position of the United Kingdom, while expressed constructively by Minister of State David Davis, was, to put it carefully, going to be "distinctive".

Sixth, there was no sense of an agenda being driven from any particular direction. At that stage, for example, I had no sense of a clear overall Franco-German approach which in the past has often acted as a "motor" for the development of the European Union.

In short, there appeared at the first meeting of the Reflection Group to be a recognition of the challenges ahead as well as the stirrings of a common searching for the best way forward. The Belgian delegation at that first meeting quoted Kissinger's comment that "if you don't know where you're going, any road will take you there". There were roads all over the place. The common challenge for the Reflection Group was to help to identify the direction in which we should be travelling.

The work and role of the Reflection Group: Survival of the Fittest Ideas

In addressing its work over the next six months, the Reflection Group was by no means operating in a vacuum.

First, the Maastricht Treaty of 1992, in providing for an IGC to be convened in 1996, had already identified some specific issues for consideration:

(i)   a review of the Common Foreign and Security Policy

(ii)   a possible extension of the number of areas in which the European Parliament acts in "co-decision" with the other arm of the legislative authority of the Union, namely the Council of Ministers

(iii)   the possibility of extending the explicit competence of the Union to act in the areas of energy, tourism and civil protection

(iv)   consideration of the nature of the legislative instruments of the Union (a possible "hierarchy of norms", in the ghastly jargon of Brussels – Norman Lamont, Norman Fowler and Norman Tebbit, I suggested to a British colleague).

The mechanism whereby one IGC can identify items for consideration at a future IGC is in effect one of the European Union's many forms of compromise. If some Member States wish to go further on an issue than others are prepared to go, the identification of the issue for further consideration at a future date goes at least some way towards meeting the concerns of the disappointed delegations, if not substantively then presentationally and with some procedural comfort for the future.

A second given element in the work of the Reflection Group was that several European Councils subsequent to Maastricht, influenced by the growing and shifting challenges facing the Union, had identified further items for consideration by the IGC, including further institutional reform with a view to the prospective further enlargement of the Union to include the countries of Central and Eastern Europe as well as Cyprus.

Third, as a contribution to the preparation of the Conference, each of the Union's institutions had, earlier in 1995, prepared reports on the functioning of the Union. These now also formed part of the background as the Reflection Group set about its work.

Fourth, the challenges faced by the Union (summarized in Chapter 1) which the IGC was to help to address were real challenges of the greatest importance, and not random imaginings from the "heat-oppressed brain" of Brussels bureaucrats.

All in all, the IGC would have plenty to chew on.

However, none of this background constituted in any sense a formal agenda for the IGC which was due to open in 1996. At an IGC each delegation can propose changing the Treaties in any way it considers appropriate. An IGC is not bound to change the

Treaties on issues previously signalled for consideration. Equally it is entirely free to change the Treaties in relation to matters which have not been signalled in advance.

The Reflection Group was set up precisely to help to give shape to the agenda of the IGC. It set itself the task of preparing what it called an "annotated agenda" for the Conference.

Technically speaking, the Group was, as indicated above, set up for the purpose of reflection rather than negotiation. Its members were "personal representatives" of the 15 Foreign Ministers and of the Presidents of the Commission and the European Parliament. The Reflection Group did involve a somewhat more flexible floating of ideas than would have been possible within the constraints of a formal negotiating process. But it would be an illusion to think that national interests could simply have been set aside in such a process. National interests are not a minor irritant in the European Union, to be lightly dismissed. They are not a sad anachronism to be wearily condescended to. They are at the heart of the process. The great challenge for Member States is to define those national interests not narrowly but with a wider European vision and in a longer-term European perspective.

Some spirits at the Reflection Group were freer than others. The European Parliament's Representatives, for example, as well as the Commission played an important role in highlighting the broader picture and the common interest. Indeed, some of the Member State representatives (a few of whom were academics rather than politicians or officials) appeared less bound by a detailed national position than others. But in the case of every Member State, it is fair to say that the choice of its representative and the negotiating flexibility afforded to that representative reflected that Member State's perception of its own interests. No national position of importance was conceded in the course of the work of the Reflection Group.

The nature of the negotiating process from beginning to end, from the beginning of the Reflection Group to the end of the IGC, was what I call *the survival of the fittest ideas*. The process through which the myriad ideas and proposals ultimately found their way into the Treaty of Amsterdam some two years later, or more often fell by the wayside, was a form of diplomatic Darwinism.

Some of the ideas seeking to survive in the Reflection Group, in the first round of the evolutionary cycle, were strong, well-formed creatures with every prospect of emerging from the miasmic lake. Other shapeless, amoeba-like creatures, unable to fend for themselves, were doomed from the start. Yet others were to pass through several mutations and evolutionary phases and, by adapting themselves to their environment, to find their way almost unrecognizable into the Treaty of Amsterdam.

The Spanish Presidency, as indicated above, had identified eight broad topics for consideration by the Reflection Group. Meetings of the Group were held about three times a month, usually in Brussels but on occasion elsewhere (Strasbourg and Madrid). Meetings lasted necessarily the best part of two days.

For the first two months, June and July 1995, the topics were addressed on the basis of questionnaires prepared and circulated in advance by the Presidency. In August the Presidency prepared, on its own responsibility, an interim report which formed the principal basis for the subsequent discussions of the Group. A number of papers were also tabled by individual delegations.

The work of the Group was directed essentially towards its final report to the Madrid European Council on 15 and 16 December 1995. The closer the report came to finalization, the more the "reflection" gave way to a detailed drafting exercise in the course of which each Representative sought to ensure that the point of view of his or her government or institution was adequately reflected in the report. Part of the final drafting exercise was carried out at the level of deputies under the chairmanship of Westendorp's deputy, Emilio Castano.

The Reflection Group's final report, submitted on 5 December 1995, was in two parts. The first, shorter part was called "A Strategy for Europe". The second, longer part was entitled "An Annotated Agenda". The report identified three main areas for the work of the IGC:

(i)   making Europe more relevant to its citizens

(ii)   enabling Europe to work better and preparing it for enlargement

(iii)   giving the Union greater capacity for external action.

The report set out under those three broad headings the views of the Reflection Group on the wide range of issues it had considered. The report was an "agreed" report, but only in the sense that there was agreement on how to deal in the report with issues on which there was no substantive agreement. While much of the report is couched in terms of the views of the Reflection Group as a whole, on all the most sensitive points differences of view remained. This reality is reflected in the report either by the setting out of alternative options or by formulations such as "a broad majority", "some members", or indeed "one member" (more often than not the United Kingdom).

The European Council in Madrid concluded that the Reflection Group report constituted "a sound basis for the work of the Conference".

After the last meeting of the Reflection Group early in December, I asked an official from the Spanish Presidency for his assessment of what the relationship would be between the Reflection Group's report and the subsequent work of the IGC. He said, without hesitation, "historical". This remark was candid (coming from a Presidency which had done a very good job in chairing the Group) and at the same time perceptive. The Reflection Group had not shifted Member States from their basic positions and its report was not set to become a reference document for the IGC itself.

What purpose can the Reflection Group then be said to have served?

Any assessment of the work of the Group must take account of the magnitude of the challenge it faced. It is no mean task to begin to sketch out a direction for a Europe which is being pulled in the potentially opposite directions of widening and deepening, a Europe in which significantly competing interests remain at stake, a Europe in which the support of a public with heterogeneous priorities must be retained and strengthened. That task was made no easier by the somewhat artificial timing of the IGC as explained above.

The importance and effectiveness of the work of the Reflection Group should not be exaggerated. The question of whether somewhat different preparatory mechanisms should be considered for future IGCs is touched on in the last chapter of this book. However, the Group served a number of useful purposes.

First, the Reflection Group clarified the issues and brought them together sufficiently to facilitate the opening of the IGC in the first half of 1996. Importantly, it did this in a way which left all Member States comfortable with the process. Any attempt to have forced premature agreement on individual issues would have soured the atmosphere and served no useful purpose.

Second, it facilitated the development of good personal relations between many of those who would later have to work together at the IGC and helped to create a good atmosphere for the IGC negotiations. This was due in considerable measure to the able and correct chairmanship provided by Carlos Westendorp and the Spanish Presidency. (The correctness of a Presidency, namely the neutral conduct of its chairing function and its alertness to the concerns of all, is not something which can always be taken for granted despite the fact that any other approach inevitably has a negative effect on Europe and usually also on the Presidency concerned.)

Third, the work of the Reflection Group forced national administrations and the European institutions concerned, and the individuals working in them, to start the lengthy process of coming to grips with the complex issues involved and developing positions on them. It gave each delegation a clear picture, in advance of the IGC, of the priorities and concerns of others. The involvement of the European Parliament (for the first time in such a process) proved constructive and useful.

Fourth, it represented the first phase in the slow evolutionary process, referred to above, in which only the fittest ideas would survive. Life was breathed into certain species of proposal which would be good for Europe and at the same time have some prospect of gaining unanimous agreement at the Conference. Such healthier species began to take root and adapted themselves gradually in order to survive in their negotiating environment. At the same time, many less healthy specimens were encouraged to slope off towards their natural demise.

Through this process of diplomatic Darwinism, some proposals received growing support at the Reflection Group – such as limiting the size of the European Parliament to a maximum of 700 in an enlarged Union, spelling out the principle of fundamental rights in the Treaty, providing for the possibility of sanctions in respect of a Member State in serious and repeated breach of those rights, and strengthening the Treaty's non-discrimination provisions. The possibility of incorporating new flexibility provisions in the Treaties developed as a particularly significant issue. Perhaps the most important trend emerging from the discussions of the Reflection Group was the emphasis on addressing the direct concerns of citizens in areas such as employment and the fight against international crime.

Other proposals, however, started to drift back into the quicksand of time and must have begun to contemplate their prospects for survival at the IGC with the optimism of a dodo – including, for example, the extension of explicit Community competence to act in new areas such as energy and tourism, the development of European "citizenship" as such, and the idea of altering significantly the balance between the institutions to the detriment of the Commission.

A number of other issues, although their importance was recognized, were clearly signalled as not being appropriate for consideration *by the IGC*. These included the existing treaty provisions on Economic and Monetary Union as well as questions relating to own resources and the development of the Union's main common policies.

The Reflection Group can be said to have carried out efficiently the difficult mandate set for it. Some limited progress was made. I leave the last word on the Reflection Group to the two lists on the following page, which I drew up during a quiet moment at the Group.

Sounds heard at the IGC Reflection Group
Alarm bells ringing
Axes being ground
Dead horses being flogged
Fiddling while Europe burns
Hobby horses breathing heavily
Jean Monnet turning in his grave
Sabres (and begging bowls) being rattled
Cans of worms being opened
Red herrings splashing
Some Personal Representatives singing from the same hymn sheet
The cries of hostages being taken (but not given)
Lip service being paid
Pandora's box being slammed shut
Antes being upped
Common denominators being lowered
Bets being hedged
Deckchairs being rearranged
Nits being picked
Wheels being reinvented
Hairs being split
Spare paddles being stored in the bottoms of canoes
Angels jostling each other in a very confined space
Grandmothers sucking eggs (under instruction)

Sounds definitely not heard at the IGC Reflection Group
Heads being banged together
Floodgates being opened
Cards being laid on the table
Blank cheques being written
Chickens being counted
Circles being squared
Bombshells being dropped (or pennies beginning to do so)
Swords being beaten into ploughshares
Bridges being burned
Brass tacks being got down to
Turkey being talked
Parsnips being buttered

Chapter 4

The Human Factor

How can we know the dancer from the dance?
(W.B. Yeats, *Among School Children*)

Negotiations involve people. The issues addressed, the positions taken and the solutions reached are not free-floating notions in an elaborate mindgame. A negotiation, such as that leading to the Treaty of Amsterdam, consists as much of the people involved as of the ideas they bring to the negotiating table.

The dancer and the dance are, in a sense, inseparable. In the European Union, of course, it takes 15 to tango.

A summary account of the IGC negotiations, which is all that is possible in this book, tends inevitably to focus on underlying ideas and trends. It tends to present the wide-lens shot of the emerging pyramid rather than zooming in on the army of workers who are labouring on its construction. For someone involved in the construction, however, it is the people that are at the forefront. It is the people that constitute the sights and the sounds, the conflicts and the friendships, the reality of the experience. When I look back at the two years of negotiations I see people, not paper.

Apart from confidentiality considerations, there is an obvious constraint in describing individuals involved in the negotiations. The singling out of some for admiration could wrongly be interpreted as implicit criticism of others. The present book would, however, represent a quite incomplete picture were I not to say something about the people involved in the IGC.

The human factor, of course, had many dimensions reaching deep into each national administration and, indeed, the media. I will, however, focus my brief comments on the negotiators themselves.

The IGC Representatives

The IGC Representatives Group was the pivot around which the negotiations turned. At the outset there had been much discussion as to what category of people should be appointed to this Group. The choice was rightly left to each Member State, since the appointment in each case had to respond to different pressures and to meet a different set of requirements. The appointment of a mixture of Ministers of State, Permanent Representatives and others worked smoothly. A list of the IGC Representatives is given in Annex 2.

The Representatives Group brought together, and was seen to bring together, an effective mixture of technical expertise and political nous. No apartheid was practised between different classes of Representative. Indeed, Ministers demonstrated a grasp of a level of detail which is usually left to officials, and the officials were capable of being every bit as political as the Ministers.

It takes all types, of course. Some Representatives took a broader view of the issues at stake and defined and presented their specific concerns accordingly. Others tended to focus on more narrowly defined national concerns. While some had a relatively straightforward job, for others it was trickier. One in particular, with a general election in prospect, had to cope with the possibility of being required to switch horses in midstream.

Some Representatives were content to remain in the lowlands of ambition. Others on occasion wandered so high up the moral high ground that, if they stood on their tiptoes, they could just about catch a glimpse of cloud-cuckoo-land. Some based their interventions on carefully prepared speaking points. Others didn't have a note in sight. Some were kept on a tighter rein by their capitals than others. The succinct and the long-winded. Graduates of the various schools of international diplomacy, including the distinguished Mike Tyson academy.

Every single intervention involved its own tactical choices. Intervene *early* to set the tone for the discussion (or because there was an early plane to catch). Intervene *late* to make it possible to take the temperature before speaking or to provide cover – it's sometimes more comfortable to intervene in support of previously enunciated positions. Intervene comprehensively on every aspect or focus on key concerns only? Low-key or tough? Whether to risk a joke?

It is fair to say that the Representatives brought an exceptional array of talents to the negotiations. Some of the Representatives were *outstanding intellects* – individuals as bright, razor-sharp and articulate as one could meet. Another category, overlapping with the first, is what I would call the particularly *effective negotiators*. Effective negotiation requires a subtle mix of skills.

Although the Representatives had strong and distinctive personalities, they also had a great deal in common: an ability to explain, a willingness (usually) to listen, an exceptional capacity for hard work. Each Representative brought to bear a mastery of complex detail on a vast array of issues, an ability to present in a coherent way evolving and sometimes internally incoherent national positions, and indeed a commitment to the process above any obvious call of duty.

The camaraderie between negotiators may, just on occasion, reflect a little touch of what one might imagine was the mixture of profound empathy and edgy respect between gladiators of old, girding up for a mortal combat not of their making.

Together, the Representatives, applying their skills as much to persuasion and presentation at home as to the bargaining and huxtering in Brussels, managed to do the difficult business of transforming the dogged pursuit of conflicting national interests into something which could serve the collective interests of Europe.

I cannot pass without brief comment on my own opposite numbers, the deputies to the IGC Representatives from other Member States and the Commission. Breach-fillers, Foible-handlers, Human Filofaxes, Creatures of the Shadows – thanks for the help, the understanding and especially the humour. See you at the next *Jeux sans Frontières*!

The political level

The human factor was, of course, important at every level, and much of what I have said about the IGC Representatives Group applies to other levels also.

The negotiation was a political one. The 15 Heads of State or Government, in addition to their preparatory discussions and to their involvement in the launch of the IGC at Turin, met to advance the work of the Conference no fewer than five times in 15 months. It was they who eventually struck the key deals at Amsterdam.

Perhaps surprisingly, the personal relations between individual members of the European Council seem to count for more in negotiating terms than such personal relations at any other level (see also Chapter 2). To an extent this may reflect the fact that, at the highest level, there is greater scope for adapting or even abandoning national positions with a view to an overall deal or indeed with an eye on some wider picture beyond the scope of the particular negotiation. Personal sympathy or irritation as well as the negotiating skills of individuals can play a very significant part in determining the outcome of a European Council.

Foreign Ministers devoted great amounts of time and skill to advancing the work of the IGC at their monthly Ministerial meetings. At that level, which involved the refinement of the emerging package rather than the striking of deals, what mattered most was the coherent, constructive presentation of national positions. Of course, the relationship between personalities counts at Ministerial level as at every level, but personality at that level is often to an extent indivisible from the presentation of firm and detailed national positions. Although many of the Ministers are particularly colourful and humorous individuals, the interplay of character at formal Ministerial sessions is at times somewhat akin to the profound but stylized dialogue of Greek tragedy.

The interplay between different levels

One sometimes hears it suggested about a European negotiation that the level of ambition has been dampened by bureaucrats. If only the politicians had been allowed to act "politically", we are told, the story would have been very different. If only the real negotiations had been conducted at the level of Heads of State or Government instead of at Ministerial level. If only they had been conducted at full Ministerial level instead of at the more technical level of IGC Representatives (which brought together officials as well as politicians).

This sort of wishful thinking portrays a misleading, or at best a very partial, picture.

Those negotiating at a more technical level do not operate in a vacuum. They act under the political guidance and control of their Governments. If anything, their instinct, if given a freer hand, would probably be to go further than the political level. Whatever their starting point may be, they are at the daily interface in Brussels of competing ideas. The ideas which they hear from others are often convincing and sensible. They can come quickly to see the weaknesses in their own positions and the strengths in those of others.

At the same time, Ministers are in their own way guided by those working at a more technical level. Ministers cannot decide their approach in a vacuum. They must be given the facts. The options and their consequences, the possibilities and the constraints, must be explained to them. In our democratic system it is the politicians who must face their electorates and who must sell the deals. It is therefore they who must call the shots. When the European Union is perceived by some to lack ambition, it is likely to say more about what the public at large wants (or what politicians think it wants) than about the hesitations of insiders.

The relationship between the political and official levels in the European Union is necessarily a symbiotic one.

Of course, politicians – unlike officials – may on rare occasions decide to throw caution to the wind. They can opt to take a significant leap forward. If they do, it is not their officials they have to bring with them, but their voters. That's democracy. Politicians know it. They are all too conscious of the human factor.

The accommodation of difference

It should be recalled that the collective ethos in the European Union combines the pursuit of interests with the accommodation of difference. It is not an ethos according to which the race is always to the swift, the battle to the strong; or where the weak are expected to go to the wall (although you should never turn your back for too long).

Of course, by definition, the eventual agreement at the IGC – which required unanimity – would have to be acceptable to every delegation. However, the ethos of accommodation goes much deeper in the European Union than any formal unanimity requirement. The spirit of attempting to reconcile differences applies even where decisions do not have to be agreed unanimously. This reflects the wider interest of every Member State in obtaining the understanding of others. It is a question of "there but for the grace of God". More profoundly, the ethos of accommodation reflects also the tentative flowering in individuals of a sense of being European. The surest thing one could do to nip such flowering in the bud would be to overestimate the depth of its roots.

Negotiators in the European Union are the human shock-absorbers between strongly and naturally competing views. They are the reconcilers of contradictory wish-lists, the fudgers of incompatible bottom lines. Their work constitutes the decompression chamber between Original Sin and the Brave New World, the paradox at the heart of this book.

"O brave new world/That has such people in't!"

PART II

TAKING SHAPE

Chapter 5

The Italian Job

The time is out of joint
(Shakespeare, *Hamlet*)

The IGC was to span three Presidencies and to trickle into a fourth. It opened during the Italian Presidency in March 1996, continued during the Irish Presidency in the second half of that year and was brought substantively to completion by the end of the Netherlands Presidency in June 1997. The texts were tidied up and finalized in all languages between July and September 1997, the first months of the Luxembourg Presidency.

The central problem for the Italian Presidency was the timing of the IGC. At one and the same time it was being held back and expected to move faster. The Tour de France and the slow bicycle race were rolled into a single event.

The Italian Presidency had drawn the shortest straw in the scope it was given for advancing the work of the IGC. Its central difficulty was the view of many Member States that there was no urgency about either opening or concluding the negotiations. Time pressure concentrates minds wonderfully. It forces delegations to think strategically, to focus on a limited number of key concerns and to move towards compromise. In the absence of time constraints, there is little if any incentive for delegations to begin to engage in negotiations.

It will be recalled that the IGC was set to take place in 1996 because the Maastricht Treaty had provided that that should be the case. Beyond that procedural requirement there was no substantive reason or fundamental concern that the IGC should proceed with particular urgency during the Italian Presidency in the first half of 1996.

Moreover, informally there was a growing recognition in many delegations that the IGC could not conclude until after the general election in the United Kingdom which was due to be held no later than May 1997. With the Conservative Government lagging behind in the opinion polls, the widespread expectation was that it would run its full course. Some Member States looked forward to what was expected to be a more constructive approach to Europe by a new Labour Government. However, the anticipated Labour victory was to an extent irrelevant to the growing belief that the IGC could not conclude until the British election had taken place. The essential point was the perception that a deal could not be struck with a British Government of either political hue until the election was out of the way. (The British delegation, while recognizing the likelihood that the IGC would have to last some time, did not itself seek to establish any linkage between the duration of the IGC and the timing of its own impending general election.)

There was also a minority contrary view that the IGC should be short and sharp. This reflected a wish to leave the Union free, as soon as possible, to move ahead to address some of the other major issues on its agenda, including enlargement and EMU, as well as a desire to have the IGC out of the way in advance of electoral rendezvous in certain other Member States. However, a short IGC – in advance of a British general election – presupposed a lowering of ambition which would not have been acceptable to many delegations. An artificial and unnecessary time-limit on the work of the Conference should not, it was argued, be allowed to determine its level of ambition.

Thus, far from there being pressure for the IGC to be completed as soon as possible, there was a growing understanding that a lengthy Conference was inevitable. The dilemma for the Italian Presidency was that it would be judged, including by the media, on its stewardship of the Tour de France although many of the cyclists were under instructions to treat it as a slow bicycle race.

Against the background of those constraints, the Italian Presidency could not have been run with greater vision, efficiency or charm. The Presidency reflected the essential qualities of commitment to advancing the European agenda combined with a genuine sensitivity to the concerns of all. These qualities, which for some Presidencies represent an astute tactical choice, seem to come naturally to Italy.

The European Council in Madrid in December 1995 had taken note that the IGC would be officially opened in Turin on 29 March 1996; that is, already halfway through the Italian Presidency. The Italian Presidency was thus divided into two three-month phases: the first phase, from January to March, leading up to the launching of the IGC by the European Council at Turin; the second phase, from April to June, consisting of the first three months of the Conference itself leading up to the European Council in Florence in June.

January to March 1996: preparations for launching the IGC

Certain formalities for the launching of the IGC had to be completed during the first quarter of 1996. Formal opinions on the convening of the IGC were to be issued by the European Commission, the European Parliament and the Council of Ministers. While the preparation of those opinions involved a considerable amount of debate within the Commission and the Parliament, leading to a fine-tuning of their respective approaches, the opinion of the Council of Ministers was a formality.

During that period, Member States proceeded to nominate their respective members of the IGC Representatives Group – a mixture of five Ministers of State, six Permanent Representatives, three senior or retired officials, and one Member of the European Parliament (representing Greece). The European Commission nominated one of its Members to the Representatives Group. (The full list is given in Annex 2.)

During those first three months of 1996, the interval between the Reflection Group and the IGC itself, there were no weekly meetings of the Fifteen relating to the work of the Conference. This offered delegations an opportunity to focus on developing their own national positions on the complex array of issues that was emerging. It should be recalled in this context that, while this book focuses essentially on negotiations *at the level of the Fifteen*, there were also positions to be developed and refined (in a sense, "permanent negotiations") *within* each Member State throughout the Conference. Indeed, significant differences of view persisted within some delegations until the final hours of the Conference at Amsterdam.

The stated positions of delegations in the negotiations can be understood as the tips of a flotilla of icebergs – the relatively small portion of individual national positions which could be seen above the surface. Many national concerns and aims and dilemmas are not intended for wider consumption, at least in undigested form. Moreover, it is a safe bet that individual negotiators rarely, if ever, convey every detail of the briefs with which they have been provided.

The mind of a negotiator is focused not just on the impact of his or her interventions on other delegations, but also on the perception of those interventions at home. The precise nature and tone of an intervention often reflect an attempt to reconcile competing interests on the domestic front. Paradoxically, the expression of an "opposing" point of view in the negotiations can sometimes be music to the ears of a negotiator hoping to kill off some doomed notion which he or she has been asked to plug. Some negotiators, when they wish to do so, are skilled at conveying to other delegations that they are taking a somewhat daft national hobby horse for a trot around the course. They convey this not by *what* they say but by their body language and *how* they say it. (For example, a negotiator can subtly convey in putting forward an idea that he is acting under instructions with which he is not in full agreement; or he may comment with a knowing smile, after a proposal he has put forward has been shot down in flames, that he has "noted carefully the position of other delegations".)

The relatively fallow period from January to March 1996 also offered an opportunity for delegations to conduct extensive bilateral contacts in advance of the opening of the IGC. Such bilateral contacts, which continued of course during the Conference, are an essential channel for conveying and understanding the often unspoken *reasons* for the national positions taken. It is possible to tease out national concerns in more detail and often with greater frankness in the context of such bilateral meetings.

The Italian Presidency also organized a very useful trilateral meeting in Rome with the two Presidencies set to follow it in chairing the IGC, namely Ireland and the Netherlands. This was followed by a further such trilateral meeting in the second half of the Italian Presidency. (There was always the possibility – which eventually became a reality – that the IGC could run into the Luxembourg Presidency in the second half of 1997. However, to have included Luxembourg also in Presidency-to-Presidency coordination early in 1996 would have sent unhelpfully pessimistic signals about the prospects for conclusion of the Conference at Amsterdam.)

Presidency-to-Presidency coordination is of the greatest importance from a practical and political point of view. The achievements of one Presidency are either the welcome legacy or the poisoned chalice of the next. Relations between Presidencies, of course, need to be handled delicately. The need for a smooth and strategic transition from one Presidency to the next must be combined with respect for the independence and responsibility of each. Italy's cooperation with the incoming Irish Presidency reflected the professionalism and courtesy manifested by the conduct of its Presidency as a whole.

Against this background, the Italian Presidency faced one significant task before the Turin European Council in March, and it set itself another task.

The role of the European Parliament at the IGC

The specific task which fell to the Italian Presidency was to obtain agreement on a formula for associating the European Parliament with the work of the Conference. The only *formal* role assigned to the European Parliament by the Treaties in relation to an IGC is that the Parliament must give an opinion on the convening of an IGC. After that, from a strictly formal point of view, the Parliament is out of the picture. In practice, of course, it has an opportunity to make its views known. Moreover, while it has no formal legal right to reject the outcome of an IGC, a negative verdict from the Parliament on the outcome of an IGC would have important political consequences. Indeed, rejection by the European Parliament might lead some national parliaments to refuse to ratify a Treaty.

A large majority of delegations, while recognizing that the Parliament could not appropriately be a participant at an Intergovernmental Conference on a fully equal footing with the Member States or the European Commission, considered that the Parliament should be more closely associated with the 1996 IGC than it had been with previous ones. (During previous IGCs the Parliament, while having the opportunity to make its views known at specially convened meetings outside the IGC as such, had been kept at arm's length.)

The participation of the Parliament's Representatives on an equal footing in the preparatory Reflection Group in 1995 had been accepted by all delegations because that had not been a formal *intergovernmental negotiating forum*. The Parliament's participation at the Reflection Group had proved to be a particular success and had created certain expectations on the part of the Parliament with regard to the IGC itself. Most delegations favoured, or at least could have accepted, the systematic presence and participation of the Parliament at the IGC negotiations, without according it the formal rights of a full participant at the Conference, including the formal right to approve the outcome.

However, a small number of Member States considered that such systematic presence and participation of the European Parliament would be at variance with the nature of an IGC, which is defined in the Treaties as "a conference of the representatives of the governments of the Member States". Some other delegations, which did not take that position, had some sympathy for it.

The task of the Italian Presidency was to work out a formula which would be acceptable to all the Member States and, at the same time, to the European Parliament. As a result of delicate footwork by the Italian Presidency over a period of many weeks, such a formula was eventually agreed by Foreign Ministers on the occasion of the General Affairs Council on 26 March. The formula involved the principle that "the European Parliament will be closely associated with the work of the Conference to enable it to have regular and detailed information on the progress of discussions and to make known its point of view on any matter discussed whenever it feels this to be necessary".

A series of practical arrangements were also agreed to give effect to this:

- the President of the European Parliament would have an exchange of views with Heads of State or Government and Foreign Ministers respectively on the occasion of each European Council and General Affairs Council

- at least once a month the Presidency would arrange for a working meeting between the IGC Representatives Group and the Parliament's IGC Representatives (in practice this formal monthly meeting was supplemented by a more informal monthly discussion, usually over dinner)

- moreover, the Presidency would regularly provide information to the European Parliament (in practice this meant a weekly meeting between the Presidency and the Parliament's Representatives).

These arrangements, while not going as far as some would have wished, provided an unprecedented opportunity for the Parliament to have a significant input into the work of the IGC – an opportunity which it used to considerable effect.

The Parliament's ability to influence the work of the IGC was greatly facilitated by its ability to speak with a single effective voice. This resulted in part from the reappointment, as the Parliament's two IGC Representatives, of its two Reflection Group members, Elisabeth Guigou (Socialist) and Elmar Brok (European People's Party), a combination reflecting the two main political tendencies in the Parliament. Apart from that balance within the Parliament's delegation, the personal contribution of those Representatives to the presentation of a coherent Parliament strategy should not be underestimated. The Parliament's IGC Representatives, of course, received essential support from many others in the Parliament at political and official level, including President Hänsch and later, more briefly, President Gil-Robles. The Parliament's effective and experienced back-up team included Richard Corbett, a theologian of the Union's institutions, soon to be elected as a Member of the European Parliament himself.

The Parliament's strategy was at once upbeat and realistic, involving a targeted focusing on key issues rather than a scatter-gun approach. The Parliament's striking sensitivity to the concerns of all Member States, including smaller Member States, enhanced its credibility.

The preparation of conclusions for the Turin European Council

The second task, which the Italian Presidency set itself during its first three months, was to work towards substantive conclusions at the European Council in Turin on the occasion of the launch of the IGC. Its problem in that regard was that it had no negotiating forum for the preparation of such conclusions. The Reflection Group had run its course. The IGC Representatives Group would come into existence only with the IGC itself. The challenge the Italian Presidency set itself was thus to work towards unanimously agreed conclusions during a period when in effect negotiations had been suspended.

The Presidency needed, therefore, to invent a procedure to address this challenge. It decided to set about the task through bilateral meetings with each Member State, either in Rome or in the respective capitals. The Irish delegation, for example, had three such meetings with the Italian Presidency. The Presidency understandably decided that, while it would show delegations at bilateral meetings a draft of the conclusions on which it was working and invite comments, it would not allow delegations to retain a copy of those draft conclusions. It is difficult enough, dealing bilaterally with 15 delegations, to develop unanimous agreement on a text. It would, in the Presidency's view, have become impossible if that text had been put into circulation and become subject to specific detailed drafting comments from 15 delegations unaware of the comments being made by the other delegations.

In the event, the Presidency succeeded in producing conclusions which could be accepted by all delegations at Turin. The draft of those conclusions was handed over to delegations and discussed multilaterally for the first time at an informal meeting of IGC Representatives (the first time they had met as a group) in Turin on 28 March, the eve of the European Council.

The Turin conclusions represented a further step in shaping the work of the IGC and provided an appropriate impetus on the occasion of its launch. As in the case of the Reflection Group, however, Member States inevitably were not prepared to concede positions in advance of the negotiations. This is reflected in the nature of the Turin conclusions which did not prejudge the scope or substance of the negotiations in any significant way. While the Turin conclusions represented an advance on the "one/some/most Member State(s)" formulation of the Reflection Group report, they reflected the continuing lack of agreement on substance either by remaining relatively general or by requesting the IGC to "examine" certain issues (sometimes even *whether* and how to achieve certain aims).

On 29 March the European Council formally adopted the conclusions without difficulty. At the first formal meeting of the IGC that afternoon, which took place at Ministerial level, delegations set out in broad terms their key concerns in relation to the negotiations. Practical modalities developed by the Presidency for the conduct of at least the initial phase of the IGC (e.g. frequency of meetings, linguistic regime, arrangements for briefing the applicant countries to join the EU) were also implicitly agreed.

April to June 1996: the opening months of the IGC

The Italian Presidency arranged an intensive work programme for the first three months of the IGC, covering the period from the beginning of April 1996 to the European Council at Florence on 21 and 22 June.

Meetings of the IGC Representatives Group (normally lasting two days) were scheduled every week and a Ministerial IGC meeting was scheduled every month. The Presidency organized the work under three broad topics: (i) citizenship (including the direct concerns of citizens); (ii) institutions; (iii) external action. It scheduled two "readings" at Representative level and one reading at Ministerial level of each of the topics.

The IGC Representatives Group sets sail

The IGC Representatives Group was to meet for the next 15 months, on a more or less weekly basis. Virtually all those meetings took place in Room 50.4 on the fifth floor of the cavernous Justus Lipsius building in Brussels. The room was chosen for its compact size. An oval table. Eye contact comfortable. Strictly two places per delegation at the table, including both the Presidency delegation and a delegation representing the Member State holding the Presidency. Three places for the Council Secretariat. Two more seats per delegation at the back. A small number of interpreters, their lips moving silently in their discreet fish-tanks.

Many familiar faces. Half of the members of the Reflection Group had been reappointed to the IGC Representatives Group. One deputy in the Reflection Group, Francisco Seixas da Costa, now Minister of State, had been appointed as Portugal's IGC Representative. One member of the Reflection Group, Franklin Dehousse, was now the Belgian deputy in the IGC Representatives Group. The supporting cast was largely unchanged.

The seating arrangement had been ratcheted one further notch in a clockwise direction. The whirligig of time which had placed Silvio Fagiolo in the chair, now flanked by the Council Secretariat, had also moved the Irish and Netherlands delegations closer to the hot seat as our Presidencies approached.

We were on the Presidency's right. The Irish IGC Representative – Noel Dorr, a former Secretary General of the Irish Foreign Ministry – was one of several newcomers to the process. He combines an exceptional breadth of vision extending far beyond the IGC with a meticulous attention to detail which accords to every point of view the respect it deserves, and to every individual the dignity that is their due. With only three months to go to our Presidency, we were already in discussions with the Council Secretariat and others about our Presidency programming, and beginning to try out for size the mindset of a Presidency.

The Netherlands delegation to our own right was led by Michiel Patijn. The IGC Representatives Group would be in safe hands in moving towards its conclusion a year later. The Netherlands had etched in its memory its experience of "Black Monday" during the Maastricht IGC negotiations in 1991 when the then Netherlands Presidency, with the best will in the world, had brought forward proposals that went beyond what the system would bear. Faced with no alternative, they had backed down. As they gradually approached a new Presidency of a new IGC, it seemed unlikely that they would get drawn again into a "federalist" war that could not be won.

An enormous amount of experience around the table. Many Permanent Representatives with a lifetime's knowledge and lore of the Brussels scene. A few delegations to our right, for example, Stephen Wall, whose delegation would need all its professionalism to steer the United Kingdom's path through the minefields ahead. A few delegations to the Presidency's left – the Danish Representative Niels Ersboell, the highly regarded former Secretary General of the Council of Ministers, who knows every gambit in European negotiations. Another man with a sticky wicket.

Even the new kids on the block, Sweden, Finland and Austria, had delegations laden with experience. Led by Gunnar Lund, Antti Satuli and Manfred Scheich respectively, they were like old hands.

As always, only the Commission's seating position at the table remained unchanged – Commissioner Marcelino Oreja's back to the door, directly facing the Presidency.

Initial discussions

For the first readings at the IGC Representatives Group, starting in April 1996, the Italian Presidency circulated notes on each of the sub-issues falling under the topic in question. In a number of cases it annexed to those notes possible draft treaty language (reflecting the fact that at some point the IGC would have to begin to move from discussing a range of theoretical options to the negotiation of specific treaty changes in legal treaty language).

For the second readings at Representative level the Presidency prepared further papers on each of the three topics (citizenship, institutions and external action), taking account of the first round of discussions. The stated purpose of these second-phase papers was to give an overview of the current state of play and to provide guidance for further discussions by focusing on the basic issues as well as on the main schools of thought on how those issues should be resolved.

For Ministerial meetings the Presidency circulated a series of specific questions on the relevant topic in order to focus discussions.

The various papers prepared by the Presidency helped to provoke more considered and focused responses at both official and political level than had been possible in the course of the preparatory process. Although Member States exercised to only a very limited extent the option of addressing the specific draft treaty texts annexed to the Presidency's notes, the Italian Presidency represented a step forward in the evolution of the Conference.

However, principally because of the timing factor outlined at the outset of this chapter, it was still rarely possible to begin to translate useful discussions into even preliminary conclusions either at the end of individual meetings or in the documentation to be submitted to the Florence European Council in June. The key unanimity requirement applied at every stage of the Conference. Thus, even where a large majority of delegations favoured a particular approach, no *agreement* was possible and no emerging agreement could be proclaimed if even one delegation was not on board. On the other hand, even where only one delegation was advocating a pet proposal, it could keep that proposal alive – albeit in most cases on a life-support machine.

The painstaking analysis of issues and setting-out of positions during the Italian Presidency, based on focused preparatory work, was a necessary stage in the IGC process. That phase could have been more compressed only if Member States had wished to spur the negotiations into a gallop rather than to keep them under a fairly tight rein.

The Florence European Council

The Presidency convened an additional meeting of Foreign Ministers (a "conclave") in Rome on 17 June 1996 to evaluate progress and to consider the best way of approaching the IGC issue at the Florence European Council on 22 and 23 June.

The Presidency decided to submit to the European Council a "progress report" on the IGC. In order to ensure the agreement of delegations to its being submitted, the report itself specified that it was "drawn up on the responsibility" of the Presidency (i.e. it was not an agreed report). It stated that it was "mainly intended for the incoming Presidency". The report made clear that it did not claim to be exhaustive and that "its content does not commit delegations as to future discussions". An addendum to the report contained "the draft texts drawn up by the Presidency to illustrate some of the options presented to the Conference". Without qualifications such as these, Member States would have seen the report and addendum as prejudging substantive issues at the Conference and would not have agreed to their submission to the European Council.

More significant than the report submitted to the Florence European Council were the conclusions of the European Council. Those conclusions, drawn up in draft form in the normal way by the Presidency and agreed on the second day of the European Council, were significant particularly from a procedural but also from a substantive view.

Procedurally, the Florence European Council stated that the analysis of the issues was sufficiently advanced and that "the Conference can turn now to seeking balanced solutions to the main political issues raised". It stated that it expected its meeting in Dublin in December 1996 "to mark decisive progress" towards completing the Conference by mid-1997. Most importantly, it gave the Irish Presidency its mandate by asking that "a general outline for a draft revision of the Treaties" be prepared by the Irish Presidency for the Dublin meeting.

Substantively, it also asked that the Irish Presidency draft should address in particular a number of aims. Those aims came closer than previous efforts had done to defining the real agenda of the IGC.

The Reflection Group's "annotated agenda" was coming into tighter focus. While it was not, of course, possible to prejudge the substance of what would later be agreed, and some issues would continue to fall by the evolutionary wayside, the list of aims identified at Florence bears a significant similarity to the contents of the eventual Treaty of Amsterdam.

In summary, the main aims identified by the Florence European Council for pursuit at the IGC were as follows.

- Bringing the Union closer to its citizens (the specific areas mentioned were employment, environmental protection, transparency in the Union's work, strengthening European citizenship, fundamental rights, the fight against crime, and the issues of asylum, visas and immigration).

- Strengthening and enlarging the scope of the Union's Foreign and Security Policy (improved preparation and implementation with reference to the "actors" involved, better coherence between the political and economic aspects of external policy, improved decision-making, more rapid budgetary arrangements, the Union's security and defence dimension and in particular the so-called Petersberg tasks, closer links with the WEU, and a possible political solidarity clause).

- Ensuring the "good functioning" of the Union's institutions while respecting their balance (the scope of qualified majority voting and the weighting of votes in the Council, the manner of appointing and composition of the Commission, the role of the European Parliament and Court of Justice, subsidiarity, the question of adequacy of resources, strengthened cooperation (or "flexibility"), and the role of national parliaments). The possibility of simplifying the Treaties was also referred to.

After the European Council, as members of the Irish delegation waited impatiently on the street for their minibus to make its way slowly through the Carabinierei's security cordons, Noel Dorr commented "*de minibus non curat lex*". It was not a charge which, in its correct Latin form (*de minimis non curat lex* – the law does not concern itself with trifles) could have been be laid against the painstaking negotiations at the IGC.

This account of the Italian Presidency has necessarily been a summary one. It cannot convey fully either the volume of the work which was processed or the complexity of the tactical choices involved, as for every Presidency, at every twist and turn of the negotiations. What may seem now like simple choices on the part of the Italian Presidency were subtle judgements in the face of conflicting pressures. What may seem in retrospect to have been inevitable was the result of complex decision-making machinery and no shortage of contradictory advice and exhortation.

At the end of the Italian Presidency, the IGC was ready to move into its next phase.

Chapter 6

The Irish Presidency: Mandate, Challenges, Approach, Work Methods

Though this be madness, yet there is method in't.
(Shakespeare, *Hamlet*)

The sensation on assuming a Presidency is like walking into a sudden pool of light – the spotlight on a stage or the searchlight in a prison yard, depending on whether the giddy excitement or the cold fear predominates.

The first tentative toe is dipped into the spotlight many months before the Presidency itself. Other delegations start turning to the incoming Presidency looking for answers. For a small Member State like Ireland the change is very perceptible. Your thoughts and priorities and plans gradually begin to attract significant interest. The number of incoming bilateral visits steps up significantly.

Presidency preparations, which have begun several years in advance, become intense in the eight weeks before the first night. You have to start thinking like a Presidency (about the vastly complex and ultimately crucial array of questions concerning the organization of work) and acting like a Presidency (by demonstrating an openness to the concerns of others, a neutral approach to the business at hand and a level of ambition for the Union as a whole).

The Intergovernmental Conference was, of course, only one part of the Irish Presidency's responsibilities in the second half of 1996. The Presidency had to deal with a wide agenda of ongoing Union business, including some key responsibilities relating to the preparations for Economic and Monetary Union and the management of the Common Foreign and Security Policy.

The Irish Presidency's mandate in relation to the IGC

The Florence European Council in June had given the Irish Presidency its mandate for the IGC. We were to prepare, for the

European Council in Dublin in December 1996, "a general outline for a draft revision of the treaties". This was intended to "mark decisive progress" towards completing the Conference by mid-1997 (at Amsterdam). The Conference was to turn "to seeking balanced solutions to the main political issues raised".

Lurking implicitly in that mandate was a tension. On the one hand, decisive progress was expected during the Irish Presidency. On the other hand, the IGC was to continue for six months beyond our Presidency. The Conference was not only expected not to conclude during our Presidency; it was instructed not to do so. As St Augustine might have put it: "Give me agreement, but not yet".

This tension reflected two underlying competing forces which had already emerged during the Italian Presidency and which are explained in the previous chapter. On the one hand, there was a fundamental concern that the IGC should not drag on for too long. The Conference was part of a necessary sequence of events. Until its completion, other key issues on the Union's agenda – notably the opening of enlargement negotiations, the reform of the common policies and agreement on the Union's financing arrangements for the early years of the new millennium – would be in abeyance. On the other hand, many delegations continued to insist that the IGC could not conclude until after the UK general election expected in May 1997, and this had come to be the working assumption of the Conference.

Our mandate also contained an ambiguity in the phrase "a general outline for a draft revision of the treaties". If the words "general outline" were emphasized, the mandate for the Irish Presidency could be seen as relatively unambitious. It could mean almost anything. If, on the other hand, the words "draft revision of the treaties" were emphasized it implied a vastly more ambitious target.

As Presidency, we were very happy with that ambiguity. To have been asked starkly to produce a "draft treaty" would, in football parlance, have been a "hospital pass" – you have to go for it but you have no hope of winning the ball cleanly. A "draft treaty" would not have been a fully achievable target. Others would have prevented us from attaining the target and blamed us for the failure. Equally, to have been set an objective as vague as a "general outline" would have removed the necessary dynamism from the negotiations for our six-month Presidency. The "decisive progress" requested would not have been made and we would, in this scenario also, have taken the rap.

The challenges facing the Irish Presidency

At the most basic level the challenge facing us as Presidency was to produce the requested "general outline for a draft revision of the treaties". However, within that framework, the challenges were very complex. I will mention four aspects of that complexity.

First and most obviously, the "general outline for a draft revision of the treaties" would have to be unanimously endorsed, in appropriate language, by the European Council in Dublin in December 1996. It would have been child's play to produce for December, off our own bat, a draft of what we considered ought to be in a new Treaty. But that would have been to miss the point entirely. The aim of the exercise was to take a further step in *shaping agreement among all 15 Member States*. While, as indicated above, there was no question of definitive agreement to a Treaty in December, the objective was to get every Member State in December to endorse an emerging package as a basis for further work. The significance of that objective was two-fold. The *striving for the objective* during our Presidency would force delegations to negotiate seriously for the first time. The *achievement of the objective* would provide a basis for work in the final stage of the Conference and enable it to conclude during the Netherlands Presidency in the first half of 1997.

The obvious fact that unanimous agreement was necessary at every stage of the Conference is worth recalling only because there is apparently no shortage of armchair visionaries who could have written a better Treaty of Amsterdam before breakfast.

Second, apart from their differing views on every detail of the substance of the Conference as well as on its overall level of ambition, there was no shortage of conflicting advice from Member States to the Presidency on *how* to implement our shared mandate. Some favoured the maximalist interpretation of the mandate. Others thought that little progress would be possible in advance of the British general election. There was even a suggestion that the work of the IGC might be suspended for some months. Yet others favoured selecting certain specific areas for progress during the Irish Presidency with the objective of obtaining agreement to one or more "mini-packages" in December.

Third, the decision that the Conference would conclude only in the middle of the following year meant that the key trade-offs could only be made long after the end of our Presidency. This in turn meant that on a small number of the most sensitive issues it would not be possible to get agreement in Dublin even on an outline treaty text as a basis for further negotiations.

Fourth, the position of the UK delegation constituted in itself a significant element of complexity. The task of moving towards agreement between the other 14 Member States was difficult enough. While the position of the UK was not as isolated as some media coverage would suggest (it had some "company" for virtually all its minority views), its overall approach was certainly at one end of the spectrum of so-called "ambition" for the Conference. Its position and room for manoeuvre were further complicated by the uncertainty about what British Government would be involved in the endgame of the IGC in 1997. The challenge for the Irish Presidency in this regard was how, in these circumstances, to bring the United Kingdom along with a significant step forward in the negotiating process, a step to which the UK would be prepared, along with other delegations, to give its assent at Dublin in December. This meant squaring the circle of maintaining the overall level of ambition of the Conference while at the same time allowing the UK delegation to cling to its comfort-blanket of cuddly if somewhat dog-eared views. We were greatly facilitated in our task by the constructive and professional approach of the British delegation.

The Irish Presidency's approach: the upper end of realism

We approached our Presidency of the IGC against the background of those challenges. Our approach reflected neither impulsive flashes of inspiration nor a pre-cooked and unalterable plan of campaign. Like the challenges it was designed to address, our approach evolved day by day with the pressure and progress of the negotiations. The description that follows of the main elements in our approach brings more than a little of the clarity and detachment of hindsight.

First, we decided to aim for the maximalist interpretation of our mandate. It was impossible, at the outset, to predict the precise nature of the document which could be submitted to the Dublin European Council in December. Indeed it would have frightened the horses and been counterproductive to do so. We nevertheless set *ourselves* the aim of taking the negotiations forward in such a way that the document submitted at Dublin would, as far as possible, resemble a draft treaty. We therefore decided early on to try to move the negotiations to the stage of focusing on draft treaty texts (see below). As our Presidency progressed and we had reason to grow more confident, we started using the shorthand description "Outline Draft Treaty" for the document we would submit at Dublin.

Second, we recognized that our key strategic aim was to have our Outline Draft Treaty accepted by the Dublin European Council as the basis for negotiations in the final phase of the Conference. (Whether it would be described as "a basis" or "the basis" or "a good basis" would merely be a presentational nuance.) This in turn meant that it would be necessary to advance the *negotiations as a whole*. Trying to advance only on some key points would have begged the insoluble question of what those key points should be. To have aimed for definitive agreement on a mini-package of issues at Dublin, as some had suggested, would have reflected a misunderstanding both of the global nature of the negotiation and of the dynamic of concession-making within a negotiation.

Third, as well as advancing the work of the Conference from a procedural point of view, we decided that we had a particular responsibility to maintain a level of ambition for the substantive outcome of the Conference. Substance, we considered, must not be sacrificed on the altar of speed. While this commitment to a degree of ambition was in line with the approach of the Irish national delegation, it also reflected our perception of our Presidency responsibilities. We shared the recognition of many that the Dublin European Council should aim reasonably high, especially since the level of ambition was likely to be dragged down rather than increased in the final phase of the Conference. At the same time we considered it essential that the level of ambition should not lose touch with reality. The incorporation in the December Outline Draft Treaty of elements which had no prospect whatever of winning ultimate agreement would have undermined its usefulness and indeed probably have prevented its adoption as the basis for further work. We came to describe our level of ambition as "the upper end of realism" (my only contribution to ephemeral Eurospeak).

Fourth, we decided, above all, to be fair. Fairness to all delegations is not only proper in itself; it is also an important element in winning the confidence necessary for a successful Presidency. No special deals to win favours or to buy off pressures. It can make life difficult at times. Fairness, to borrow the words of the shortest sermon I ever heard delivered (by an American Franciscan priest in Bonn) – "well, it's kinda tricky".

Fifth, we decided to be as open as possible, as the Italian and Spanish Presidencies had been, about the conduct of the Conference. Our press conferences after every meeting offered a detailed and candid account of the negotiations.

Work methods of the Irish Presidency

We evolved work methods to facilitate our chosen approach to the implementation of our Presidency mandate.

We decided that the IGC Representatives Group should continue to meet for two days almost every week (maintaining the mixture of formal sessions and more informal discussions over dinner). This proved absolutely necessary given the length of time it takes 16 delegations to address a wide and varied range of complex issues, and given that meetings with the European Parliament's IGC Representatives also had to be programmed regularly on the same occasions. We had resisted gentle suggestions, in the run-up to our Presidency, that meetings should be less frequent – although we understood the pressures on IGC Representatives, who tended to be either Ministers with very considerable domestic responsibilities or Permanent Representatives in Brussels with an enormous ongoing workload.

We decided to launch our Presidency of the IGC with an informal meeting of IGC Representatives in Cork. Apart from the contribution that such a meeting could make to developing good working relationships, we saw this as a way of developing consensus on our broad approach to the Presidency while at the same time drawing on the collective wisdom of partners in that regard.

Most importantly, by offering the opportunity for a more informal exchange of views, the Cork meeting was designed to move discussions beyond formalized statements of position in the form of *tours de tables*. We saw Cork as an opportunity to convey a sense that the negotiations were moving into a new phase. We considered that if we could win recognition of the *concept* that the negotiations were moving into a new phase, this would help to create its own reality. In practice, this proved largely to be the case.

Ministerial meetings would continue to take place on a monthly basis. We decided to try to foster more of a negotiating atmosphere at Ministerial level by creating a psychological distinction between the IGC Ministerial sessions and the ongoing business of Foreign Ministers at the General Affairs Councils which took place on the same occasions. We did this by arranging the IGC Ministerial sessions in a different meeting room, by limiting the size of delegations and by introducing the innovation of an oral report to Ministers by the Chairman of the IGC Representatives Group, Noel Dorr.

The evolutionary process goes on: successive approximations

The work of the Conference during the Irish Presidency was constructed around three broad phases. Noel Dorr christened this process "successive approximations". Each phase made it possible to take one further step in developing an approach which would approximate more closely to what might be the ultimate basis for agreement.

In the first phase, broadly from July to September 1996, we tabled for discussion by IGC Representatives what we called Introductory Notes on every subject under consideration at the Conference. In preparing these, we drew as we considered appropriate on proposals which had been tabled by individual delegations. Each meeting, during the first phase of our Presidency, discussed anything between two and six such Introductory Notes which we had prepared.

The Introductory Notes summarized the issues for discussion and, wherever possible, also contained in annex draft treaty language, often in the form of alternative drafts. On a limited number of sensitive subjects (notably flexibility and certain institutional questions), on which there was nothing resembling agreement on the overall approach to follow, it was not possible for us to annex draft treaty texts. The tabling of draft treaty texts on those issues, rather than more general options for discussion, far from bringing delegations closer together, would have moved them further apart.

In a large majority of the areas of work of the IGC, on the basis of the Introductory Notes, delegations for the first time at the Conference began to engage in discussing the specific wording of possible treaty changes. To a limited but important extent delegations, encouraged by Noel Dorr, also began to enter into exchanges which were more flexible than the rigid format of 16 successive formal interventions. (It should be noted, however, that the limited extent to which such flexible exchanges are possible, in a negotiation involving delegations with 16 different points of view to express, remained a significant factor throughout the IGC).

For the reasons outlined in earlier chapters, it was not possible for the Presidency to conclude formally at meetings that any specific wordings had been agreed. We could, however, form our own judgements on how the evolutionary process was working, on which ideas and wordings would be most likely to survive that process. We could and did reflect those judgements in the next round of papers we would table.

In the second overlapping phase, broadly from October into November 1996, on the basis of the first discussions in the Representatives Group, we tabled papers for further discussion by Representatives which we called "Suggested Approach". This change in the title of the papers was itself aimed at nudging forward the nature of the negotiation. These second-phase papers contained, wherever possible, treaty language refined on the basis of the first round of discussions. This language was now cast in the form of "suggested" treaty language.

The third overlapping phase, from November into early December 1996, which will be dealt with in later chapters, was devoted to the preparation of the Outline Draft Treaty for the Dublin European Council in December. It represented a further "successive approximation", this time taking account of the second round of discussions.

The three phases of "successive approximation" during the Irish Presidency were not in practice as clear-cut as the schematic explanation in this chapter suggests. For example, discussion at Ministerial level of a different topic each month, which had to be dovetailed with the phasing of work at IGC Representative level, represented a further and important layer in the "approximation" process. The role of the special meeting of the European Council in Dublin in October 1996 ("Dublin 1") is dealt with in Chapter 8.

The Council Secretariat

A summary of the work methods of the Irish Presidency of the IGC would be incomplete without reference to the fact that we worked very closely with the Council Secretariat, composed of permanent European civil servants, which supports each six-monthly Presidency. These professional work-programmers, mood-judgers and compromise-formulators are sidelined by a Presidency at its peril. Virtually every document tabled at the IGC during the Irish Presidency was a collaborative effort between the Presidency and the Council Secretariat – a first Secretariat draft initially guided and subsequently adapted by the Presidency. In the European Union it is a Presidency that exercises political responsibility, that provides direction, that ultimately makes the procedural and substantive judgements. In exercising that role it relies significantly – if it is sensible – on the expertise, legal knowledge, experience and commitment of the Council Secretariat.

Chapter 7

The Union and the Citizen

Salus populi suprema est lex. (The good of the people is the chief law.)

(Cicero, *De Legibus*)

The Irish Presidency inherited, as explained in previous chapters, a solid body of work representing more than a year of preparatory work and preliminary negotiations. Our challenge during the six months of our Presidency was to shape and structure that material into an Outline Draft Treaty, wherever possible in the form of actual treaty language, which could be accepted by all delegations as the basis for negotiations in the final phase of the Conference.

One of the questions we faced was how many Sections there should be in our Outline Draft Treaty. Put another way, the question was how best to carve up the somewhat unusually shaped chicken which was emerging from the communal oven. In close consultation and full agreement with the Netherlands Presidency which was to follow us, we decided in the course of October 1996 that we would present our Outline Draft Treaty in December divided into the following five main "Sections":

- Section I: An Area of Freedom, Security and Justice
- Section II: The Union and the Citizen
- Section III: An Effective and Coherent Foreign Policy
- Section IV: The Union's Institutions
- Section V: Enhanced Cooperation – "Flexibility".

This presentation continued to provide the overall structure for the work of the Conference until its substantive conclusion at Amsterdam in June 1997.

"The Union and the Citizen" (Section II) is the subject of this chapter. Later chapters are devoted to each of the other four main components of the work of the Conference (one of which – "An Area of Freedom, Security and Justice" – like Section II, addressed directly very specific public concerns. It was, however, considered to merit a Section in its own right.)

As explained in the introduction to this book, rather than analysing the substantive issues separately from the progress of the negotiations, I have opted for what I hope will be not too confusing a mixture of sequence and substance. Accordingly, while I have emphasized that the Conference was a single negotiation and that the challenge of each Presidency was not to win definitive agreement on individual Sections of the Treaty but rather to move the whole mountaineering expedition on to the next camp, I have chosen – as far as "The Union and the Citizen" is concerned – to focus in particular on how work was carried forward during the Irish Presidency.

The citizen moves centre-stage

In recent years there has been a significant shift in emphasis in the European Union from the aim of pursuing the process of integration as such to addressing the most direct concerns of citizens.

This shift is, to some extent, presentational. The process of integration has, from the outset, been pursued and supported precisely because it was seen to be in the interests of ordinary people. The existing Treaties address those interests in many practical ways. Moreover, the new explicit emphasis on the concerns of citizens is in itself a significant step in the process of European integration. However, the shift in emphasis is far more than presentational. It represents, in my view, an important development in the nature of the European Union and in its relationship with the man and woman in the street whose interests it is designed to serve.

That such a change in emphasis is taking place is beyond doubt. It has seeped into the very language of the European Union. Over the past dozen years, the vocabulary of speech-making about Europe in every Member State, not just those traditionally considered more sceptical, has been transformed. References to Political Union and to the "ever-closer process of European integration" are now few and far between. "Federalism", the touchstone of political correctness just a few years ago in the Maastricht negotiations, the famous "F-word", now seems a quaint anachronism. It was absent from the 1996/1997 IGC, somewhat like the much-but-not-universally-loved uncle who kicked up such a fuss a few Christmases ago that he was not invited back. The buzzwords today are subsidiarity, transparency, flexibility and the direct concerns of citizens.

The stated overall priorities of recent individual EU Presidencies also illustrate this trend. For example, in the case of the Irish Presidency in 1996, the Taoiseach, John Bruton, spoke of secure jobs, safe streets and sound money. More recently, the British Presidency in the initial presentation of its programme for the first half of 1998 gave a higher profile to the issues of employment, environment and the fight against crime than to the future of the Union's main common policies and to the further enlargement of the Union.

This change in emphasis has taken place everywhere in the European Union, albeit in varying degrees. The change could be said to represent an important manifestation of democracy. It is what voters want to hear, or at least what politicians think that voters want to hear (which is the most appropriate and usually the most accurate available barometer of those wishes).

The new focus on the concerns of citizens is not a statement for or against European integration. It is a statement about the nature of that integration. The demonstration of the relevance of the actions of the European Union to citizens can no longer be considered an incidental benefit, an important afterthought. Relevance must now be the motive of action rather than its consequence. Relevance must not only be assumed but be demonstrated from the outset.

The public response in some Member States to the Maastricht Treaty had, more than anything, brought home the fact that public support could not be taken for granted. It would no longer be enough that a European Treaty should be right for Europe, indeed no longer enough that it should be right for its citizens. In future any European Treaty would have to demonstrate convincingly its relevance to those citizens.

The IGC and the citizen

The Treaty of Amsterdam is the first European Treaty in which the citizen is centre-stage. The new treaty provisions which address the concerns of citizens reflect not a windfall but a deliberate choice on the part of the IGC.

It was evident from the very first meeting of the Reflection Group in June 1995 (see Chapter 3) that the IGC would be expected to take a significant step in addressing the priorities of citizens. It set about doing this in the way it operated as well as in the substance of its work.

As far as its *operation* was concerned, the Conference was conducted in a transparent manner throughout. Every effort was made to ensure that it could not be seen as a secret negotiation behind closed doors as, in some quarters, the Maastricht negotiations had been seen. Press conferences and briefings were systematic and comprehensive. Documentation flowed like milk and honey. If there was any barrier to public understanding of developments it was due to an excess rather than to an absence of information.

As far as the *substance* of the IGC is concerned, the significant focus of its work on issues of immediate public concern may well, in the longer run, be seen as the most significant underlying trend reflected in its work. Perhaps no revolutionary breakthrough was made on any individual issue. However, significant practical improvements were agreed in very many areas of direct public concern (including employment, public health, social exclusion, consumer protection, the environment and the fight against crime). The cumulative impact of these treaty changes will, I think, come in time to be seen as representing a fundamental shift in the nature of the European Union.

The Union and the Citizen – the main issues

It seemed clear at the outset of our Presidency that *three* issues (apart from those relating to fundamental rights and the fight against crime dealt with in Section I of our Outline Draft Treaty) should lie at the heart of the aim of developing Treaty provisions in relation to the Union and the Citizen: *employment*, the *environment*, and *transparency in the operation of the Union*.

Why these three issues in particular? First, because of the priority clearly attached to each one by several (although not necessarily the same) delegations; second, because there seemed to be a good objective case for strengthening the treaty provisions in those areas; and third, because there seemed to be no *a priori* reason why it should not eventually prove possible to reach unanimous agreement on improvements in the areas concerned (a necessary consideration, since even the most enthusiastic support from many delegations for a particular treaty change would lead to nothing if faced with the implacable opposition of even one).

To these three issues should be added the fourth issue of *subsidiarity* (the principle which helps to regulate the level – European or national – at which decisions should be taken). This was another area where the insistence of some delegations meant that some development of the existing treaty provisions was likely to be necessary.

The overall work methods of the Irish Presidency are described in Chapter 6. The aim was gradually to shape agreement on each topic through a process of "successive approximations", the emerging agreement wherever possible taking the form of specific treaty language. As explained, the "successive approximations" involved generally a three-phase process as regards each topic: an Introductory Note; a Suggested Approach; reflection of the issue in the Outline Draft Treaty at the end of the Presidency. Each successive draft took account of the discussion which preceded it. The Presidency's approach to each of the four issues in question reflected those overall work methods.

The following summary gives an impression of the rhythm of work involved on these and other issues at the level of IGC Representatives.

	Introductory Note	Representatives' discussion (1)	Suggested Approach	Representatives' discussion (2)
Employment	9 July	16/17 July	17 Sept	23/24 Sept
Environment	17 Sept	30 Sept	22 Oct	29 Oct
Transparency	16 July	3/4 Sept	8 Oct	22 Oct
Subsidiarity	26 July	3/4 Sept	8 Oct	15/16 Oct

This timetable (concerning the key aspects of Section II of the Outline Draft Treaty) reflects only a small part of the overall IGC Work Programme during the period in question. Similar discussions took place during the same period on all other main aspects of the work of the Conference. This timetable is included merely to provide an illustration of the general rhythm of work.

The initial Introductory Notes on the various topics, underpinned by the mandate from the Florence European Council and by the recognition at the informal meeting in Cork that the Conference should move into the negotiating phase, succeeded for the first time at the IGC in provoking serious discussion and engagement on draft treaty texts. Those first discussions in turn enabled the Presidency to produce revised texts as part of its subsequent "Suggested Approach" on each topic.

While some delegations did not yet accept even the principle of the texts in question (and indeed in some cases did not do so until well into the Netherlands Presidency), they could see that the nature of the game was beginning to change. There comes a point in a negotiation where a delegation, unless it is resolved in the end simply to veto something strongly supported by partners, must recognize that proposing specific amendments to a text about which it may be unenthusiastic serves its interests more effectively than general grumbling.

Employment

The task of maintaining and creating jobs has been recognized for many years as the most important challenge facing the European Union. The Union's Treaties have until now, however, contained no employment chapter to provide a solid basis for action at European level.

There is a widespread public expectation that the European Union should address the issue of unemployment more effectively. At the same time the levers for addressing the problem remain essentially in the hands of Member States. This illustrates the dilemma which the Union faces in many areas of particular sensitivity for citizens. The sensitivity creates the paradoxical expectation of both action and non-interference at European level.

It was clear that a large majority of Member States considered that a strengthening of the treaty basis for action at the European level in relation to employment should be a priority of the Conference. For some it was the highest priority. Several ideas in that regard had been floated and discussed over many months. Some Member States, notably Sweden, had tabled specific proposals. It was equally clear from discussion that a minority of Member States were either opposed to or deeply unenthusiastic about new treaty provisions on employment. This more negative view appeared to reflect three concerns: first, that the introduction of new treaty provisions would not in itself create any jobs and that unrealistic expectations should be avoided; second, that any new treaty provisions should not lead to significant new expenditure programmes; third, that competence for employment matters should essentially be retained at national level (a point not contested by any delegation).

The initial challenge, therefore, for the Irish Presidency in preparing its Introductory Note on employment dated 9 July 1996, taking account of the preparatory material, was to produce a coherent treaty text. This text would, on the one hand, have to provide a more effective basis for action by the Union on employment and thereby address the concerns of most delegations. On the other hand, it would have to accommodate the opposition or reticence of other delegations sufficiently to make it possible for discussion to begin to focus on the content rather than merely the principle of the draft text.

Accordingly, our Introductory Note contained in annex a draft Treaty Chapter (or "Title") on employment which represented a practical application of the "upper end of realism" for which we were aiming. The essence of the proposed approach was encapsulated in one provision:

> The Community shall contribute to a high level of employment by encouraging cooperation between Member States and by supporting and supplementing their action, while fully respecting the primary responsibility of the Member States.

The approach contained the following principal elements: (i) the establishment of a high level of employment as an objective of the European Union; (ii) a brief definition of the respective roles of Member States and of the Union in relation to employment policy; (iii) the establishment at the level of the Treaty of a detailed procedure (drawing on more informal existing procedures) to ensure an appropriate degree of coordination at European level; (iv) provision for the possibility of the adoption of "incentive" measures in the employment area (e.g. to improve knowledge of the labour market and to encourage innovation); (v) the establishment of an Employment Committee to promote the coordination of employment and labour market policies.

We used a number of drafting techniques to help to facilitate the implicit acceptance of the draft text in our Information Note as a *de facto* basis for negotiation. For example, we recalled in the introduction that the question of the incorporation of a new Chapter on employment into the Treaty remained one of the "main issues" for the IGC. (In other words, discussion of the annexed text did not necessarily imply that the principle of such a text had been agreed.) The provision on "incentive measures" – particularly sensitive for some because of potential budgetary implications – was placed in square brackets and thus given a more tentative flavour (with the aim of tempering any initially negative reactions to the text as a whole).

Reactions to the Introductory Note at the IGC Representatives' meeting on 16/17 July were predictable. The broad majority of delegations welcomed the text (subject, of course, to drafting concerns). The reluctant minority maintained their positions of principle. However, the significant development was that even the reluctant minority did not reject the text out of hand and, while formally reiterating and maintaining their positions of principle, began to address points of detail and to dabble in drafting suggestions.

After the lengthy discussion, we were not able as Presidency to draw even tentative formal conclusions. To have tried to do so would have provoked negative and indeed counterproductive reactions from some delegations. There was no explicit agreement to any provision or even to the principle of such a text. What there implicitly was, however, was the beginning of a basis for negotiation. Negotiations at the IGC on employment would never again be about abstract concepts. The sculptor's lump of stone was in place. It was now a question of chiselling away to give it its shape.

When we came in September to the second phase of producing a "Suggested Approach" on employment, we amended our first draft in the light of the first discussion. The second draft, for example, made clear that it was taking account of the following considerations which had emerged in July: the primary competence of Member States in the matter of employment should be acknowledged more clearly; the consistency of employment policy with the broad guidelines of economic policy should be ensured; the procedures for coordination should be streamlined and reflect more closely the existing informal procedures. We also acknowledged that some of the detail did not need to be set out in the Treaty.

The process of refining the proposed employment provisions continued through a second discussion at Representative level, a first discussion at Ministerial level on 1 October, preparation of our Outline Draft Treaty in November and finalization of the text under the Netherlands Presidency right through to the Amsterdam European Council in June 1997. While the *wording* of each of the provisions in the text on employment which was annexed to our initial Introductory Note in July 1996 was amended or adapted in one way or another in the course of the remainder of the Conference, the key *elements* and broad balance of that first draft remained at the heart of the evolving text and provided the basis for ultimate agreement.

Environment

Common sense tells us that environmental issues involve a significant dimension which should, and indeed can only, be addressed at the European level. As we put it in our Outline Draft Treaty: "Environmental problems do not respect borders. At its most simple they can follow the flow of a river or the direction of the wind."

The European Union Treaties already contain important provisions on the environment. The challenge for the IGC was to identify and agree appropriate ways of strengthening those provisions. Some delegations, from the outset, regarded the environment as one of the key issues at the IGC. Others, while fully agreeing on the importance of environmental protection, were unconvinced that the issue needed to be addressed by means of treaty change.

In our Introductory Note dated 17 September (drawing, of course, on the discussions which had taken place during the Italian Presidency and at the Reflection Group) we put forward draft treaty texts covering two environmental issues: the incorporation of sustainable development among the explicit objectives and specific tasks set out in the Treaties; and the highlighting of the need to integrate environmental protection requirements into the definition and implementation of all Community policies. Again both of these ideas remained, through the process of successive approximations, at the heart of the new environmental provisions eventually agreed in the Treaty of Amsterdam.

The Introductory Note also listed a number of other environmental proposals which had been made by individual delegations. We did not table specific draft treaty texts on these as it was not clear to what extent any of them – some had not yet been discussed – would be likely eventually to gain sufficient support or at least acceptance to make possible the necessary unanimous agreement at the Conference.

Of the additional environmental proposals then listed, one creature – which appeared weak in those early stages of the evolutionary process – proved itself a surprisingly resilient species (perhaps its essentially Scandinavian design helped it through the Ice Age!). This was the aim of strengthening, clarifying and tightening-up the internal market provisions as they relate to the environment. The relevant article in the existing EC Treaty (100a(4)) contains a delicate balance, painstakingly negotiated, between the right of a Member State in some circumstances to maintain higher environmental standards and the need to ensure that the maintenance of such standards does not constitute "a means of arbitrary discrimination or a disguised restriction on trade between Member States".

There appeared at the outset of the IGC to be a wide measure of reluctance, because of the delicate balance in the existing Treaty, to re-open those provisions in any substantive way. However, in the course of the Irish and Netherlands Presidencies – including, importantly, in the final weeks of the Conference – agreement emerged on amending the relevant provisions in ways which, while continuing to provide for an appropriate balance, met the concerns of those delegations emphasizing the importance in certain circumstances of higher environmental standards.

Transparency

The institutions of the European Union have in recent years become significantly more transparent in their operation. The tabloid image of "faceless Eurocrats" (like the secret, black and midnight hags in Macbeth stirring up an incomprehensible, apparently random but profoundly threatening cauldron of trouble for an unsuspecting European public) could not be further from the truth. However, more can and should be done at both European and national level to make information about Europe more easily accessible.

The instincts of European institutions are generally more "transparent" than those of national administrations. In my four years working for two Irish Members of the European Commission, I do not recall a single visitor to the Commission expressing anything other than satisfaction, and sometimes surprise, at the access they had received to a wide range of Commission personnel and thinking.

At the same time, for reasons of effectiveness, a degree of confidentiality has to be maintained in relation to aspects of the Union's work. While the work of the Council of Ministers is often part of the legislative process, which might imply a case for full public access, its work also constitutes an international negotiation (often on matters of great sensitivity to third countries). This means that full and continuous public access would be both unprecedented and inappropriate. Selected set-piece Council debates are now televised. If all such debates were televised, however, the real negotiations would not take place in the Council at all. Similarly, the Commission – like any collegiate body – maintains a degree of confidentiality about its deliberations.

As on every other issue at the IGC, transparency was the subject of a range of views. Discussion centred on the attempt to identify an appropriate mix of openness and effectiveness. Three ideas in that regard began to be refined in the course of the Irish Presidency. Subject to further refinement in the course of the Netherlands Presidency, these were eventually reflected in the Treaty of Amsterdam: (i) recognition in the Treaties of the principle that the decisions of the Union should be taken as openly as possible; (ii) incorporation of provisions concerning the right of any citizen to have access to Parliament, Council and Commission documents subject to appropriate conditions; (iii) confirmation that when the Council acts as legislator the results of votes and explanations of vote shall be made public.

Subsidiarity

The principle of subsidiarity recognizes, on the one hand, that where things can be better done at national level (or indeed by implication below that, at regional level), action should not be undertaken at the level of the Union. On the other hand, it recognizes also that where the Union can, within areas of its competence, act more effectively than would be possible at national level, it should do so. The principle of subsidiarity, involving this delicate balance, had been incorporated in the Maastricht Treaty only after lengthy and difficult negotiations.

The overwhelming view at the Conference was that any development of the treaty provisions on subsidiarity should leave the *nature and definition* of the principle unchanged. The issue for the IGC was, therefore, whether the detailed guidelines for the *application* of subsidiarity, agreed by the Fifteen at the Edinburgh European Council in 1992, should be elevated to the level of the Treaty (by means of a "protocol" or a non-legally-binding "declaration"); and, if so, whether those rules should be reflected in summary, in full, or in an amended form.

The conclusion of the Irish Presidency, after the various phases of discussion, was that the incorporation of the existing guidelines on subsidiarity in summary form in a Protocol to the Treaty might provide the basis for agreement. The wording of the suggested Protocol contained in our Outline Draft Treaty was significantly elaborated in the course of the Netherlands Presidency before its eventual incorporation as a Protocol in the Treaty of Amsterdam.

Other issues relating to the Union and the Citizen

Another issue dealt with by the Irish Presidency according to the same method of Introductory Note and Suggested Approach was the issue of *European citizenship* as such – a concept already incorporated in the Maastricht Treaty – which confers certain specific rights additional to those deriving from national citizenship. It was an issue to which a number of delegations initially attached particular importance at the IGC.

However, apart from confirming explicitly that European citizenship complements and does not replace national citizenship, the range of proposals on citizenship tabled by various delegations did not include any which appeared to meet the twin requirements of practicality and acceptability. Some delegations were concerned *inter alia* about the potential legal or financial consequences of new citizenship provisions. Accordingly, in tabling our Introductory Note on "citizenship", we listed some of the ideas which had been floated by delegations to test whether any of them would run. We did not, however, table specific treaty texts for discussion. The idea of developing the European citizenship provisions in the Treaties in any significant way, on the occasion of this IGC, gradually drifted into the swamp through the process of natural selection.

In parallel with the structured timetable for discussion of the main issues at the Conference, delegations continued to table an array of proposals on disparate issues. Some of these creatures never had any hope of survival. Others would manage to fend for themselves and eventually found a home in the Treaty. We christened these proposals "Other Issues". They were handled, as far as possible, during our Presidency as a single package according to the same three-phase approach as the principal issues.

One such issue which surfaced, initially in the form of a Finnish proposal relatively late in our Presidency, was a possible strengthening of the treaty provisions on *consumer protection*. The initially not-unwelcoming response to that Finnish proposal made it possible for us to incorporate in our Outline Draft Treaty in December provisions to establish more clearly in the Treaties the objective of the promotion of the interests of consumers and to provide a basis for addressing that objective more effectively. These provisions, after further refinement, also found their way into the Treaty of Amsterdam.

The Netherlands Presidency

I have, for the reasons outlined, addressed the area of the Union and the Citizen principally as it presented itself in the course of the Irish Presidency. As in every other area, the preparatory work of the Spanish and Italian Presidencies had been important.

The role of the Netherlands Presidency was, of course, crucial to success. The Netherlands Presidency had the difficult and delicate task of moving from general acceptance of the Outline Draft Treaty as the basis for further work, to unanimous and definitive agreement on treaty amendments, essentially down to every last comma. The area of the Union and the Citizen was one of those in which, at the beginning of 1997 at the outset of the Netherlands Presidency, the possible area of agreement was already emerging most clearly. However, the Netherlands Presidency – while it felt confident enough to leave the area of the Union and the Citizen to one side for the initial months of its Presidency – had to preside over the final refinement of the treaty texts in this area also.

Moreover, a number of other important provisions in relation to the Union and the Citizen came to fruition during the Netherlands Presidency.

The Maastricht Treaty had incorporated, by means of a Protocol, a "Social Agreement" which applied to all Member States other than the United Kingdom. This arrangement had been accepted at the time (reluctantly by all other than the UK itself) as the only way of making progress in the social area. The Social Agreement meant that there was no single, coherent and effective legal framework for Community action in the social area. There was a risk of a developing schism. All Member States, other than the UK, strongly wished to see the *Social Agreement incorporated into the Treaty proper.*

The issue hinged solely on the outcome of the UK general election. There wasn't the remotest prospect that a Conservative

Government would abandon its favourite mantra about the effect of European Community legislation in the social area on competitiveness. The Labour Party, on the other hand, had already indicated that in Government it would sign up to the Social Agreement. In the event, it did – a first proof of its European credentials. (The role of the Irish Presidency on this issue, which could only be settled in the final weeks before Amsterdam, was to find a formula for demonstrating that the issue remained alive on the agenda of the Conference without provoking a backlash from the then British Government.)

Furthermore, agreement also emerged in the course of the Netherlands Presidency for some *further strengthening of the treaty's social provisions.* Support, for example, developed, notably at the informal Ministerial IGC meeting in early April 1997, for an earlier Irish proposal to incorporate in the Treaties an explicit legal basis for the adoption of incentive measures to combat *social exclusion.* (As Presidency we had judged that, on the basis of the positions expressed by partners some months earlier, it would have been both inappropriate and counterproductive to have pressed the issue prematurely in our Outline Draft Treaty beyond the level of support that had emerged up to that point.)

Among a range of other issues dealt with under the heading of the Union and the Citizen on which agreement emerged in the course of the Netherlands Presidency were the following.

- An important strengthening of the treaty provisions on *public health* (including an improved basis for measures to protect people against animal and plant diseases). The new provisions in this regard were based initially on a proposal tabled by the Belgian delegation relatively late in the Irish Presidency.

- A strengthened basis for addressing the concerns of the Community's *"outermost" regions.*

- A Protocol on the *funding of public service broadcasting.*

The Treaties have also, as a result of the IGC, been made slightly more readable by the deletion of a number of their obsolete provisions (so-called "simplification"). On the basis of a mandate developed during our Presidency, largely by the Council Secretariat, the detailed work in this regard was carried out by a working party, under the authority of the IGC Representatives Group, in the course of the Netherlands Presidency. The treaty articles have also been renumbered in a more logical sequence.

It did not prove possible to agree a more radical restructuring and recasting of the Treaties ("codification"), partly due to the concern of some delegations that this might lead to an unnecessary extension of public debate to issues, long since settled, which substantively were to remain unchanged. Some delegations had pressed the issue of "codification" as representing potentially a significant step in popularizing the Treaties. Others had seen the exercise as being of little public interest and having the potential to lead to confusion.

The first words of the Explanatory Memorandum accompanying the Irish Presidency's Outline Draft Treaty in December 1996 were: " The European Union belongs to its citizens. The Treaties establishing the Union should address their most direct concerns." The end product of the IGC marked a limited but significant step in that direction. The Treaty of Amsterdam reflects many of the concerns of the citizens whom it is designed to serve – in the detail of many of its contents, in its underlying trend and in the new direction it traces for the European Union of the future.

Chapter 8

Streets Broad and Narrow: Dublin 1

A map-maker, according to the fable, unsatisfied that his map of a particular city contained sufficient detail, enlarged the map again and again until eventually the map was as large as the city itself.

The European Council, the so-called "Summit", is the supreme decision-making body of the European Union. The buck stops with the Heads of Government or, in the case of France and Finland, the Heads of State. Theirs is the authority within national Governments to arbitrate between conflicting views. Theirs is the scope at European level to move towards compromise on key issues.

The regular six-monthly meetings of the European Council take place towards the end of each Presidency. The success or failure of each Presidency is largely measured by the achievement of its end-of-term meeting. The European Union's work programme is established from one regular European Council to the next. They are the most recognizable milestones in the development of the Union. For those involved in European Union business, the litany of European Councils – Fontainebleau, Maastricht, Venice, Edinburgh, Amsterdam – suggests not so much the dream package holiday, but more the painstaking pilgrimage towards the Europe of tomorrow, each location retaining its inherent connotations and its long-term significance.

The almost invariable practice has developed that each Presidency now convenes also a second meeting at the level of Heads of State or Government. The decision to convene these supplementary meetings reflects several factors including the view held by political leaders themselves, as well as by the media and the public more generally, that the increasingly important business of the Union requires more frequent meetings. However, these supplementary Summit meetings sit less comfortably with the natural six-month rhythm of Union business. Unless they are devoted to one specific issue, as was the case with the Employment Summit in November 1997 during the Luxembourg

Presidency, they are normally characterized as "informal" or "special", involving an exchange of views but no formal conclusions.

While such informal meetings serve a useful function, they can lead to a certain tension between the necessary absence of conclusions and an understandably media-fed public expectation that specific decisions will be taken. A discussion that is by prior definition "unconcludable" may be misinterpreted as inconclusive.

The Florence European Council in June 1996 had agreed that such a supplementary special meeting of the European Council would take place in the second half of that year, during our Presidency. After much difficulty the meeting was scheduled for 5 October. (The difficulty of finding, even at several months' notice, a date on which all 15 Heads of State or Government and the President of the Commission can clear their diaries for a meeting has to be experienced to be believed.) While a specific agenda for the meeting had not been identified at Florence, it was always clear that the IGC would be one of the items for discussion. As 5 October approached, it became increasingly evident – since no other items were bubbling to the surface of the Union's agenda – that the IGC was likely to be the substantive item for discussion.

This posed a dilemma for the work of the IGC. The work programme of the Conference, as will be evident from earlier chapters, was elaborate and tight. It was designed to lead, through carefully planned phases, to the submission of an Outline Draft Treaty in early December. It was clearly materially impossible to telescope the work of the Conference with a view to submitting such a document to the special meeting of the European Council in October (which came to be known as "Dublin 1"). Our dilemma was to organize Dublin 1 in a way which could inject some political adrenalin into the work of the Conference and at the same time avoid cutting across its work programme. Wrongly handled, the effect of Dublin 1 on progress in the negotiations could have proved negative.

Each delegation at the Conference was gradually forming an impression of the sticking points and bottom lines of the other delegations. The informal meeting of IGC Representatives in Cork, at the outset of our Presidency, had offered us a particularly useful opportunity to assess, in the case of each delegation, on the one hand the elements it considered essential for inclusion in the new Treaty and, on the other hand, the most sensitive points whose inclusion could create significant difficulty for it.

One thing had emerged quite clearly at the Cork meeting. While there was no shortage of delegations urging that the work of the Conference should concentrate on only "a few key issues", there was no agreement whatsoever as to what those key issues were. The sum total of "key issues", if the priorities of all delegations were taken into account, amounted to precisely the emerging agenda of the Conference. The Presidency, like the map-maker referred to at the opening of this chapter, would have to include all the main topographical features of the Conference if our emerging map was to be accepted as the way forward. Ultimately, our presentation of the "agenda" of the Conference, both in our ongoing Work Programme and in our Outline Draft Treaty, would have to correspond to the *real underlying agenda.*

A Presidency cannot *invent* a way forward out of thin air. It must, at the same time, *guide* and *shape* the direction of the Conference. It is not a scissors and paste job. Defining the real underlying agenda – identifying the European interest, recognizing what will run and what will not, developing language which will be both effective and acceptable – is a complex and subtle challenge. It is an art form rather than a science. The task was complicated by the inevitability that the key positive points *required* by some delegations were also, for others, the most sensitive negative points *to be avoided at all costs.* Indeed, the sum total of neuralgic issues to be avoided also amounted, if the sensitivities of each delegation were taken into account, to something not far off the emerging agenda of the Conference!

As Dublin 1 approached, two conflicting views emerged at the Conference about the extent of the "map" which should be submitted for consideration by Heads of State or Government. Whether the agenda for Dublin 1 was to be broad or narrow may have carried faint echoes of Molly Malone.

One strongly urged view was that the agenda should be narrow. A limited number of key topics should be selected for discussion at that meeting so that Heads of State or Government could give a particular push to them. This approach, however, necessarily begged the question of what those topics should be. It also presupposed a more formal decision-making Summit than was envisaged or indeed would have been appropriate at that point in the negotiations.

The alternative, majority, view was that the agenda for Dublin 1 should be broad. According to this view, progress in the negotiations was satisfactory and the main task – for the Presidency and for the IGC as a whole – was still to produce a balanced overall Outline Draft Treaty for Dublin 2 in December. The priority was therefore to organize Dublin 1 in a way that would not derail or delay that underlying work programme. Those holding this view attached importance to avoiding untimely confrontation or an unnecessary crisis for any delegation. It was a question not of not offending anyone, but of how to advance the negotiations effectively. (In the United Kingdom, the Conservative Party Conference was due to take place just a few days before Dublin 1. A premature confrontation at the IGC would have served no purpose whatsoever. It would have forced the then British Government, and indirectly any new British Government, into a *less* constructive negotiating approach.)

The first of these two views, the "push a few key issues" view, could be seen as stemming from a perception that the precise direction of the Conference could and should be determined, in a somewhat arbitrary way, at a high political level and handed down to the negotiators. In a sense, of course, a decision *by officials in advance* to limit the items on which Heads of State or Government would be expected to give a push could be seen as restricting rather that maximizing the real political input from the highest level.

The second view, the "advance the single package" view, could be seen as based on the perception that what was needed, within the general political remit given to the Conference from a high political level, was a careful build-up from lower levels, working on texts, to a stage where the major political choices could be addressed at a high political level and a final deal struck on the basis of trade-offs.

As Presidency we were under conflicting pressures. We understood the two points of view and sought, as was our function, to organize Dublin 1 in a way which would advance the work of the Conference and at the same time be acceptable to all delegations.

Our sole aim was to advance the work of the Conference as effectively as possible while keeping up its level of ambition. No delegation, in the normal course of a European Union negotiation, has a greater interest than the Presidency of the day in advancing the work at hand. That is the natural aim of a Presidency, which will have to carry the can if there is seen to be lack of progress. Advancing expeditiously the work at hand is not an aim that needs to be urged on a Presidency.

After very careful reflection, we decided that the best course would be to provide for substantive discussion on the IGC at Dublin 1 subject to two principal considerations. First, there would be no identification in advance of a limited number of specific agenda items to be addressed. Heads of State or Government would be free to emphasize whatever IGC issues they considered to be of particular importance. Thus, rather than having an artificial selection of issues in advance, the European Council would itself contribute to the ongoing process of "natural selection". Second, the informal nature of the meeting, without conclusions, would be maintained.

Moreover, we decided that the discussion by Heads of State or Government would be set against the background of the historic challenges facing the European Union on the wider European continent, and presented as a *preliminary* one in the context of the longer-term negotiating process. That longer-term process would later involve *intermediate discussion* at Dublin 2 in December 1996 and *ultimate decisions* at Amsterdam in June 1997.

There is never a formal "agenda" for a European Council. Rather its President, in this case John Bruton, sends a letter to his colleagues a few days before the meeting outlining what is to be discussed and how it is to be handled. The letter in this case required particularly careful drafting to reflect, in a way that would be acceptable to all delegations, the approach to the meeting on which we had decided.

The meeting took the form of separate lunches and dinners for Heads of State or Government and for Foreign Ministers with, in between, during the afternoon, a single working session of the European Council involving all. The afternoon session and the lunch of Heads of State or Government were devoted essentially to discussion of the IGC. (The separate discussions at the Foreign

Ministers' lunch were, as is the practice at Summits, devoted to a range of foreign policy issues on which the Union often has to react at short notice. In this case, developments in the Middle East pushed their way to the top of the Foreign Ministers' agenda, and indeed also required some discussion at the European Council itself.)

The afternoon session on the IGC was preceded by the traditional discussion with the President of the European Parliament. The session itself was kicked off by a detailed report on the progress of the Conference by the Chairman of the IGC at Ministerial level, the Irish Foreign Minister, Dick Spring. This procedure emphasized the role of Foreign Ministers as the principal IGC negotiators.

Although there were no formal conclusions from the meeting, Dublin 1 can, I think, be said to have served five purposes.

First, it was seen to give a certain impetus to the work of the IGC. The need to maintain a high level of ambition and to conclude the Conference at Amsterdam in June 1997 was confirmed. The importance of this aspect should not, however, be exaggerated as the general view within the Conference had been that work was, in any event, generally on course. Nevertheless, against the background of a certain media perception that negotiations had stalled, it provided public reassurance that all was well. In terms of keeping the negotiations on track, Dublin 1 represented, in the end, less a victory than a comfortable scoreless draw.

Second, Dublin 1 gave the members of the European Council, who would ultimately have to become sufficiently immersed in the detail of the IGC to strike the final deals, a very useful opportunity to begin to come to grips with both the substance of the negotiations and the nuances of each other's positions.

Third, while there were no agreed conclusions, each Head of State or Government would return home with his own personal conclusions which he could input into the developing position of his own delegation. This in turn would help to advance the work of the Conference.

Fourth, it provided the Irish Presidency with a significant opportunity to develop its most valuable resource, namely its insight into the priorities of the different delegations.

Fifth, the natural selection process provided for in the organization of discussion at Dublin 1 served a useful purpose. While virtually all IGC agenda items were touched on by one delegation or another, the priority attached spontaneously by virtually every Head of State or Government to strengthening cooperation in the Justice and Home Affairs area, in particular in the fight against international crime, gave a significant political impetus to the further consideration of this issue at the IGC. To a certain extent the same could be said about the employment issue. These two issues were clearly to the forefront of thinking at the highest political level, no doubt reflecting domestic public concerns. This represented a more genuine *political* input than the prior identification of specific issues for the meeting would have done.

Most importantly, after Dublin 1, the show was still on the road. The wheelbarrow was on track.

Chapter 9

Outline Draft Treaty

All government, indeed every human benefit and enjoyment, every virtue, and every prudent act, is founded on compromise and barter.
(Edmund Burke, *Speech on Conciliation with America*)

The mandate set for the Irish Presidency, described in more detail in Chapter 6, was to produce what the Florence European Council had described as "a general outline for a draft revision of the treaties". The challenge was not to produce a theoretical academic masterpiece. It was to draw together the strands of the negotiation. It was to meld the disparate views into a document which could be accepted by all as a good basis for the final phase of the negotiations and make it possible to conclude the IGC during the Netherlands Presidency. The *Financial Times* described the mandate as "Mission Impossible".

The Irish Presidency had decided, as far as the *substance* of the IGC was concerned, to aim for the "upper end of realism". As far as the *nature of the document* was concerned, the Presidency had intended from the outset that it should resemble as closely as possible a draft treaty rather than merely a schematic outline. As the negotiations developed, the Presidency felt sufficiently confident of progress to start speaking of an "Outline Draft Treaty".

The Presidency had recognized from the outset that it would be necessary to provide itself with a space for taking stock, for reflection, for designing the shape and nature of the document on which its stewardship of the IGC would be judged. Exceptionally, therefore, we scheduled no IGC meetings for the first week in November.

Although the work programme and working methods of our Presidency had from the start been geared to the preparation of the Outline Draft Treaty, it was not possible to start the actual process of designing and drafting it before the initial phases of negotiation during our Presidency had cast their light. By the beginning of November, the second phase of discussions, based on our "Suggested Approach" papers, had been completed. Foreign Ministers had given political direction on many of the key points. The Dublin 1 Summit had provided a modest shot in the arm for the work of the Conference. In late October we had held a first round of bilateral consultations ("confessionals"), with each delegation focusing in particular on some of the sensitive institutional questions.

Kilkea Castle

During the week we had set aside at the beginning of November, we arranged a four-day informal think-in and drafting session at the Kilkea Castle Hotel in Kildare. The Irish team for the session was a small one – four officials with secretarial back-up. A few other officials attended parts of the meeting of direct concern to them. The think-in was chaired by Noel Dorr, the Irish member – and at the time Chairman – of the IGC Representatives Group.

Apart from the Presidency, the session involved a small number of officials from the Council Secretariat (including the Secretary General, Jurgen Trumpf, his *chef de cabinet*, Eckart Cuntz, Jacques Keller-Noellet and, my own most regular interlocutor, the human whirlwind Giorgio Maganza). The exceptional ability of these and other Council Secretariat officials, including the formidable and friendly head of the Legal Service, Jean Claude Piris, does not need my testimony. What I would like to record, however, is the quite exceptional and unfailingly patient and good-humoured commitment of all the Council Secretariat officials, including the secretarial staff, with whom I had the pleasure of working during our Presidency.

Certain key Commission officials were also invited to attend the think-in. At every stage of our Presidency, we attached particular importance to the expertise and advice of experienced Commission officials such as Carlo Trojan (the then Deputy Secretary General and now Secretary General) and Jim Cloos (the *chef de cabinet* of President Santer), who had played a central role in the Luxembourg Presidency's chairing of the Maastricht negotiations. The Commission had decided to play a somewhat more low-key role at this IGC, for example in the number of proposals it tabled, than it had in the Maastricht negotiations. Its wisdom and insights were always appreciated.

The tension at the heart of the task in hand was that, while unanimous agreement would not be obtainable in a single area of the work of the Conference in December (six months before its conclusion), the mere setting-out of options would have represented scant progress. The think-in offered us the opportunity of teasing out possible ways of squaring this circle.

Our meetings in the hotel's conference centre lasted all day. Discussions continued informally each day over lunch and dinner. Having first discussed our broad approach to the drafting of the document, we then tried to identify possible ways forward in each of the main areas, drawing diagrams where necessary to tease out the complexities in areas such as decision-making under the Common Foreign and Security Policy. In parallel, various participants began to try their hands at drafting individual sections in the light of the broad approach to the document that was emerging. In some areas, including the sensitive and important area of external economic relations, numerous drafts were attempted. All drafts were subsequently refined significantly, but the exercise helped to clarify our thinking.

As I have emphasized elsewhere, the exercise was a practical rather than an academic one. Our task was not to produce the "perfect" Outline Draft Treaty by ourselves or for ourselves. The task was rather to take the raw material of the negotiations – the concerns and priorities of each Member State, the emerging trends in the discussion, the treaty texts which were beginning to take shape – and to give that material a coherence and a shape which would address effectively the principal challenges and, at the same time, be acceptable to all delegations as a basis for the final phase of the Conference.

Broad approach to the Outline Draft Treaty

In the course of the discussions at Kilkea Castle, the broad approach that we decided on was the following.

- We would produce a comprehensive Outline Draft Treaty covering all aspects of the work of the Conference.

- The Outline Draft Treaty would, wherever possible, take the form of draft treaty texts. In most cases, this was the natural extension of the process of refining treaty texts which had been under way since the beginning of our Presidency.

- Ambitiously, we decided that, wherever possible, the proposed treaty amendments would take the form of "clean" texts without sub-options or the contagious "square brackets" which too often spread like wildfire in international negotiations.

- However, the necessary corollary of this decision to include "clean" treaty texts, none of which could receive definitive unanimous agreement in December, was that other ways would have to be found to accommodate points of view other than those reflected in the proposed texts. Every delegation would have to "find itself" sufficiently in the Outline Draft Treaty. Producing an "immaculate" document which was not accepted as the basis for further work by every delegation would have served no purpose whatever. It would have represented a setback for the Conference.

The problem of reflecting adequately the view of each delegation posed itself most awkwardly in the case of the British delegation (which not only was distinctively minded but faced the difficulty of not knowing what Government would be in power – and therefore what the broad approach of its delegation would be – during the final stage of the IGC). However, not a single delegation could accept the premature cutting-off of any of its pet concerns.

Apart from a very occasional square bracket, necessary to prevent volcanic eruptions, several ways were identified of appearing at least to "keep alive" options other than the texts we proposed (e.g. appropriate references in the "introduction" accompanying each treaty text; alternative approaches set out in "comment boxes" in each section; a general statement in the introduction that the document was "not binding in its detail on any delegation").

- We decided also to include a "Part B" in the Outline Draft Treaty. Part B was to contain a *brief description* of proposals "which have been tabled by delegations at the Conference but which do not fall easily under any of the Chapter headings" in the main body of the document (Part A). There was a necessary ambiguity about Part B. Some of the issues would ultimately be reflected in the Treaty of Amsterdam. Many others would drift into oblivion. We considered, on the one hand, that sufficient support had not yet emerged for any of the issues in Part B to justify the proposal by us of draft treaty texts. On the other hand, we recognized that "death by silence" would be too blunt and premature for proposals whose owners still had some affection for them and would be more likely to go along with a gentle natural death.

- In a limited number of important areas of the work of the IGC it was self-evidently not opportune to table treaty texts. A large majority of delegations urged the Presidency not to do so. It had always been evident that certain key issues, while they were discussed in detail during our Presidency, could only be settled in the final phase of the Conference when the trade-offs would take place. On certain sensitive institutional questions in particular delegations had been reluctant to place their cards on the table. Similarly, the issue of flexibility, which was linked to progress in many other areas of the work of the Conference, was unripe for the tabling of texts in treaty language.

  Even if the Presidency could have formed a reasonable judgement of where the ultimate compromises were likely to lie in these sensitive areas, it was clear that the tabling, almost out of the blue, by the Presidency of proposals in textual form – on which no consensus was emerging through the process of "successive approximations" – would have been hotly contested. Such texts would have provoked quite pointless confrontation and called into question the acceptability of the document as a whole as a basis for the further work of the Conference. One would have been, in the French phrase, *parti pour la gloire*. In this limited number of areas we decided therefore to set out clearly and comprehensively the state of discussions and, where appropriate, options for further consideration by the Conference.

- Finally, as a particular priority, we decided to aim to make the Outline Draft Treaty as comprehensible and readable as possible. Any members of the general public interested in following developments at the Conference should, we believed, be able to do so. This meant in the first place that the treaty changes themselves should be drafted as simply and clearly as possible. However, the extent to which treaty provisions can be expressed in simple language is severely limited both by their necessarily legal nature and by the fact that the process of compromise inevitably involves the art of fudge. The main element, therefore, in making the document capable of being understood by non-initiates was the use of an *overall* introduction and explanatory memorandum, as well as *separate introductions* to each chapter of the Outline Draft Treaty. These would explain in layperson's language the issues at stake and how the proposed treaty changes were designed to address them. This attempt to explain to the public what was involved at the IGC represented a significant innovation.

The negotiations continue

The informal think-in at Kilkea Castle proved essential for the Presidency. It gave us an opportunity to think through and sketch out our broad approach to the preparation of the Outline Draft Treaty. In relation to the main substantive issues under consideration at the Conference it also gave us an opportunity to reflect on how best to proceed, drawing on the experience of both the Council Secretariat and the Commission. A number of elements in our draft, and indeed in the eventual Treaty of Amsterdam, were significantly shaped by our discussions at Kilkea Castle.

We were now ready to enter the third and final phase of our Presidency with a clear, if still evolving, view of the possible shape of the document we would submit to Dublin 2.

The regular pattern of weekly meetings of IGC Representatives continued throughout the rest of November. Two discussions having already taken place on all the main topics, we devoted the November meetings to certain issues on which we considered that further discussion would facilitate the refinement of our Outline Draft Treaty. These included in particular the further development of the draft provisions on the fight against international crime, in the light of the clear priority attached to this aspect by the Dublin 1 Summit. The monthly IGC Ministerial meeting took place on 25 November.

In parallel with these ongoing multilateral meetings during November, for which we tabled new papers, we continued to work, with the Council Secretariat, on the gradual refinement of our Outline Draft Treaty.

Further bilateral "confessionals" which we held with each delegation in the last week of November helped significantly in that process of refinement. Although they were not formally participants in the IGC, we also held a "confessional" with the European Parliament's IGC Representatives.

The "confessionals" took place in one of the Presidency rooms opposite Room 50.4 in the Justus Lipsius building. The last week of November. On one side of a small table, Noel Dorr accompanied by a few Presidency and Council Secretariat officials. On the other side of the table, the stream of penitents.

One by one, each IGC Representative. Usually just one accompanying official. "Bless me, father, for I have sinned. This is my legal adviser."

A useful opportunity for Noel Dorr to outline the key elements of the approach we intended to take in the preparation of our document. Test the waters. Avoid surprises.

Beyond that, listen. It is in listening that the value lies for the Presidency. "What's weighing on your mind?"

The drafting of the Outline Draft Treaty during November and early December was not, of course, an exercise separate from the negotiations. The Outline Draft Treaty was nothing other than our attempt, as Presidency, to give shape and direction to the ongoing negotiations. We continued, in our drafting of it, to draw on the discussions that were taking place.

For the moment, however, it was under wraps.

Chapter 10

An Effective and Coherent Foreign Policy

> At the still point of the turning world
> (T.S. Eliot, *Four Quartets*)

The general structure of this book, as explained at the outset, mixes the sequence of the IGC with its substance. I have opted not for an academic analysis of the Treaty of Amsterdam as eventually agreed but rather to give a snapshot of the various issues from the perspective of different periods in the evolving negotiations.

The work of the IGC was divided into five broad Sections. Chapter 7 deals with the substance of one of those Sections, "The Union and the Citizen". The present chapter is devoted to a second of the Sections, namely "An Effective and Coherent Foreign Policy". All I can attempt here, as in the other Sections, is to give some flavour of the negotiations and what was at stake. Each substantive area of the Conference's work will be the subject of many articles and books analysing it in much greater depth.

I have chosen to present this area – the external dimension – from the perspective of the Irish Presidency's Outline Draft Treaty. This choice of perspective is, as for other areas, inevitably somewhat arbitrary. It does, however, offer the opportunity of illustrating, with reference to one particular area (namely the external area), the practical implementation of our broad approach to the drafting of the Outline Draft Treaty. Moreover, the Common Foreign and Security Policy is probably one of the areas in which the contents of the Outline Draft Treaty most closely resemble the provisions eventually agreed at Amsterdam.

The external challenge

The European Union does not exist in a vacuum. It faces opportunities, challenges and responsibilities in the wider world which it must be equipped to address. The Union cannot afford to be lulled into complacency by its own remarkable internal stability and security. It has to adapt itself continuously to respond to the evolution of its external environment.

Apart from the issues dealt with specifically under the heading of external policy at the IGC, external considerations extended into virtually every aspect of the Conference's work. The prospect of the further enlargement of the Union and the stability of the wider continent formed the backdrop to our work as a whole, in areas such as institutional reform and Justice and Home Affairs. There are inevitably differing views as to whether, in the heel of the hunt, adequate account was taken of that backdrop.

Three principal aspects of the Union's foreign policy were under consideration at the IGC.

The *first* aspect was the development of the Union's Common Foreign and Security Policy (CFSP), established by the Maastricht Treaty of 1992. Through the CFSP, the Member States agree common positions and joint actions on an array of foreign policy issues (e.g. the Middle East peace process, disarmament and human rights). The CFSP, which had evolved gradually from the system of European Political Cooperation introduced in the early 1970s, remains in a sense "intergovernmental" in nature. Its decisions are taken by unanimity. However, it involves commitments and treaty obligations. As the so-called "second pillar" of the three "pillars" that constitute the Union, the CFSP is fully part of its single institutional framework.

The *second* aspect (in effect a subset of the first) was the development of the security and defence dimension of the CFSP.

The *third* aspect was to try to strengthen the European Community's ability to act in external economic relations, a quite different kettle of fish. Economic aspects of external policy are generally part of the "first" (Community) pillar of the European Union. For the most part, external economic negotiations are conducted by the European Commission and decisions taken in the Council by qualified majority vote (rather than unanimity). It can thus be said to be more supranational than inter-governmental.

During our Presidency and particularly in presenting our Outline Draft Treaty, we strongly emphasized the importance of ensuring coherence between these different aspects of the Union's external policy.

The Common Foreign and Security Policy

The Common Foreign and Security Policy (CFSP) is a remarkable, limited and delicate instrument.

It is *remarkable* because of the extent to which 15 independent states, with distinctive histories, different popular priorities, and often conflicting perceptions of their interests, manage to speak and act with one voice in the minefield of international relations. Of course, the Union's relative inaction can on occasion be an easy target for criticism. It should not, however, obscure the fact the CFSP is by a long way the most ambitious and effective attempt ever undertaken between free democratic nations to coordinate their foreign policy positions. To measure its achievement, one only has to imagine how difficult, if not impossible, it would be for a much smaller and perhaps less diverse group of countries – say the United States, Canada and Mexico – to coordinate their positions on a similar range of foreign policy issues.

The CFSP is at the same time *limited* precisely because of the diverse perceptions of interest and different popular priorities. Unless and until those perceptions of interest and priorities merge – at best a lengthy process largely coterminous with the achievement of Political Union – the Union cannot act in foreign policy matters as if the existence of individual Member States were a thing of the past.

The CFSP illustrates well the paradox at the heart of this book – Original Sin in a Brave New World. Foreign policy cooperation is a microcosm of the development of the European Union as a whole. On the one hand, in the genuinely exciting "Brave New World" of the European continent on the verge of a new millennium, the Member States share profound external interests and responsibilities. There is not only a political but also a moral responsibility on the Union to address those challenges as effectively as possible. On the other hand, one cannot simply ignore the continued political reality of the pursuit of perceived national interests. One cannot wish a Political Union into existence. One cannot act as if one already exists. The simple fact is that, at the present stage of the Union's development, there is a limit to the extent to which any Member State is prepared to submerge a perceived important foreign policy interest within a single European position. There is also a limit, in our democratic societies, on the extent to which a Government can cut across a view strongly held by its electors.

Classic foreign policy issues are often not susceptible to the type of compromise which applies to most Community business. You can easily split the difference on importing 75 tonnes of tomatoes. It is less easy to do so when it comes to condemnation of human rights abuses or to the recognition of a Government.

The CFSP is thus also *delicate* because it is the process through which a national perspective and a European perspective on foreign policy issues can, painstakingly and sometimes imperceptibly, move closer together. The development of the CFSP has to be based on reality. It has to be gradual. To act as if the perception of national interests could suddenly be dismissed, as if we had reached the promised land of a brave new European world, far from representing a leap forward for the CFSP, could undermine it fatally. As long as national interests are perceived to exist, to ride roughshod over them would be to strengthen the pursuit of them rather than the reverse. Perhaps one day the same degree of shared perception of interest will be reached in the foreign policy area as now exists for much of normal Community business but, as the Supremes song puts it, "you can't hurry love".

Against this background, discussion of the CFSP at the IGC focused principally on the possible adaptation of its decision-making process. All CFSP decisions currently require unanimity (although in theory the Fifteen can decide unanimously that certain implementing decisions can be taken by qualified majority). There was a subtle range of views at the Conference reflecting different degrees of reluctance or enthusiasm for adapting that principle of unanimity.

In suggesting, in our Outline Draft Treaty, a draft treaty text on improved CFSP decision-making, we drew on the various rounds of discussion that had taken place, most recently at the IGC Ministerial meeting devoted to external policy on 28 October 1996. It was an issue to which particular attention had also been devoted at our Presidency think-in in the first week of November, described in the previous chapter. We attempted in the Outline Draft Treaty to cast some of the emerging ideas in a new and coherent form. At the same time, as in other areas, in order to facilitate the acceptance of our proposal as a basis for discussion, we recalled in a "comment box" the range of other options still on the table.

We hoped that the approach suggested could represent meaningful progress and at the same time provide a basis for compromise. The approach involved *preservation of the unanimity requirement* subject to the following *adaptations*.

(i)   It would be explicitly confirmed that abstention by one or more delegations would not prevent the adoption of a unanimous decision.

(ii)   Provision would also be made for what came to be known as a "constructive abstention" mechanism whereby a Member State, in abstaining, could make a formal declaration. In the event of making such a declaration, a Member State would not be obliged to implement the decision in question but would accept that the decision binds the Union. It would refrain from action likely to conflict with the decision and the other Member States would respect its position.

(iii)   The most sensitive decisions (including the adoption of all joint actions and all decisions with defence implications) would remain subject to unanimity, with the new constructive abstention mechanism providing a degree of flexibility. However, a new procedure was proposed for the adoption of other decisions, including the adoption of common positions and all implementing decisions. The mechanism envisaged was that such decisions would be taken by qualified majority subject to the right of any Member State to prevent a vote being taken "for stated reasons of national policy". However, in such a case, a qualified majority in the Council could refer the matter to Heads of State or Government for decision by unanimity. (Thus, while the right of an individual Member State ultimately to block a decision would remain intact, the conditions for exercising such a veto would be significantly tightened up.)

The approach to CFSP decision-making that we put forward was subject to extensive further discussion well into the Netherlands Presidency. Member States will always continue to express their preferences as often as you offer them an opportunity to do so. However, the essence of what was proposed in relation to CFSP decision-making in the Outline Draft Treaty saw its way, after a few vicissitudes, into the Treaty of Amsterdam. The one significant change was that, while the mechanism in (iii) above (qualified majority for certain decisions subject to a right to invoke stated reasons of national policy to block such a decision) was maintained, it was decided to apply it *not* to the types of decision outlined in our Presidency draft but *rather* to all decisions (other than those with defence implications) adopted on the basis of any "common strategy" decided unanimously by the European Council. (The concept of a "common strategy" was one for which agreement emerged in the course of the subsequent Netherlands Presidency.)

A colleague in another delegation described the new decision-making procedures as "from consensus to nonsensus", but he was joking. I think.

The Outline Draft Treaty also contained proposals for a CFSP policy-planning and early warning unit to be established in the Council Secretariat, for which a very wide measure of support had emerged. This unit, which is now provided for in the Treaty of Amsterdam, is expected to improve significantly the preparation of CFSP decisions. It is designed to play a role, somewhat akin to that of the Commission in relation to normal Community business, in addressing issues and in identifying policy options from a European perspective.

Another issue, stemming from a French proposal, that was discussed extensively at the Conference was the appointment of what came to be known popularly and with political correctness as "Mr or Ms CFSP", a new post designed to enhance the continuity and profile of the CFSP. (After the British general election in May 1997, it was suggested to the British delegation, which had earlier floated the concept of a "Baroness CFSP", that a "Comrade CFSP" might now be more appropriate.) The spectrum of options put forward on this issue extended from strengthening the role of the Council Secretary General in the formulation, preparation and implementation of policy decisions to the more ambitious idea, espoused by France, of appointing a powerful and independent personality outside the existing structures to exercise the role of High Representative of the CFSP.

In our Outline Draft Treaty we proposed a strengthening of the position of the Secretary General, an approach which accorded with the centre of gravity of opinion at that time. We also recalled the alternative options. The concept continued to be refined in the course of further discussion during the Netherlands Presidency. The Treaty of Amsterdam provides for strengthening the position of the Secretary General "who shall exercise the function of High Representative of the Common Foreign and Security Policy", a not untypical European compromise.

A number of other ideas for improving the operation of the CFSP set out in the Outline Draft Treaty worked their way, after further (in some cases substantial) amendment in the course of the Netherlands Presidency, into the Treaty of Amsterdam. These included: a highlighting of the role of the European Council in laying down general CFSP guidelines or strategies; closer association of the Commission with the CFSP; adaptation of the arrangements for the external representation of the Union; a tighter definition of the instruments available to the CFSP; a provision to facilitate the conclusion of international agreements; and provision that, in general, operational CFSP expenditure would be charged to the European Community budget.

Security and defence

Perhaps the most important and sensitive issue in relation to the CFSP under consideration at the IGC was the possible adaptation of the Union's objectives on security and defence matters as well as of the means for pursuing those objectives. Apart from the provision in the Maastricht Treaty that these issues should be revisited, the issue was, it seemed, driven by two impulses. First, the European Union incontrovertibly faced new security challenges. The Outline Draft Treaty put it as follows: "As part of a credible foreign policy, the European Union must be able to respond effectively to the new and complex security challenges of the post Cold War world, which require multifaceted approaches and solutions. The achievement of its foreign and security policy objectives increasingly requires the Union to draw on the full range of instruments at its disposal."

The general recognition of this reality led, without substantial difficulty, to the incorporation, proposed initially by Sweden and Finland, into the Treaties of the so-called "Petersberg tasks", the essence of the current security challenges in Europe (humanitarian and rescue tasks, peacekeeping tasks and tasks of combat forces in crisis management, including peacemaking). There was also ready agreement to the general principle of developing the relationship between the European Union and the Western European Union by fostering closer institutional relations. The Western European Union is already described by the Maastricht Treaty as "an integral part of the development" of the European Union. To carry out the "Petersberg tasks" the European Union would have to have recourse to it.

Second, more controversially, a large number of Member States – many of which regarded defence as the unfinished business of Maastricht – wished to take a further significant step in developing the defence dimension of the European Union. Their objective was the merger of the EU and the WEU. Some favoured also in this regard an optional EU Treaty Protocol setting out the mutual defence commitment (of those who would sign it) which at present applies within the WEU to full WEU members. These more far-reaching ideas faced an insurmountable double hurdle at the IGC. First, there was no agreement among NATO countries themselves on the respective roles of NATO and the European Union. It was evident that, for the United Kingdom at least, the non-subordination of the WEU to the EU would be a sticking point. Second, the traditionally neutral countries were unwilling to envisage such a significant step.

Some of the security issues were of such sensitivity that it was obvious that they could be settled only at Amsterdam. We tried nevertheless, as Presidency, to move forward the work of the Conference towards the area of possible agreement. We had scheduled discussion of security and defence issues at our very first meeting of IGC Representatives in Cork. When it came to preparing our Outline Draft Treaty we sought to address the issues in a way that could be accepted by all Member States as a basis for further work.

As regards the Union's objectives in security and defence, for example, we suggested amending the relevant existing article (J.4(1) TEU) as follows:

> The common foreign and security policy shall include all questions relating to the security of the Union, including the *progressive* [present wording: eventual] framing of a common defence policy *in the perspective of* [present wording: which might in time lead to] a common defence.

The Outline Draft Treaty went on to specify that the questions referred to shall include the Petersberg tasks, which it listed. In the commentary which accompanied the treaty text proposed, we pointed out that the formula suggested represented a middle course between contrasting points of view.

The suggested text served its purpose of being accepted as part of the overall basis for negotiation and indeed remained unchanged right up to the discussions which took place at the Amsterdam European Council itself in June 1997. However, the compromise reached in the final trade-offs at the Amsterdam meeting resulted in a significantly adapted compromise. While the Amsterdam Treaty retains the word "progressive", it also retains the present Treaty wording "which might in time lead to a common defence", with the addition of the words "...should the European Council so decide. It shall in that case recommend to the Member States the adoption of such a decision in accordance with their respective constitutional requirements."

As regards the relationship between the EU and the WEU, the Presidency also sought to find a compromise between those delegations that wished to retain the existing treaty wording, which underlines the separate nature of the two organizations ("the Union *requests* the WEU"), and those that ideally wished to see a merger of the two organizations and therefore favoured wording spelling out the EU's authority over the WEU ("the Union *instructs* the WEU"). While recalling the main alternative wordings on the table, we came up with the formulation "the Union *will avail itself of* the WEU", which eventually found its way into the Treaty of Amsterdam.

The provision for fostering closer institutional relations with the WEU was also retained in the Treaty of Amsterdam, complemented by the clarification that this was "with a view to the possibility of the integration of the WEU into the Union, should the European Council so decide" (in which case it would "recommend" to Member States the adoption of such a decision "in accordance with their respective constitutional requirements"). A Protocol to the Treaty of Amsterdam also specifies that the EU and the WEU are to draw up arrangements for enhanced cooperation between them within a year of the entry into force of the Treaty.

The above is necessarily a summary account of the security and defence issues at the IGC. The issues were discussed on numerous occasions at both political and official level at the Conference, teased out at myriad bilateral meetings and worried over within national administrations before agreement was ultimately reached at Amsterdam (see Chapter 16). They will no doubt be analysed in much greater detail elsewhere.

The snapshot of the issue in the present chapter focuses, for the reasons explained, particularly on early December 1996. This may tend to exaggerate somewhat the role of the Irish Presidency. The final deals were struck under skilful Dutch chairmanship some six months later. What the Irish Presidency tried to do, as in other areas, was to provide a basis for negotiation which could lead to eventual agreement.

External economic relations

The third aspect of the Union's external policy considered by the IGC was the issue of strengthening its ability to act in external economic relations. The outcome on this issue, while not negligible, was arguably one of the most disappointing aspects of the Conference. There was no issue to which the Irish Presidency devoted more of its time or energy in seeking to find a basis for substantial progress.

One of the key features of the European Community since its inception has been its ability to act effectively and to speak with one voice on international trade matters. The original EEC Treaty provided mechanisms in that regard which, until recently, had been considered broadly adequate. Essentially, the Commission conducts negotiations within a framework set by the Council. At the close of negotiations an agreement is concluded by the Council on a proposal from the Commission, the Council generally acting by qualified majority rather than unanimity.

The issue became a significant one at the IGC not because the existing treaty provisions had been found to be inadequate in their original conception, but because the trading environment in which the Community must operate has changed radically in recent years. The original EEC Treaty was drafted with a view to trade in *goods* at a time, 40 years ago, when the focus was on goods. In recent years, new areas such as *services, direct foreign investment* and *intellectual property* have grown, and continue to grow, very significantly in importance. In recent judgements, the Court of Justice has held that the provisions of the existing EC Treaty do not generally apply to such areas.

There was a strongly held majority view that the current situation undermines the capacity of the Community to act effectively in defence of its own interests and the interests of its Member States in an evolving and highly competitive international trading environment. The lacunae in the Treaty were considered to inhibit the Community, notably in the World Trade Organization, in negotiations which are now of central importance to it. The opposite, equally firmly expressed, view was that in practice no significant problems had been experienced by the Community in the conduct of international trade negotiations and that any problems could be ironed out by means of a non-binding Code of Conduct. The former view reflected a willingness to expand the role of the Commission. The latter view appeared, apart from a sensitivity about cutting across national prerogatives, to reflect a mistrust of the Commission on the part of some Member States, based on their perceived experience of some previous trade negotiations.

Drawing on earlier discussions, including at the IGC Ministerial meeting on 28 October, we presented in our Outline Draft Treaty an ambitious text which, while not otherwise affecting internal competences within the Community, would have made the Commission the sole external negotiator in the areas concerned, within the framework of mandates adopted by the Council. This approach went considerably beyond what several Member States had indicated that they could accept. However, the Presidency considered it appropriate to try to maintain a significant level of ambition. The external trade area seemed to us a perfect example of one in which, to borrow from Benjamin Franklin, if the Member States did not hang together they would assuredly hang separately. We retained some hope that a further detailed exploration of the issues might eventually allow a significant breakthrough at the highest level.

In order to soften our relatively controversial approach in a hotly contested area, we recalled in the introduction to the proposed text the continuing wide range of views on the matter. We also, exceptionally, left in square brackets the issue of whether the Council would act by unanimity or qualified majority but made clear, in the introduction to the text, our firm view that provision for decisions to be taken by qualified majority would clearly enable the Community to defend the interests of its Member States more effectively.

The text in the Outline Draft Treaty was accepted, as part of the overall document, as a good basis for the remainder of the negotiations. However, the continuing resolute opposition of some Member States meant that the substance of possible strengthened treaty provisions in the external economic relations area was gradually whittled away during the remainder of the IGC. Despite its determined efforts, the Netherlands Presidency, as it brought the remnants of possible new external trade provisions into port at Amsterdam, looked increasingly like the Old Man and the Sea.

In the event, despite passionate pleas from some Heads of Government at Amsterdam, all that was salvaged was a new enabling provision which would in effect allow Community procedures to be extended later to some of the "new areas" of international trade by unanimous Council decision, without recourse to a further IGC.

Conclusion

I have attempted to give some sense of the external relations issues as they presented themselves at the time of our Outline Draft Treaty in December 1996, in the run-up to Dublin 2. If our suggested approach prefigured in many respects what was agreed at Amsterdam, the IGC negotiations, of course, remained global and nothing could be agreed until everything was agreed. All of the issues, including those in the external area, were revisited and refined in the course of the Netherlands Presidency. The final outcome on the defence issue in particular inevitably remained part of the endgame described in Chapter 16.

The proof of the new external relation provisions of the Amsterdam Treaty will, to a large extent, be in the eating. If the political will is forthcoming, the new CFSP decision-making procedures in particular provide a basis for significantly more effective action. If the political will is not forthcoming, it is probably just as well that the essentially intergovernmental nature of the CFSP has been preserved.

Chapter 11

The Rocky Road to Dublin: Dublin 2

Not chaos-like, together crushed and bruised,
But, as the world, harmoniously confused:
Where order in variety we see,
And where, though all things differ, all agree.
(Alexander Pope, *Windsor Forest*)

The natural desire of each Presidency to be seen to have done a good job is an important catalyst in advancing the business of the European Union. A Presidency is judged largely on the outcome of its end-of-term European Council. Even if it has conducted the broad mass of its business efficiently and decisively over six months, it is normally on the handling of the priority high-profile issues at its regular European Council that a Presidency is deemed to have met with either success or failure.

A European Council brings with it a media circus, several thousand journalists waiting to deliver their verdict on events. Inevitably there are different versions of a European Council. If that were not the case, the national press officers would not be doing their job. On occasion, indeed, one has the impression that at least two different meetings have taken place – what happened in the meeting room and what gains currency in the press centre. Maybe even 16 different meetings if the press officers from the Member States and the Commission have been working overtime. In some respects, the media's perception can be more important than the events themselves. Appearance has its own reality.

The European Council on 13/14 December 1996 – "Dublin 2", as it was called – represented the culmination of the efforts of the Irish Presidency. As the meeting approached, the range of issues for consideration fell into place, including employment (the Dublin Declaration on Employment would be adopted), the enlargement of the Union (a meeting with the Prime Ministers of the Central and Eastern European applicant countries and Cyprus would take place on the second day), Justice and Home Affairs, and several external relations issues.

However, it became clear that two issues in particular would dominate the meeting itself and determine how it would be judged: first, a nexus of key decisions relating to Economic and Monetary Union (Finance Ministers were due to meet separately in Dublin as well as to participate at the European Council itself for the relevant discussions); and second, the IGC.

The former became the more dominant issue, including in the media coverage. While the EMU issues required substantive negotiation at Dublin 2, it had been clearly established that the trade-offs at European Council level in relation to the IGC would take place six months later at Amsterdam.

Order in variety

The challenge for the Irish Presidency in relation to the IGC at Dublin 2 remained what it had been from the outset, namely to mark decisive progress at the Conference by producing a "general framework for a draft revision of the treaties" *which could be accepted by all delegations as a basis for working towards final agreement at Amsterdam*. We had decided, as I have explained in previous chapters, to interpret our mandate with a degree of ambition as regards both the substance ("the upper end of realism") and the nature of the document we would produce ("an Outline Draft Treaty" – wherever possible in the form of "clean" treaty texts).

The crux was that no delegation could get everything it wanted; yet each delegation would have to "find itself" sufficiently in the document to accept it as a basis for further work.

The principal political problem we faced in the run-up to Dublin 2 was a notion, which had refused to die off fully, that the Conference could and should try to bypass the evolutionary nature of the overall negotiating process and press a number of issues at Dublin towards a level of specific agreement. This concept reflected neither the state nor the global nature of the negotiations. It required a quite different understanding of the very nature of the negotiating process than that of the Presidency and the majority of delegations. If the Outline Draft Treaty had purported to reflect a level of agreement, in any areas, significantly beyond that which had been reached, it would have had no prospect of being accepted, even tacitly, as a basis for the further work of the Conference.

As Presidency we had essentially only one shot at producing our Outline Draft Treaty. Once tabled, it could not be subject to negotiation *prior to or at Dublin 2*. Any suggestion that the detail of the document, once tabled, was open to such negotiation, or any provision for a drafting session on it, would have allowed every single issue to be opened up with no prospect of agreement on any of them. For the Irish Presidency, there was one issue – whether we could produce a coherent and ambitious document which, taken as a whole, would be accepted by all delegations as the basis for the final phase of the negotiations. (Of course, in that final phase during the Netherlands Presidency, the *detail* of every aspect of the document would remain subject to significant further amendment and refinement.)

We attached, as we had throughout our Presidency, particular importance to fairness, without fear or favour. We listened very carefully to the concerns of every delegation and sought to accommodate those concerns to the maximum extent possible within the framework of our task. No special deals for any delegation, even for our own national delegation.

Apart from our approach to the substance of the document (set out in Chapter 9), we had to make a sensitive choice, taking into account as always the views of partners, about the *timing* for the tabling of our document in the run-up to the European Council on 13/14 December.

The IGC Representatives Group continued to meet every week. Its last meeting was scheduled for 3 December. The second round of bilateral "confessionals" at IGC Representative level had taken place on 26/27 November. Following the IGC Ministerial meeting on 25 November, Foreign Ministers were due to meet again for a special IGC "conclave" in Brussels on 6 December. The Taoiseach, John Bruton, was carrying out, over a period of weeks, the usual Presidency pre-European Council tour of capitals for preparatory discussions with his fellow Heads of State or Government.

The Presidency and the Council Secretariat continued, in parallel, the preparation of the Outline Draft Treaty. The document was not nestling in our back pocket ready to be sprung on partners, like a rabbit out of a hat. It was not to be plucked out of thin air. Rather it was an attempt to introduce a degree of acceptable coherence into a common exercise. We therefore continued, in preparing the document, to draw significantly on the ongoing multilateral and bilateral discussions.

At such periods, time is a very precious commodity, especially for a Presidency. My most abiding memory of the last weeks before Dublin 2 will be of drafting and redrafting various parts of the Outline Draft Treaty. This process continued late on the evenings of Sunday 1 December and Monday 2 December and made it possible to finalize the Outline Draft Treaty when Noel Dorr and I met with the Council Secretariat after the IGC Representatives' meeting on 3 December and for final drafting sessions with the Secretariat in the course of 4 December.

We had reached the decision that the finalization of the document should be held back as long as possible, both to take maximum account of ongoing discussions and to minimize any risk of attempts by others to amend it. We also saw an advantage in preserving a certain "freshness" about our draft. At the same time we came to the view that, at the latest, it would have to be made available for the Conclave of Foreign Ministers (the principal IGC negotiators) on Friday 6 December. Having debated various options, including distributing it at the Conclave itself, we decided to make it available shortly in advance of that meeting, allowing sufficient time for each delegation to make a first assessment of it.

In putting the final touches to the Outline Draft Treaty, we decided to present it to delegations in a somewhat more formal, and therefore "authoritative", physical format than the almost inevitable A4 sheets stapled at one corner. A limited number of very simply bound copies were therefore produced for delegations, essentially by the addition of front and back covers (in the traditional colour for each language version) and by binding the document in a "book" format. Presentational points of this nature can make a small but important difference to the perception of the substance and significance of a document.

Our aim was to produce a document which, in both its substance and its presentation, was more than an amalgamation of working texts, more than a collage of "photographs" of different parts of the negotiations. Our aim was to produce a document which, for the first time, would bring overall coherence to the negotiations, make sense of the disparate elements, explain to the public what was at issue, and allow participants to hold physically in their hands a document which could, with justification, be described as an Outline Draft Treaty.

The drafting of the document was finalized with the ever-patient Council Secretariat at about 11 p.m. on 4 December, leaving sufficient time for the final amendments to be incorporated overnight in all the language versions by the Council Secretariat translation services. The document was made available simultaneously to all delegations at 3 p.m. on 5 December.

Conclave of Foreign Ministers

Foreign Ministers gave their first reaction to the Outline Draft Treaty at their Conclave on 6 December. A decision on acceptance (or not) of the document as a basis for the further work of the Conference would ultimately be for Heads of State or Government in Dublin the following week, but the reaction of Foreign Ministers could be make-or-break. To our relief, virtually all Foreign Ministers warmly welcomed the text. There seemed little doubt, from their initial reaction, that the document would be broadly accepted by virtually all delegations as a basis for further work. We were particularly reassured that the Netherlands delegation, which would shortly take over the chairing of the IGC, was happy with it and that the British delegation – whose positions at the time were at greatest variance (by a long way) with the treaty texts proposed in the Outline Draft Treaty – accepted the overall presentation as fair.

The document was the fruit not of the Presidency working in isolation, but of the collective efforts of negotiators from all Member States. Most delegations appeared to share in a sense of satisfaction that there was now a comprehensive, coherent and balanced document, somewhere near "the upper end of realism", which offered the prospect for agreement at Amsterdam.

However, the French Foreign Minister took the view, as he informed the media, that while the draft represented an accurate picture of the stage the negotiations had reached, it was lacking in ambition and could not be seen as the outline of a new treaty.

While he emphasized that his criticism was not of the Presidency, his reaction to the document qualified its initial welcome and cast at least some doubt on the likelihood of its acceptance by the European Council as a basis for further work. Another delegation, which was not satisfied with the way a few specific points had been reflected in the document, was also cool in its response.

Dublin 2

During the days remaining before the European Council on 13/14 December, the Taoiseach, John Bruton, completed his tour of capitals (London on 9 December and Paris on 10 December). Chancellor Kohl and President Chirac sent a detailed joint letter to their colleagues setting out their views on IGC.

Telephone contacts, reflecting different advice for and conflicting pressures on the Presidency, continued. Delegations were to assemble in Dublin on the evening of 12 December.

The key, as always, would be the European Council "Conclusions". (As explained in Chapter 2, these are drafted in advance by the Presidency with the assistance of the Council Secretariat, adapted in the light of discussions on the first day of the European Council, distributed to other delegations (for the first time) early on the morning of the second day, and then finalized by the European Council itself.)

In this case, the stage that the IGC had reached was reflected in the Outline Draft Treaty itself. The key aim for the European Council Conclusions, if it could be achieved, was therefore always going to be a statement to the effect that the Outline Draft Treaty constituted the basis for further work. (Whether the words to be used were "a basis" or "the basis" or "a good basis" was of no real significance.)

Several separate pages of detailed Conclusions for the European Council could, of course, also be drafted. However, if those Conclusions were to be both "substantive" and unanimously accepted, they could amount to little more than a summary of the stage the negotiations had reached – namely the Outline Draft Treaty itself.

The dilemma facing the Presidency was that the initial signals from a few delegations at the Foreign Ministers' conclave had been that they might not be comfortable with our Outline Draft Treaty as the basis for further negotiations.

In the light of conflicting pressures in the period immediately before the European Council in Dublin, we came to two decisions about the Conclusions.

First, we would try to facilitate agreement by expanding our draft of the Conclusions (which had, of course, not yet been seen by other delegations) to highlight some of the elements in the Outline Draft Treaty, to identify explicitly certain issues for further consideration, and to build up assertive statements about what was still to be negotiated. However, this would be done without calling into question in the slightest degree the document as the basis for further negotiations, and without having the European Council set definite *new* directions or priorities or policy choices (on which, in any event, there would have been no prospect of agreement).

Second, we decided to stick firmly with the orthodox and well-proven method for preparing European Council Conclusions, described above, which leaves the Presidency in the driving seat until the point at which the draft conclusions are tabled for consideration by the Heads of State or Government themselves. Although a large majority of delegations as well as the Commission supported our approach in this regard, we came under strong pressure, both before and during the European Council, to convene a special drafting group to prepare "substantive" Conclusions on the IGC. However, this would not only have seriously undermined the effective functioning of the European Council in Dublin, but also have set an unwelcome precedent for the future. It would moreover have pandered to the illusion that the state and aspirations of the IGC at that stage could have been set out in a form which differed in any significant substantive way from the Outline Draft Treaty itself. A calling into question of the Outline Draft Treaty as the basis for further work would have marked a setback for the Conference and undermined the significant progress which it represented.

The Presidency did, however, as part of the delicate exercise of accommodating the sensitivities of all delegations, convene an informal dinner of IGC Representatives in Dublin on the evening of 12 December to tease out the state of play. We conveyed signals both at that meeting, which was not conclusive, and bilaterally on how we intended to handle the drafting of Conclusions.

Discussion on the IGC on the first afternoon of the European Council, on 13 December, proved, if I may invert T.S. Eliot, to be a whimper rather than a bang. All the Heads of State or Government, as well as the President of the European Commission, were positive in their overall reaction to the Presidency document, each emphasizing points of particular concern for the future negotiations. President Chirac, as he subsequently was to inform the media, was kind enough to say "bravo" to the Irish Presidency.

Late that first evening, the Presidency met in the usual way with the Council Secretariat and the Commission to finalize the draft Conclusions covering all aspects of the work of the European Council. Early the following morning, we distributed our draft Conclusions to other delegations in the normal manner.

Apart from the IGC, these Conclusions reflected important progress in several areas. Most notably, the necessary agreement had been reached to keep Economic and Monetary Union on track.

The Conclusions relating to the IGC, which ran to just over three pages, were approved by the European Council – along with the rest of the Conclusions – on the second morning of its meeting, subject to some minor adjustments. The Conclusions on the IGC welcomed the Outline Draft Treaty which "makes it possible for the negotiations to move now into their final phase" as "a good basis for the final phase of the Intergovernmental Conference which should conclude at Amsterdam in June 1997". The European Union moves in strange ways.

The media assessment of Dublin 2 was broadly positive. Both appearance and reality were on this occasion satisfactory.

For the Irish Presidency – mission accomplished.

PART III

TAKING DECISIONS

Chapter 12

Dutch Masters: the Netherlands Presidency

In der Kunst ist das Beste gut genug
(In Art the best is good enough)
(Goethe, *Das Italienische Reise*)

The Outline Draft Treaty inherited by the Netherlands Presidency on 1 January 1997 was an outline sketch in a picture-frame. The skilful brushstrokes of the Dutch Masters would be required to complete and give life to the picture. Some parts of the tableau would require more work than others. Their task would be made no easier by the continuing attempts of 15 different artists to hold the paintbrush.

The principal challenge of the IGC fell to the Netherlands Presidency. The Dublin 2 European Council had set a clear mandate for the new Presidency. It had reaffirmed "the importance of completing the Conference at Amsterdam in June 1997". The task now was to move to definitive and detailed agreement on a treaty – quite a different kettle of roll-mops.

The Netherlands Foreign Minister, Hans van Mierlo, travelled to Tralee in Kerry for a useful handover discussion with the Irish Foreign Minister, Dick Spring, on 6 January 1997. There is a fundamentally empathetic relationship between succeeding Presidencies if they avoid trying to tell each other what to do. We were determined to reciprocate the constructive support which we had received from the Netherlands during our own Presidency.

The stakes had now become higher both for the Netherlands Presidency and for the Union as a whole. The prize was agreement at Amsterdam. The shadow was the risk that failure to reach such agreement would be seen as a significant setback for the Union. Failure would delay, and might actually call into question, a range of important developments including the opening of enlargement negotiations and possibly even the move to a single currency.

The Netherlands Presidency, however, had been given one vital weapon – confirmation of an agreed target that the Conference should conclude at Amsterdam. The slow bicycle race had long since been abandoned. There was no longer an artificial constraint on the rate of progress of the Conference (other than the impending British general election, which in some areas prevented it moving fully into top gear). From now on, if the negotiations stalled, the fault would lie "not in our stars but in ourselves".

My account of the strategy and conduct of the Netherlands Presidency will be comparatively brief. Holding the Presidency offers an exceptional opportunity to comprehend the workings of the Union during the period in question. If I could have the same insight into the IGC in the first half of 1997 that I had during the Irish Presidency in the second half of 1996, I would be, quite literally, a Dutchman. Maybe the following imperfect account of the Netherlands Presidency will at least serve the purpose of encouraging Tom or Mathias to clarify the record.

The mandate given to the Netherlands Presidency would require two things.

First, it would require the continued development over six months of an overall package through the process of "successive approximations". In the few sensitive areas in which it had not been possible for the Irish Presidency to propose treaty texts, such texts would have to be tabled on the basis of emerging options and developed towards the area of possible agreement. In other areas, the texts accepted as the basis for further work would have to be refined.

Second, the Netherlands Presidency would have to ensure, on the basis of that overall package, a successful outcome to the final poker game at Amsterdam on 16/17 June 1997.

The shape of the Presidency's work programme was always going to be significantly determined by the date of the British general election which had to take place no later than early May 1997. Although the final deals in every area could only be struck at Amsterdam itself, in some areas it would not even be possible to move in earnest to locking the main elements of those deals firmly into place until a British Government, of either hue – which could ultimately strike those deals – was in position.

In the event the British general election took place at more or less the last possible moment, on 1 May. In practice, allowing a minimum time for the members of the new British Government to find where to hang their coats, this was to leave significantly less than six working weeks for the intensive final phase of the negotiations (which is dealt with in Chapter 16).

The work programme, January to April

The initial work programme distributed by the Netherlands Presidency, which surmised accurately the electoral inclinations of John Major, covered the first four months of 1997.

The work programme was launched with an informal meeting of IGC Representatives in Amsterdam which followed broadly the format of the informal meeting in Cork at the outset of the Irish Presidency. The impressive setting for the meeting – the converted St Olof's Chapel which now constitutes the conference centre of the Barbizon Palace Hotel – ensured appropriate godspeed for the work of the Presidency. The tour of the Maritime Museum in Amsterdam organized for delegates served as a reminder that the Netherlands Presidency would require all the navigation skills of their ancestors to avoid the reefs ahead.

The informal meeting offered the Presidency an opportunity to present and build a sense of shared commitment to its aims, its methods and its work programme. It also made possible a more informal exchange of views on some of the most sensitive outstanding issues.

The rhythm of meetings up to the end of April was to be maintained, with monthly Ministerial IGC meetings and weekly meetings of IGC Representatives in the weeks when Ministers were not meeting.

While maintaining this formal rhythm, the Presidency also sought in a number of ways to increase the intensity of the negotiations. It emphasized that fulfilment of the mandate to conclude at Amsterdam required the firming up of national positions as well as a greater engagement in serious negotiation. It focused discussion in the initial months almost entirely on some of the more difficult and sensitive issues.

As had been the experience of the Irish Presidency, the very assertion that the negotiations were moving into a new phase and pace helped to create its own reality.

In summary, the tactic of the Netherlands Presidency, in footballing terms, was to "put 'em under pressure".

The looming British election continued to pose a strategic dilemma. On the one hand, the Conference could not afford to tread water for four months. On the other hand, it was clearly in nobody's interests that the Conference be handled in a way which would allow it to become a divisive issue in the British election. The more controversial it became from a domestic UK point of view, the more the hands of a new British government of either complexion would be tied. The successful handling of this aspect was in no small measure due to the sensitive approach of the Netherlands Presidency and, of course, to the very professional British negotiators themselves. It is not, I think, without significance that no delegation – including the British delegation – sought at any stage to transform an inherent tension into a public crisis.

The Netherlands Presidency initially concentrated work on three issues (which are the subject of the next three chapters of this book): (i) flexibility, i.e. a treaty basis to allow reinforced cooperation, within the Union's institutions, between a number of Member States less than the full membership; (ii) sensitive institutional questions; (iii) Justice and Home Affairs.

On the first two of these issues, the Presidency had to try to move towards the development of draft treaty texts in the light of the emerging analysis and options. On the third, the texts contained in the Irish Presidency's Outline Draft Treaty were used as the starting point of discussion. For two months, the Conference discussed virtually no issues other than these three. Even into March and April, there was a heavy focus on these issues, especially on Justice and Home Affairs.

Wisely, the Netherlands Presidency "parked" the remaining issues for varying periods of time. The issues thus left in abeyance, which were gradually revisited for the purposes of refinement, included two of the five Sections of the work of the Conference (the Union and the Citizen, and Foreign Policy), the less sensitive institutional questions, and issues, other than Justice and Home Affairs, falling under the heading of Freedom, Security and Justice (including fundamental rights and non-discrimination.) The re-examination of these issues, using as a starting point the texts in our Outline Draft Treaty, started essentially in March. Several of the issues were revisited for the first time in April.

The growing pressure of work meant that a very large number of issues often fell to be addressed at a single IGC Representatives meeting. For example, twelve issues (seventeen views per issue!) were scheduled for discussion at the IGC Representatives meeting on 21/22 April.

In addition to the regular Ministerial IGC meetings, a supplementary Conclave of Foreign Ministers was convened in Noordwijk on 6/7 April to try to make progress in particular on some of the sensitive institutional questions, as well as on CFSP decision-making and the social dimension.

The Presidency, moreover, was not dealing with a finite in-tray. There is no formal deadline for the tabling of new proposals at an IGC. At its first meeting in January, the Netherlands Presidency had recognized that the dimensions of the IGC had been determined, and appealed for "no new surprises". However, this did not stop delegations from submitting new proposals and papers – some in core areas of the work of the Conference and others in areas not yet addressed. These proposals were largely irrelevant, other than for domestic consumption, except in so far as they influenced the papers tabled for discussion by the Presidency. A few issues, such as public health and social exclusion, were gradually subsumed into the emerging package. Others found some foothold in the package only in the final weeks, usually in the form of non-binding declarations. Many fell by the wayside.

To examine the technical issues of simplification and consolidation of the existing Treaties, the Netherlands Presidency set up an expert working party, under the authority of and to work in parallel with the IGC Representatives Group. *Simplification* meant essentially the deletion of treaty provisions which over 40 years had become obsolete. *Consolidation* meant examining the scope for restructuring and reordering the complex patchwork of treaties which had developed. The expert working party, chaired by the Presidency, held its first meeting on 15 January 1997 and continued to meet on a weekly basis over the following months. The legal service of the Council Secretariat provided the raw material for its work.

40th anniversary of the Treaty of Rome

The Ministerial IGC meeting on 25 March, which took place on the Campidoglio in Rome to mark the 40th anniversary of the Treaty of Rome, was the pivot of the first half of the Netherlands Presidency. The Presidency tabled for that meeting an "Addendum" to the Outline Draft Treaty containing new or revised treaty texts in the areas on which work had focused since January. While the "Addendum" provided the basis for a useful exchange of views in Rome, the Presidency did not seek to have it endorsed and the meeting adopted no formal conclusions.

The formal commemoration ceremony to mark the 40th anniversary, on the afternoon of the Ministerial meeting, took place in the Aula di Giulio Cesare. The eponymous dignitary, who had some centuries before tried his hand at a different form of European integration, might have pondered whether the ambition of the IGC "should be made of sterner stuff".

Ambition is one of the most precious resources in the European Union but, like other things which glister, it is not always what it seems. Without ambition Europe is lost. But excessive ambition, out of touch with reality and public support, must be treated with caution. One must be on the look out for national interest trying to masquerade as ambition for Europe. One must beware of cheap appeals to a precious commodity.

Place your bets

In the course of April, as the grinding work on texts continued, there was already much discussion of how to handle the final furlong of the IGC after the British general election. The Presidency indicated its intention of convening a special (additional) European Council on 25 May.

The corridor talk was about the prospects for completion of the Conference at Amsterdam in June. Insiders said that at the equivalent stage of the Maastricht negotiations, work had been more advanced. Everything remained to play for.

Chapter 13

Flexibility

When I consider every thing that grows
Holds in perfection but a little moment
(Shakespeare, _Sonnet 15_)

The word "flexibility" is used to describe the scope for a number of Member States – less than the full membership of the Union – to cooperate more closely in certain areas within the Union's institutional framework. In some respects, flexibility was the most important of the five main Sections of the IGC's work. Whatever the Conference would agree or would not agree on flexibility would be of the greatest significance for the future development of the Union.

It was also the most difficult issue for the IGC to come to grips with. In every other area of the work of the Conference, the basic question for delegations was whether they could accept what was proposed on specific issues. In relation to flexibility, the additional parallel challenge for delegations was to define the issue itself. To say that flexibility meant different things to different people would be to put it mildly.

The concept of flexibility in the European Union is not a new one. The existing Treaties, for example, provide for Member States to move at different speeds towards Economic and Monetary Union and some Member States do not even consider themselves bound to move to that objective. The Social Agreement, agreed at Maastricht, had provided a basis for action in the social area in which one Member State (the UK) would not participate. Moreover, Community legislation regularly allows temporary exemptions or a gradual phasing-in of measures for some Member States.

However, the essential thrust of existing flexibility arrangements is that the coherence and common endeavour of the Union should be preserved. Apart from the exceptional cases of EMU and the Social Agreement – the latter widely regarded as having been a mistake which the IGC should take the opportunity of rectifying – existing flexibility relates not to objectives, which should remain shared, but to the speed at which Member States will move towards agreed objectives.

The issue at the IGC was whether the Treaties should provide for more far-reaching flexibility mechanisms, whether recourse to the possibility of flexibility should become an orthodox way of doing business in the Union, whether flexibility should itself be consecrated as a principle of the Union rather than tolerated as a deviation from its principles.

The concept of flexibility gained currency in the course of 1995, including in discussions in the Reflection Group. The Reflection Group's report contained a significant section on flexibility which stated that "if a common will is ultimately found to be lacking, that should not prevent those who wish and even need to make the Union progress from doing so subject to clear limits".

Two other developments gave a significant push to the impetus for developing flexibility mechanisms in the Treaties. First, the pre-Madrid European Council letter from Chancellor Kohl and President Chirac on 6 December 1995 emphasized that both Germany and France would be pressing for a general flexibility clause in the Treaty. Second, some of the principal theologians of Community orthodoxy – the Commission in its formal opinion of February 1996 on the convening of the IGC and the three Benelux countries in their IGC Memorandum of March 1996 – came out in support of such flexibility mechanisms.

This second development was particularly significant. The positive support for flexibility from several of the players who traditionally defend the "community" method and the integrity of Community institutions meant that the most likely natural counterweight to the impulse for flexibility – priority for the preservation of coherence – was unlikely to develop as significantly as would otherwise have been the case.

Up-and-under

For a long time it remained very far from clear what was meant by the holy grail of "flexibility" or how precisely the Treaties might be developed in that regard. The concept of flexibility was still, in rugby terms, an up-and-under or Garryowen (a *ballon-à-suivre*).

Although discussions continued during 1996, the two delegations that were its principal authors – France and Germany – did not table detailed ideas on how flesh might be put on its bones until October 1996. The relatively slow development of thinking on the issue of flexibility at the Conference reflected two principal factors.

In the first place, it was clear from the outset that a mishandling of the flexibility issue could undermine the coherence of the European Union and conceivably even lead to its disintegration. All delegations recognized that it was a concept which would, therefore, have to be developed gingerly. The Reflection Group report had rejected "any formula which could lead to an *à la carte* Europe", as had the Benelux Memorandum. The Commission Opinion had firmly rejected any idea of a "pick-and-choose" Europe, which "flies in the face of the common European project". It was not entirely clear if and how flexibility could be fully reconcilable with coherence. Nevertheless, with the aim of reconciling the two concepts, every presentation advocating flexibility identified several limitative criteria to apply in its application.

A second reason for the gentle pace of progress at the IGC on the general issue of flexibility *as such* was its inextricable link with several of the other substantive issues under consideration at the Conference. The need for and nature of any new general flexibility provisions would have to take account of the substantive provisions likely to be agreed in areas such as the Common Foreign and Security Policy, and Justice and Home Affairs ("the "second pillar" and the "third pillar" respectively). The extent to which provisions in such other areas would themselves contain a degree of "flexibility" would largely determine the need for general flexibility provisions. The extent to which general flexibility would be considered necessary for normal Community ("first pillar") business depended to a significant degree on the willingness of the Conference to substitute the flexibility of majority decision-making mechanisms for the more inflexible unanimity requirement.

Moreover, the extent of lack of consensus on the direction for the future development of the European Union, the core justification for flexibility, could be fully assessed only in the light of progress in the other main areas of the work of the IGC. That in turn was an issue not entirely unrelated to the outcome of the British general election.

Flexibility: form, purpose, application and implications

The dossier on flexibility bequeathed to the Netherlands Presidency was a fluid one. The issue had been discussed on a number of occasions during our Presidency, notably on the basis of the ideas tabled jointly by France and Germany in October 1996. However, we had taken the view, shared by most delegations, that it would have been premature to table a treaty text on the matter in our Outline Draft Treaty. Instead we had set out in some detail the state of play on the issue, including areas of emerging common ground, as well as some of the key questions remaining to be addressed.

The magnitude of the task facing the Netherlands Presidency in nudging the Conference gradually towards agreement on new flexibility provisions can be illustrated by recalling some of the areas of continuing difference between the Member States as regards flexibility: its *form*, its *purpose*, its *application*, and its *implications for the Union*.

Three broad, not necessarily mutually exclusive, *forms* of flexibility were under consideration in different areas of the Conference's work, as follows.

(i) *Case-by-case flexibility*: This form of flexibility would apply when individual acts or decisions were being adopted. An example of this type of flexibility was the new constructive abstention mechanism eventually agreed as regards the Common Foreign and Security Policy (see Chapter 10).

(ii) *Pre-determined flexibility*: Such flexibility would take the form of providing for flexible cooperation in a specific area by detailing all aspects in the Treaty itself, possibly in the form of a Treaty Protocol. In the event, the only example of this type of flexibility eventually reflected in the Treaty of Amsterdam, in a hybrid form, is in the Justice and Home Affairs area.

(iii) *An enabling clause approach*: The third form of flexibility was referred to as an "enabling clause" approach because, rather than setting out in the Treaty itself detailed provisions for flexibility in a specific area, the idea was to include in the Treaty general provisions *enabling* the development of enhanced cooperation in areas unspecified in advance, but subject to certain conditions.

This third form of flexibility, the enabling clause approach – which might be termed "general flexibility" – was essentially the one dealt with under the specific heading of "flexibility" at the IGC, the other forms being dealt with in the context of consideration by the Conference of different substantive areas of its work.

Views on the *purpose* of flexibility were not only various but contradictory. For some, the principal purpose of additional flexibility was to provide for an appropriate degree of differentiation in the context of the further enlargement of the Union. For others, flexibility was already increasingly necessary in a Union of 15 Member States. For some, the purpose was to allow the faster ships to move more quickly, certainly not an excuse for the slower ships to drop out of formation. For others, the attraction of flexibility was precisely to allow a degree of opting-out or hanging back, certainly not an excuse to allow the leaders of the convoy to disappear over the horizon.

The different perceptions of the purpose of flexibility were reflected in the other terms used interchangeably to describe the concept of flexibility, namely "enhanced cooperation" and "differentiated integration".

As to precise areas in which the *application* of general flexibility provisions could be appropriate, there were as many views as delegations. The view that there should be no prior limitation on the areas in which general flexibility might apply was met by the view that broad sweeps of the Union's business should be ruled out of bounds. Depending on your point of view, the Common Foreign and Security Policy (the second pillar), for example, was either the most or the least appropriate area for general flexibility. Nor was there consensus as regards areas within normal Community (first pillar) business for possible application of general flexibility. Provision for the application of flexibility to a nexus of policies in and around the single currency was, depending on your point of view, either anathema or the very purpose of flexibility.

Underlying these various approaches were fundamental concerns about the *implications* of flexibility for the future development of the Union. The one option which the Union does not have is simply to stand still, to "hold in perfection".

The nature of the fully enlarged Union, a few decades from now, hinges to a considerable degree on the issue of flexibility. Only three broad long-term scenarios seem possible: an extrapolation of the current Union, largely coherent but diluted in its aspirations; a Union in which flexibility permits the development of an inner core, based in the first instance on the single currency, but risking the creation of a Union within the Union; or a Union involving a patchwork of enhanced cooperation arrangements, coherence to an extent sacrificed on the altar of flexibility. The long-term shape of the Union has by no means been resolved, nor could it have been, by this IGC.

The Netherlands Presidency

Although such differences persisted, the sense of common purpose at the IGC in addressing the issue of flexibility should not be underestimated. The importance of the issue was recognized by all. Intermingled with the pursuit of different, often evolving, views was a shared search for a way forward which could reconcile the need for both coherence and flexibility and provide a basis for agreement at Amsterdam.

As the Netherlands Presidency set about trying to draw the strands together, common ground was emerging on several important points of principle including recognition that flexibility should be used only subject to precisely defined conditions (to ensure notably the maintenance of the Union's internal and external coherence, the full preservation of its achievements and institutions, and respect for its objectives). It was accepted that flexibility in a given area should be open equally to all Member States, that no Member State should be obliged to participate, and that the position of non-participating Member States should be respected.

In so far as the IGC would wish to develop specific treaty amendments reflecting a general *enabling clause* approach to flexibility (as in (iii) above), the task fell to the Netherlands Presidency. (The other types of flexibility continued to fall for consideration, as indicated, as an integral part of other substantive areas of the work of the Conference.)

The Netherlands Presidency decided to devote its first IGC Ministerial Meeting on 20 January 1997 to the issue of flexibility, and sought the guidance of Ministers on a number of key questions. The three questions submitted to Ministers on 20 January 1997 addressed the core of the issue. While reactions on that occasion were preliminary and inconclusive, the questions remained at the heart of the IGC's deliberations on flexibility.

The Presidency focused its three questions in particular on flexibility under the "first pillar", that is in respect of normal Community business. Flexibility in respect of the Common Foreign and Security Policy, which was seen by most – although not all – delegations as being adequately and more appropriately addressed through case-by-case flexibility mechanisms as described in Chapter 10, was being addressed principally under the foreign policy heading. Flexibility in relation to Justice and Home Affairs could not be considered in isolation from the substantive consideration of that area which, in the Presidency's view, should involve a significant degree of "predetermined flexibility" as explained in Chapter 15.

The *first* question submitted to Ministers on 20 January concerned the areas of the first pillar to which flexibility should apply. Should there be a "positive list" of areas where flexibility could apply or a "negative list" of areas that would be excluded from its application?

The *second* question concerned the decision-making procedure to apply for the establishment of enhanced cooperation in a particular area. Should the unanimous agreement of Member States be required or could the decision be taken by some form of majority decision? This was and remained, until Amsterdam itself, the central political question in relation to flexibility. The ability of one Member State to veto recourse to flexibility mechanisms would obviously restrict its significance and, according to one view, render it meaningless. The ability of a majority of Member States to introduce "enhanced cooperation", in the face of opposition from one or more other Member States, would at the very least raise questions about whether such "enhanced cooperation" would in practice serve its stated intention of deepening European integration and protecting and serving the interests of the Union as a whole.

These first two questions remained intimately interlinked and the interplay between them continued throughout the remainder of the Conference. The importance of pre-defining areas in which flexibility could apply was perceived to diminish to the extent that the decision-making mechanism to be agreed would allow an individual Member State to exercise a veto.

The *third* question related to the role of the Commission. Should it, in relation to flexibility, exercise its normal *exclusive* right of initiative for (first pillar) Community business which ensures, in the interests of the Union as a whole, that it retains a firm grip on any proposals for decision by the Council of Ministers? Or rather should the Commission have something more akin to a right of approval or endorsement for proposals formulated essentially *by a group of Member States*?

Many considered the Commission's precise role a somewhat abstruse issue. The Irish delegation, with some support from others, considered that it was an issue of fundamental importance and argued that there was a world of difference between a proposal for the application of flexibility being developed by and within the checks and balances of the Commission itself and such a proposal being first developed and even drafted between a group of foreign ministries before being presented to the Commission for its possible endorsement and formal submission to the Council. (While due weight must be attached to the view, expressed by some, that it would not be in the nature of the Commission to develop proposals in respect of some Member States only, the fact is that by definition any proposals for flexibility would, as the Treaty of Amsterdam later put it, be "aimed at furthering the objectives of the Union and at protecting and serving its interests", a function for which the Commission is eminently well suited.)

In the light of the Ministerial discussion on 20 January (and taking account of a number of proposals tabled by individual delegations including Italy and Portugal), the Netherlands Presidency tabled a draft treaty text for an enabling clause approach to flexibility for consideration at the IGC Representatives' meeting on 17/18 February. The text consisted of a *general clause*, applicable to all three "pillars", setting out the general conditions and institutional arrangements for flexibility, and *specific clauses for each of the three pillars* setting out the conditions for enhanced cooperation in each of those areas.

This text tabled by the Presidency now became the basis for negotiation on flexibility, as texts tabled six months earlier by the

Irish Presidency had done on other subjects. The process of refinement ("successive approximations") could now apply in relation to flexibility also. Discussion of "general flexibility" continued to focus almost entirely on the first pillar aspect, although the proposal that it should apply to all three pillars remained on the table.

The Presidency, over the remaining months, scheduled many discussions of flexibility at official and political level, each meeting permitting a further refinement of the draft text. The task was a particularly difficult one, not only because of its inherent delicacy and complexity but also because of its interlinkage with other areas of the Conference's ongoing work.

The outstanding issues for Amsterdam

Through this process the text was gradually refined in both its broad approach and its detail. The general conditions for the application of flexibility, for example, were brought towards completion. The exclusive right of initiative of the Commission was adequately built into the draft.

However, it remained clear that two issues in particular in relation to general flexibility would remain to be settled at Amsterdam.

First, the question of the decision-making procedure for the launching of enhanced cooperation in a particular area – unanimity or something more flexible – could be settled only at the highest level. The outcome of the British general election would be significant in this regard. No British government was likely to cede a right of veto over such enhanced cooperation – indeed, a new Labour Government, keen to bring Britain back into the mainstream of European developments, was likely if anything to take an even more jaundiced view of free-ranging flexibility. A change of government in London might, however, decrease the perceived need of some others for a circumnavigation mechanism around an immovable object, and might therefore defuse the issue somewhat. Until the decision-making mechanism was agreed, the linked question of how to define areas of Community business in which flexibility might or might not apply could not be definitively settled.

The second key issue for resolution at Amsterdam in relation to general flexibility was whether the "specific" enabling clauses, permitting and at the same time circumscribing flexibility, would apply only to the first pillar (normal Community business) or also to the second and third pillars (the CFSP and Justice and Home Affairs).

The possibility of an enabling clause applying in the Justice and Home Affairs area seemed entirely secondary to the far-reaching flexibility mechanisms being negotiated separately by the Conference in that area (see Chapter 15).

As regards the CFSP, a majority of delegations remained broadly satisfied with the new case-by-case flexibility being built into CFSP decision-making process itself. They considered that provision for a group of Member States to undertake separate actions in the foreign policy area, through a general enabling clause approach, would risk undermining the external coherence of the Union. Half in jest, it was asked what the implications for US foreign policy would be if, for example, its Middle East policy was said to be supported by all States other than California, Texas and Utah. Although the notion of general flexibility in relation to foreign policy had clearly passed its sell-by date, it was retained as part of the emerging package. Indeed, it remained in the Draft Treaty eventually submitted for consideration by the European Council at Amsterdam and was removed only at that late stage.

The pieces of the flexibility puzzle for the Amsterdam endgame were slowly but surely falling into place.

Chapter 14

Institutions

Rien n'est possible sans les hommes, rien n'est durable sans les institutions.

(Jean Monnet, *Mémoires*)

The institutions conceived by the founding fathers of European integration are the Union's most original and important resource. With all their imperfections, they are the structure through which competing interests can be reconciled. They offer the context for slowly reshaping national interests in a wider European perspective. They are the fulcrum of the delicate balance between European hope and experience. Only they can make it possible to transform the reality of human nature in our brave new European world from a dangerous contradiction into a hopeful paradox. It is a paradox which still offers the best hope of addressing the concerns of citizens and must increasingly shoulder responsibility for the prosperity and stability of the wider European continent.

Institutional questions represented the fourth of the five main Sections of the IGC's work.

The principal institutions of the European Union

The European Union has four principal institutions, as follows.

- At the heart of the system is the *European Commission* which acts as the guardian of the common interest. It has the exclusive right of proposing legislation. (Moreover, unless the Commission agrees, the unanimity of all Member States is required to amend a Commission proposal.) It manages and implements policies decided by the Council of Ministers, and is responsible for ensuring that the Treaties, as well as Community legislation, are respected.

- The *Council of Ministers*, consisting of representatives of the governments of the Member States, is the principal decision-making body in virtually all areas. It adopts Community legislation through various procedures involving also the

European Parliament (including in some cases "co-decision" with the Parliament). The Council acts either by unanimity or by qualified majority (see below). It shapes Union policy under all three pillars. Along with the Parliament, it constitutes the "budgetary authority".

- The *European Parliament*, the direct election of which is without parallel or precedent in the world, constitutes the most visibly democratic aspect of the Union's institutional arrangements. Apart from its long-standing budgetary powers as part of the "budgetary authority", the Parliament's role in the legislative process has been systematically expanded by each successive IGC.

- The *Court of Justice* is responsible for the interpretation and application of the Treaties and of Community law. Its rulings, which are final, ensure that the Union is a Union of law.

Motivations for and against change

The Union's institutions need to be continually adapted and streamlined to take account of developing circumstances and new challenges. Institutional change therefore figures as a perennial subject on the agendas of Intergovernmental Conferences.

The need to address institutional change imaginatively and creatively must be balanced by a counsel of caution. While wishing any institutional bathwater on its merry way down the plug-hole of history, the Union must at the same time keep a firm grip on a rather irreplaceable baby.

The Intergovernmental Conference faced a wide range of institutional challenges. It might be useful to reflect first briefly on what seemed to be the *four principal motivations* behind the tabling at the IGC of proposals for institutional change.

The *first*, and for many the most important, motivation for institutional change was to make the functioning of the Union more effective. The IGC took place with a further enlargement in prospect which is set to make the Union larger and more heterogeneous than could have been conceived at the time the original Communities were founded. There was a widespread view at the IGC that the institutions, initially conceived for a Community of Six and already not always functioning on all cylinders in a Union of Fifteen, could grind towards a halt in a Union of Twenty-five.

The *second* motivation was to make the Union more visibly democratic in its operation, notably by expanding the role of the European Parliament. A different angle, strongly pressed by some – especially France – in this context, was that the role of national parliaments in relation to Union business should also be enhanced.

The *third* motivation shared by a significant minority, although not explicitly acknowledged, was to try to rebalance the existing institutional equilibrium in favour of larger Member States at the expense of the small and medium-sized ones.

The *fourth* motivation – reflected in a UK proposal pressed in the early stages of the Conference – was to seek to define more precisely certain powers of the Court of Justice (some would have alleged with a view to clipping its wings). This particular hobby horse stayed up with the field around the first circuit of the course before falling into a ditch somewhere out of public view on the back straight.

The motivation behind an individual proposal was often, of course, quite mixed. The motivation of countries, as of human beings, usually has more than one explanation. The insistence of some delegations, for example, that the right of each Member State to nominate a member of the Commission should be discontinued reflected, at one and the same time, the view that this would make the Commission more effective and the perception that it could increase the influence of larger Member States.

There appeared to be two principal trends working contrary to these aims. In the first place, proposals designed to make the Union more effective or to extend the role of the European Parliament had to contend with sensitivities, of one sort or another, about national sovereignty. All Member States, to some degree, shared those sensitivities. Second, attempts to rebalance the institutions in favour of larger Member States faced firm and predictable insistence from the less populous Member States that the broad institutional balances should be preserved.

The sensitivity of the issues

In the addressing of institutional change at the IGC, public concerns and sensitivities in every Member State represented a very fundamental constraint. The outcome of the Conference would eventually have to be ratified by each Member State and acceptable to its public opinion. The task was not to design flawless theoretical structures in a political vacuum. That could have been done by a firm of international management consultants. The outcome of the Conference on institutional questions, whatever it might be, would have to do two things. First, it would have to reflect the subtle and complex nature of the coming together of interests and aspirations which defines the very nature of European Union. Second, it would have to ensure that the Union's institutions would continue to deserve – and, if possible, succeed in increasing – the allegiance and support of the public in each Member State.

Of course, no delegation at the IGC approached the institutional issues with those lofty constraints always to the forefront of its mind. In the nature of a negotiation, each delegation pursued, in the first instance, its own perceived interests with its own public opinion in mind. However, while individually the delegations pursued different and often competing interests, collectively they shared the task of reconciling those interests for their common benefit. The European Union at work.

Thus, although discussions on the institutional issues were sometimes fairly close to the bone and on occasion tense, they were conducted with courtesy. The pursuit of narrow national interests was generally intermingled with a wider awareness of the interests of others. The largest Member State, Germany, for example, showed exemplary understanding of the sensitivities of the smallest Member States. The contributions in the institutional area of the Commission and the European Parliament also served as a force for equity.

Rapid progress in some areas

It was clear from an early stage, even from the first discussions in the Reflection Group, that certain institutional questions were of particular sensitivity and would go to the wire in the final trade-offs. Nevertheless, the Irish Presidency, like the Italian Presidency before it, did what it could to advance the work of the Conference on institutional questions.

First of all, progress was made during our Presidency towards agreement on some of the less sensitive institutional questions. Our Outline Draft Treaty in December 1996, for example, contained a proposal for a streamlining and speeding-up of the complex co-decision procedure on which agreement was already emerging at the Conference. It also proposed placing the Parliament on an equal footing with the Council within the co-decision procedure, a point on which at that stage there were strongly opposing views but which was eventually agreed. Among the other institutional proposals contained in the Outline Draft Treaty which found their way into the Treaty of Amsterdam were proposals for reducing the number of legislative procedures, for providing that the Parliament must formally approve the nomination of the President of the Commission, and for capping the size of the Parliament at 700.

The Outline Draft Treaty also contained a suggested Protocol on national parliaments, successfully targeting the broad area of eventual compromise in that area. The idea was, without creating any new institutions, to facilitate the role which national parliaments play at national level in relation to European Union business and to recognize the scope for the existing Conference of European Affairs Committees of National Parliaments (COSAC) to make any collective contribution which it deemed appropriate to the Union's institutions.

The triangle of sensitive institutional questions

On the sensitive institutional questions, however, progress remained very slow. Such questions were not susceptible to a process of "successive approximations". Compromises did not lie in skilful drafting or the gradual refining of texts. These were points of gut difference and fundamental importance such as cannot be resolved until the end of any negotiation. Moreover, they were interlinked.

Nevertheless, we tried as Presidency to address these issues both through multilateral negotiation and through bilateral "confessionals" to see if there might be some way of nudging them forward in a way which would not provoke unproductive confrontation.

The notion that there was a "triangle" of sensitive institutional issues gained currency during our Presidency: the extension of qualified majority voting to further aspects of Community (first pillar) business; the weighting of the votes of Member States in the Council of Ministers; and the size and composition of the Commission.

The *first* side of the triangle, the extension of qualified majority voting (QMV), was for some (including the Commission, the Parliament, Italy and Belgium) an issue of primary importance with a view to the effective functioning of the Union – now and especially with a view to further enlargement. Apart from the United Kingdom, whose stance at that time was to oppose any extension of QMV, all other delegations supported some such extension with varying degrees of enthusiasm. (A number, however, considered that the importance of the issue was exaggerated given that QMV already applied in a wide range of areas and that, by common consent, QMV would be inappropriate in some of those that remained.)

Despite the widespread support *in principle* for the extension of QMV, *in practice* when it came to identifying articles to which QMV might be extended there was scarcely a single article in relation to which there was consensus – even among the 14 Member States other than the UK – that QMV would be appropriate. With a view to teasing out the preliminary views of other Member States, as Presidency we circulated to all delegations on 18 September 1996 a detailed questionnaire concerning their attitude to QMV in all the areas of Community business to which unanimity still applied. The response to the trawl was partial and not encouraging. It confirmed that a case-by-case approach (i.e. examination Treaty article by Treaty article) to the possible extension of QMV was unlikely to lead to a satisfactory result. In the end, any satisfactory agreement on new QMV areas would have to be on the basis of a package of such areas to be agreed at the highest level.

The *second* side of the triangle related to a possible rebalancing of the weighting of votes in the Council of Ministers. At present, when QMV rather than unanimity applies in the Council, the votes of

Member States are weighted to take account of the respective sizes of the Member States (in population terms). However, the voting weights are not fully proportional to population. Broadly speaking, the smaller a Member State, is the more its voting weight exceeds what its population alone would justify.

The view was strongly pressed by some more populous Member States at the IGC that the accession which had taken place of several small and medium-sized Member States had already produced distortions by progressively reducing the proportion of the total number of votes exercised in the Council by the five largest Member States. They expressed the fear that this situation would be exacerbated by the prospective entry to the Union of several more small and medium-sized states, and that the progressive reduction in the proportion of the Union's population necessarily represented by a qualified majority of Member States would affect the legitimacy of the Union's decision-making process.

The opposing view was also strongly put, that each enlargement means the dilution of the voting strength of every Member State – including the small and medium-sized Member States which do not act as a group and derive no particular benefit from the accession of other such states. It was pointed out that, in all conceivable circumstances including any foreseeable enlargement, a qualified majority would continue to represent a majority of the Union's population. According to this view, no convincing case had been made for doing anything other than simply continuing to extrapolate existing voting weights on the occasion of each enlargement.

Two broad avenues for a rebalancing of the weighting of votes, should this be decided, began at the same time to be explored – an actual *reweighting of the votes* of individual Member States or the introduction of a *"dual majority" system* whereby a Council decision would require, in addition to a qualified majority of weighted votes (as at present), that those votes would have to be cast by Governments representing a certain percentage of the Union's population. Both of these broad avenues were the subject of a wide variety of emerging sub-options, each of which had its own logic but at the same time gave rise to its own sensitivities.

The *third* side of the triangle was the size and composition of the Commission. At present the five largest Member States each nominate two Members of the Commission and the rest nominate one each, making a total of 20 Commissioners. The Commission, in comparison with the Council of Ministers, functions with relative ease. Its decisions are taken by a simple majority of its Members and generally without interminable *tours de table*.

The Treaties provide that the Commissioners shall be completely independent in the performance of their duties. Commissioners may not operate under instructions from Governments. However, it is widely recognized as very beneficial for the Commission, which acts as a college, that it should at all times be sensitive to the potential impact in every Member State of its decisions.

It is an article of firm personal conviction for me, based in part on my experience of working in the Commission for several years, that the generally excellent quality and commendable fairness of the Commission's proposals do not stem from its miraculous arrival in a promised land of unsullied European consciousness or human perfectibility. Rather the quality of the Commission's output depends on the mundane and necessary balances and procedures which lie at its heart, as well as on the outstanding quality of many of its Members and officials.

The Commission was built by Jean Monnet and his contemporaries, solidly and creatively and effectively, on the very paradox which lies at the heart of this book. The Commission is the cockpit for the gradual development of the Brave New World on our continent. Anyone, however, who suggests that the Commission has succeeded in changing human nature is for the birds.

At the IGC, the larger Member States argued, with varying degrees of insistence, that the Commission could not continue indefinitely, especially with further enlargement, to be composed of at least one national from each Member State. They would be prepared, the argument went, to forgo their right to nominate a second Member of the Commission provided and only provided that there would be fewer Commissioners than Member States. The underlying implication was that, with a Commission capped, even after further enlargement, at 10, 12, 15 or 20 Members, the five larger Member States would continue to nominate one Member each whereas the other Member States would nominate Members on some basis of rotation. (One of the larger Member States stated that it could accept strictly equal rotation between all Member States in the nomination of Members to a much reduced Commission. However, this was entirely unacceptable to other larger Member States and was not entertained at any stage as a serious possibility.)

The principal argument adduced for a reduction in the size of the Commission was the need to preserve and enhance its efficiency and public acceptability in an expanding Union. The principal, and equally strongly expressed, counter-argument was that those very same aims could best and indeed only be served by continuing, now and for the future, to include at least one national from each Member State in the Commission. It was argued that the efficiency and effectiveness of the Commission required not an ideal "management" size, as might apply in the case of a private business, but rather a composition which would continue to reflect the sensitive and central role of the Commission in the most important pooling of sovereignty ever undertaken by independent democratic countries.

The Irish delegation, while, of course, insisting on its own continued right to nominate a Member of the Commission, did not see or express its approach in those narrow terms. Noel Dorr set out on several occasions at the IGC Representatives Group the thinking behind our approach, which was based not only on our perceived national interests but also on what we saw and continue to see as the interests of both the Commission itself and the Union as a whole. It could not be in the interests of the Commission or the Union, we argued, that there should, for example, be no French or German Members of the Commission. Several of the other smaller countries intervened in similar terms.

An eventual system of nominating Members of the Commission in which the nationality of the nominees would play no part would ultimately be in the interests of no one more than the smaller Member States. However, unless and until full Political Union exists in reality and in people's hearts – and maybe some day in the distant future it will – there can be no question of acting as if it does. There will be no unilateral institutional disarmament.

Alongside this so-called "triangle" of sensitive institutional questions, consideration continued of the areas to which the co-decision procedure, which maximizes the European Parliament's role in the legislative process, might be extended. On this issue, as in the case of the extension of QMV, it was difficult to move delegations from general support in principle to specific agreement on detail. It was another area in which a satisfactory agreement could only, it seemed, be reached on the basis of a package at the end of the process.

The tabling of specific treaty texts on the sensitive institutional questions in our Outline Draft Treaty would have served no useful purpose, and we were widely urged not to do so. We decided accordingly to set out those issues in some detail and to reflect fairly and accurately the views and the options which were emerging. In the case of the extension of QMV and the co-decision procedure we tried to maintain a high level of ambition for the Conference.

The Netherlands Presidency

One of the most difficult tasks faced by the Netherlands Presidency was to steer the difficult institutional issues towards agreement at Amsterdam. It did so, as it did other issues, fairly and in the light of its perception of the wider European interest.

One of the main difficulties it faced was the interlinkage of the three sides of the triangle. On the one hand, it seemed clear that there was such an interlinkage, although some delegations wished to downplay it. On the other hand, perceptions of the nature of the interlinkage differed widely.

Some saw the principal interlinkage as being between the weighting of votes in the Council and the composition of the Commission (the second and third sides of the triangle above). Even as regards that interlinkage, there were contrasting views on what the nature of that linkage should be – the larger Member States aiming to pick up something on both, the other Member States, broadly speaking, reluctant to concede anything on the weighting of votes unless they obtained something themselves on Commission membership.

Others saw the principal interlinkage as being between the extension of QMV and the weighting of votes in the Council, unwilling to move on the former without what they saw as progress on the latter. Inevitably, others saw this interlinkage very differently. In their view, a change in the weighting of votes would make an extension of QMV more rather than less difficult to accept.

The dilemma posed by these various interlinkages for the Netherlands Presidency was that, while it was evident that an institutional deal would be possible in the endgame only on the basis of an *overall* compromise, the issues nevertheless had to be examined *as the individual issues they for the moment remained* and refined in the direction of possible agreement.

The Netherlands Presidency devoted a great deal of time and energy, especially at the political level, to these sensitive institutional questions. Discussion of them during the first six months of 1997 could be said to have fallen into *three broad phases*. January to April saw an in-depth examination of the issues based on papers prepared by the Presidency to reflect emerging options. The next six weeks, without further paperwork, were used to tease out further a possible way through the maze. It fell, as expected, to the Amsterdam European Council in June to cut a deal. The sensitive institutional questions were the last to be resolved in the early hours of the morning of 18 June.

The very first IGC meeting of the Netherlands Presidency, the informal meeting of IGC Representatives in Amsterdam on 13/14 January 1997, opened the *first phase* of discussion on institutional questions during the Netherlands Presidency with an in-depth informal exchange of views on the three sides of the triangle of sensitive institutional questions, as well as on the extension of the co-decision procedure.

This was followed by a discussion at the IGC Representatives' meeting on 17/18 February for which the Presidency had tabled three important new papers: a possible package of areas to which QMV might be extended; a similar package with regard to extension of the co-decision procedure; and an options paper on the weighting of votes in the Council, containing in annex a detailed analysis of the issues involved. Reactions to all three papers were predictable. A broad general willingness to consider the first two packages was at odds with a series of specific reservations on the detail – amounting collectively, if maintained, to an unravelling of the respective packages. On the weighting of votes it remained impossible to start the process of moving towards a single option.

On the fourth issue, the composition of the Commission, the Commission itself tabled a Communication on 5 March 1997 which was considered by Representatives at their meeting on 10/11 March. The approach suggested by the Commission was to confine the Commission to one Member per Member State, with a procedure for reviewing the Commission's membership above a certain number of Member States, and in any event when the number of Member States would exceed 20. It also expressed the view that the number of "portfolios" as such should be reduced – the remaining Commissioners being entrusted either with "specific tasks" or "support functions". It envisaged that all Members of the Commission would be full Members of the college. (Earlier variants of the idea of appointing "deputy" Commissioners were gradually running out of steam.)

The Netherlands Presidency, reflecting the same tactical choice as our own Presidency, did not incorporate treaty texts on the sensitive institutional questions in its "Addendum" (to our Outline Draft Treaty) which it submitted to the IGC Ministerial meeting in Rome on 25 March 1997. Instead it chose to reflect the state of play on the institutional issues in a separate progress report.

The Presidency devoted two detailed Ministerial discussions in April – at the Conclave in Noordwijk on 6/7 April and at the IGC Ministerial meeting in Luxembourg on 29 April – to what might be called the two "small versus large" institutional issues, i.e. the weighting of votes in Council and the size and composition of the Commission. For each Ministerial discussion it tabled papers setting out what it saw as the evolving options on each question.

While there was no prospect of consensus emerging at that stage, the ongoing discussions offered a vital opportunity for the Presidency to test the seaworthiness of the various options. It became increasingly evident, for example, in the light of the views expressed, that any notion of placing a ceiling on the size of the Commission in a way which implied an end, now or in the future, to the right of each Member State to nominate a full Member of the Commission was untenable.

The successive discussions at political level also gave each Member State essential insights into the sensitivities of others. It was evident, for example, that whereas, generally speaking, the larger Member States attached greater importance to a rebalancing of voting weights in the Council, for the less populous Member States their continued right to nominate a full Member of the Commission was the more sensitive issue.

The Presidency tabled, for the IGC Representatives' meeting on 5/6 May, revised packages in relation to the extension of QMV and co-decision, attempting to move somewhat closer to what might eventually be agreed but still a long way from consensus.

The period from that meeting (the first since the change of government in London) until the Amsterdam European Council itself on 16/17 June is what I would consider the *second phase* of consideration of the sensitive institutional issues during the Netherlands Presidency. During those weeks no further papers on the issues were tabled by the Presidency. While discussion of them continued at every level (Representative level, Ministerial level and most notably at the special informal meeting of the European Council in Noordwijk on 23 May), the Presidency decided prudently to play its cards close to its chest. It would essentially have only one shot at tabling a compromise to provide a basis for agreement at Amsterdam. It did not wish to have whatever compromise it would table blasted out of the water or slowly unravelled in advance.

There appeared to be a growing sense, taken up by the press, after the informal European Council on 23 May that a radical reduction in the size of the Commission or a calling into question of the continued right of each Member State to nominate a full Member of the Commission was unlikely to form part of the eventual compromise at the IGC. The idea of a later review mechanism was also gaining some currency.

Prime Minister Kok's traditional pre-European Council tour of capitals offered the Presidency a crucial opportunity to fine-tune its compromise proposal.

The *third phase* of the Netherlands Presidency's consideration of these issues would be the discussion at the Amsterdam European Council itself, which is dealt with in Chapter 16.

Building on the areas of emerging agreement in some less sensitive institutional areas set out in our Outline Draft Treaty, the Netherlands Presidency had also meanwhile been developing treaty texts in some further low-key areas, including a strengthening of the role within the Commission of its President, and a limited enhancement of the roles of the Court of Auditors, the Court of Justice, the Committee of the Regions and the Economic and Social Committee. At a very late stage of the IGC, the possibility of a Protocol confirming formally in the Treaties existing decisions regarding the thorny question of the location of the Community's institutions also came into prospect and was ultimately agreed.

However, on the sensitive institutional questions all remained to play for at Amsterdam.

Chapter 15

Freedom, Security and Justice

How often have I said to you that when you have eliminated the impossible, whatever remains, *however improbable*, must be the truth?

(Sherlock Holmes – Sir Arthur Conan Doyle,
A Study in Scarlet)

The maintenance and development of the European Union as an area of "Freedom, Security and Justice" constituted the fifth main Section of the work of the IGC and became one of its principal priorities.

The issues arising under this heading, like those falling under the Section entitled "the Union and the Citizen", were matters of very direct public concern. They were considered to merit a Section in their own right. From the time of the Irish Presidency's Outline Draft Treaty through to the final Draft Treaty submitted by the Netherlands Presidency at Amsterdam itself, "Freedom, Security and Justice" was presented as the first Section of the emerging package.

The impetus for developing the Treaty provisions on Freedom, Security and Justice reflected the priority attached by many delegations to addressing the direct concerns of citizens in areas such as fundamental rights, non-discrimination, the fight against crime, and cooperation in the areas of asylum and immigration. The prospective accession to the European Union of several countries with different, or at least more recent, traditions in some of these areas – and which would benefit from the Union's arrangements regarding the free movement of persons – gave further urgency to the work of the Conference.

The work of the IGC in relation to Freedom, Security and Justice can be divided conveniently between the issues which it was possible to advance significantly during the Irish Presidency in 1996 and those which were substantively negotiated during the Netherlands Presidency.

The Irish Presidency

Two important blocks of work in relation to Freedom, Security and Justice were significantly advanced during the Irish Presidency.

Fundamental rights and non-discrimination

The first block of work, drawing on the work of both the Reflection Group and the Italian Presidency, concerned fundamental rights and non-discrimination. In this area, it was possible – through the process of "successive approximations" – to table, in our Outline Draft Treaty in December 1996, draft texts on *five* aspects which found their way, subject to some refinement, into the Treaty of Amsterdam.

The *first* aspect was the incorporation into the Treaties of a reaffirmation of the principles on which the Union is founded – liberty, democracy, respect for human rights and fundamental freedoms, and the rule of law. This was accompanied by making explicit the requirement that any country applying to become a member of the Union must respect those principles.

The *second* aspect was the establishment of a procedure for determining the existence in a Member State of the existence of a "serious and persistent" breach of those principles and allowing for the suspension of certain rights of the Member State in question. This "sanctions" clause was seen and designed as a "nuclear weapon" to be used only in a dramatic case (such as a *coup d'état*) and certainly not as an instrument for routine or regular use. The words "serious and persistent", which later slipped out of one draft, were reinserted and maintained through to the final Treaty.

The *third* aspect was a provision to confer explicitly on the European Court of Justice jurisdiction, which it was already in practice exercising, with regard to the requirement that acts of the Community ("first pillar") must respect fundamental rights. This draft provision was extended during the Netherlands Presidency so that such jurisdiction will apply also as appropriate in the area of police cooperation ("third pillar").

The *fourth* aspect was the incorporation into the European Community Treaty of a legal basis providing that the Council may, acting unanimously within the scope of the Treaty, take appropriate action to prohibit discrimination on the grounds of sex, racial or ethnic origin, religious belief (later amended to "religion or belief"), disability, age or sexual orientation. This provision, although it necessarily contains the safeguard of the unanimity requirement, establishes an important basis for action to address the direct concerns of many citizens and to enhance the human face of the Union in the eyes of the public.

The *fifth* aspect was a strengthening of the already important treaty provisions on equality between men and women, an aspect also further developed under the Netherlands Presidency.

Justice and Home Affairs

The second block of work relating to Freedom, Security and Justice that was significantly developed during the Irish Presidency was the area of Justice and Home Affairs. However, a great deal of the substantive work in this regard – what turned out, indeed, to be the most difficult aspects to negotiate – remained to be dealt with by the Netherlands Presidency.

Cooperation on Justice and Home Affairs, as established in the Treaty on European Union (the "Maastricht Treaty") under the so-called "third pillar" of the Union, was in a sense intergovernmental (like the Common Foreign and Security Policy dealt with in chapter 10). Although decisions under the "third pillar" were capable of binding Member States, the mechanisms were in several respects akin more to those of intergovernmental cooperation than to the supranational operation of normal Community ("first pillar") business. All decisions had to be unanimous. The circumscribed nature of the Commission's right of initiative prevented it from acting as the motor for progress. The role of the European Parliament was slight and that of the Court of Justice optional on a case-by-case basis. The Maastricht Treaty had identified certain general areas as being "matters of common interest" rather than setting specific objectives for the Union. The means or instruments for action in this area had in a sense been imported from the foreign policy context, and their nature militated against their effective use.

The "third pillar" encompassed two principal areas of cooperation: (i) cooperation as regards asylum, visas, immigration and the control of external frontiers (what came to be described as "free movement, asylum and immigration"); (ii) cooperation in the fight against international crime. A number of other issues, such as judicial cooperation in civil matters, were also covered.

The distinction between these two principal areas of cooperation is important to an understanding of discussion at the IGC. Enhancing the basis for action on both aspects was a priority for the IGC, but there was a significant difference as to how this should be approached in respect of the two areas. As regards *cooperation in the fight against crime*, while it became a priority for all that this should be significantly strengthened, there was a broad consensus that it should remain, at the present stage of the Union's development, essentially intergovernmental in nature (and therefore remain in the "third pillar" of the Union). As regards *free movement, asylum and immigration*, a strong majority view developed that this area should become subject – to some extent at least – to normal Community procedures (and therefore transferred to the "first pillar").

This view that *free movement, asylum and immigration* should be "communitarised" came to be seen, perhaps more than any other issue at the IGC, as the litmus test of commitment to theological orthodoxy in relation to the integration process. It was, of course, strongly contested by others. The United Kingdom and Denmark in particular had strong reservations about full "communitarisation" of such issues. Especially in the early stages of the Conference, these Member States were by no means alone in their reservations. Even when it was eventually agreed at Amsterdam to incorporate the *free movement, asylum and immigration* provisions into the "first pillar", with opt-outs for "heretics", this was done on a watered-down basis which suggested a persisting undercurrent of agnosticism even within the one true faith.

At the outset of the IGC, there was another important ghost at the *free movement, asylum and immigration* feast – the Schengen arrangements. These had arisen in the following circumstances. The Single European Act in 1985 had provided for an internal market comprising an area in which the free movement of persons (among other things) would be ensured. The 13 continental

Member States interpreted this as requiring the lifting of internal border controls within the Union. However, the United Kingdom considered that the free movement provided for in the Single European Act related only to citizens of the Member States and that it was therefore entitled to maintain border checks on persons (who could be third-country nationals) entering the United Kingdom from other Member States. The UK has left nobody in any doubt that this is an entitlement which a British government of any complexion would continue to exercise.

Faced with this situation, some of the continental Member States had developed the so-called Schengen arrangements to ensure, on the one hand, the lifting of border controls between themselves and, on the other hand, a range of so-called "compensatory measures" (e.g. control of external frontiers) to make this feasible. Eventually, all 13 continental Member States, as well as Norway and Iceland, had become involved in these arrangements.

Significantly, the Schengen arrangements had been developed *outside* the European Union Treaties. However, the Schengen arrangements overlapped very significantly with actions which could be taken by *all 15 Member States* through the existing treaty provisions of the "third pillar". Decisions taken under the "third pillar" superseded, as had already happened on a number of occasions, any Schengen decisions covering the same subject matter.

The UK would, under no foreseeable circumstances, fully accede to Schengen given Schengen's *raison d'être* of abolishing frontier controls. The Schengen Member States, on the other hand, were determined that any provisions agreed at the IGC should not cut across or water down their Schengen arrangements in any way. The prospect of further enlargement which would extend the Union's external border far to the east made the maintenance of the deeper level of cooperation attained outside the EU Treaties through Schengen a core issue for many delegations at the IGC.

Ireland was in a distinctive position. In line with our strong commitment to the process of European integration, we did not object to the transfer to the first pillar of *free movement, asylum and immigration* as such. Nor indeed did our non-participation in Schengen essentially reflect problems of principle in that regard. However, we had to have regard to our Common Travel Area with the United Kingdom which we greatly value and to which we must give priority.

That long-standing Common Travel Area constitutes an area of free movement – without the requirement of travel documents – between Ireland and the United Kingdom. It is indeed an area of free movement older and more complete than that between the Schengen countries. Much the greater part of travel out of Ireland (leaving Northern Ireland out of the equation) is to or through Britain. If Ireland were to participate in Schengen, and this were to lead to the establishment of controls (and travel documents) within the Common Travel Area, this would ironically reduce rather than increase free movement to and from Ireland. Thus – as far as we would be concerned – the very purpose of Schengen would be negated. Moreover, the level of mutual cooperation and trust regarding entry to the Common Travel Area, facilitated by the absence of land borders to be controlled, makes it possible for Ireland and the United Kingdom to forgo the more intrusive internal personal identity cards and controls which are standard in continental Member States.

Against this complex backdrop, the Irish Presidency set about developing, through "successive approximations", treaty texts to strengthen the basis and means for Union action in the Justice and Home Affairs area. Distinct sets of provisions were developed concerning the two aspects of Justice and Home Affairs – on the one hand, a strengthening of the intergovernmental "third pillar" provisions which in future would essentially encompass only *cooperation in the fight against international crime*; and, on the other hand, new provisions, moving beyond intergovernmental cooperation, as regards *free movement, asylum and immigration*.

The draft provisions on both of these aspects contained in our Outline Draft Treaty provided a basis for the remainder of the negotiations and were in large measure reflected in the Treaty of Amsterdam.

A strengthened third pillar: the fight against international crime

The strengthened "third pillar" provisions which we proposed were designed, first of all, to provide a more focused definition of areas for cooperation in the fight against crime as well as for common action in addressing those areas. These areas included:

- all forms of police cooperation, in particular for the purposes of preventing and combating terrorism and other forms of international crime, including through the development of the operational capacity of Europol

- combating trafficking in persons and offences against children

- combating illegal drug-trafficking.

The clear support at political level for action in such areas, notably at the Dublin 1 Summit in October 1996, made it possible for our Outline Draft Treaty to sketch out, at some level of ambition and in some detail, the scope of future Union action in these areas. Action in respect of racism and xenophobia was also envisaged. (Refinement of this text during the Netherlands Presidency saw, among other things, the addition of references to international arms trafficking, corruption and fraud.)

The Outline Draft Treaty also proposed to improve significantly the *instruments* available to the Union for strengthening its common action in these areas. The Commission would be given a shared right of initiative in all areas. The European Parliament would be systematically consulted. A new instrument (a "framework decision" somewhat akin to a Community directive) was provided for, which would leave to national authorities the choice of form and methods for its detailed implementation. It was envisaged that Conventions could enter into force once adopted by a certain number of Member States.

The issue of whether unanimity should be retained in the third pillar remained open, although it seemed increasingly clear that the majority view – that unanimity remained appropriate in the sensitive areas concerned – would prevail, as in the end it did. (The role of the Court of Justice in this area was settled only at Amsterdam, which decided to make acceptance of the Court's jurisdiction to an extent optional for individual Member States.)

Strengthened action on free movement, asylum, immigration: the first pillar beckons

The proposals in our Outline Draft Treaty as regards *free movement, asylum and immigration* took the form of a new treaty "Title" (a subdivision of the treaty capable of containing several "chapters"). Detailed objectives were set out in the proposed Title as regards asylum, immigration, visas, the rights of third-country nationals legally resident in a Member State, and the crossing of external frontiers. Importantly, it was proposed to set clear target dates for the adoption of measures in these areas.

There were strongly conflicting views as to whether such a new Title should remain intergovernmental in the "third pillar" or be communitarised by its incorporation in the "first pillar". Aware that for some – on either side of the argument – it was a point of such fundamental importance that it could determine their overall reaction to the Outline Draft Treaty, we did not propose explicitly where the Title should be located. We did, however, provide an unambiguous signal in that regard by commenting "that the incorporation of this Title in the Treaty establishing the European Community [i.e the "first pillar"] would provide the most effective basis for coherent action".

The sensitive institutional aspects in these areas, which were related to the location within the Treaties of the new Title, were left to be resolved during the Netherlands Presidency. As Presidency, we considered that to have made at that stage specific "proposals" on institutional aspects, which remained sensitive and entirely unresolved, would have been likely to provoke a negative reaction risking a setback for the level of the Conference's ambition. We therefore decided to confine ourselves in our Outline Draft Treaty to "comments" on the institutional aspects. (We suggested, for example, that it would be logical for the Commission to exercise the right of initiative in these areas and that consideration should be given to the introduction of qualified majority voting to apply after a transition period.)

We also suggested tentatively, having in mind the galvanizing effect which the 1992 target date had had on the completion of the internal market, that the IGC might consider whether to set an overall target date, perhaps 1 January 2001, to complete the progressive establishment of an area of Freedom, Security and Justice. Although the approach of retaining specific deadlines for the adoption of certain decisions was carried through, the particular highlighting of 2001 as an overall target date was not retained.

The Netherlands Presidency

The Netherlands Presidency thus inherited two things: (i) a series of draft treaty amendments in the area of fundamental rights and non-discrimination, which – subject, as in other areas, to subtle tweaking – could provide a basis for agreement at Amsterdam; and (ii) two important building blocks for the construction of a package of new treaty provisions in the area of Justice and Home Affairs, namely an outline of reasonably detailed draft provisions for strengthening Union action as regards both the *fight against crime* and *free movement, asylum and immigration*.

However, the most difficult work of the Conference in this area still lay ahead. The Netherlands Presidency, apart from the painstaking task which it faced – as in every area – of refining the texts now accepted as the basis for ongoing work, had to resolve, with unanimous agreement, three major political issues:

- the extent to which there would be agreement to "communitarise" the area of *free movement, asylum and immigration*, in relation to which the acid test was considered to be the location of the proposed new Title in the "first pillar"

- how to provide for the necessary flexibility within the area broadly covered by the new Title to make possible the maintenance and development, on the one hand, of the deeper level of cooperation already existing between 13 Member States *outside* the Treaty through the Schengen arrangements and, on the other hand, of the Common Travel Area between Ireland and the United Kingdom

- how to progress a proposal relating to political asylum on which draft texts had not been discussed during the Irish Presidency but which had been recognized by the Dublin 2 European Council as one for further development.

Justice and Home Affairs

The first two of those issues were related and were dealt with as part of the emerging overall package on Justice and Home Affairs. The Netherlands Presidency devoted more time to Justice and

Home Affairs than to any other area of the work of the Conference. Discussions took place principally at the level of IGC Representatives, at which level the issues had to be clarified and processed in order to present meaningful choices for guidance at political level.

The first two discussions of the issues at the level of IGC Representatives during the Netherlands Presidency, on 27/28 January and 10/11 February 1997, were based on the texts set out in the Outline Draft Treaty in relation to which the Netherlands Presidency now sought direction on a number of outstanding questions.

However, one significant new element was brought into the equation at the second of those meetings, namely a proposal for the incorporation of the Schengen arrangements *into the European Union Treaties*. A national Netherlands proposal to that effect had been presented to the IGC in July 1996. In the absence at that time of clear signals of interest from other Member States, reflecting in part significant differences of view among the Schengen countries themselves, the proposal had since then lain dormant. Now, as Presidency, the Netherlands reintroduced the proposal suggesting that there might be two ways of giving effect to it. Either the new general "enabling clause" flexibility proposals which were being negotiated (see Chapter 13) might be applied in due course to Schengen, or else Schengen could be incorporated now – lock, stock and barrel – into the Union Treaties, both its existing "acquis" (i.e. its existing corpus of agreements and decisions) and its potential for future development.

It was effectively the latter option which appeared to be of significant interest to the Presidency. There were strong attractions in the approach. In one fell swoop it appeared to offer the prospect of preserving Schengen in full, grafting it onto the Union and ensuring that its further development could take place within, rather than in potential disharmony with, the Union. The incorporation of Schengen into the Union, if pursued, would also address the concerns of continental Member States that existing cooperation arrangements (including in Schengen) should be consolidated and strengthened in advance of enlargement. It could be combined with a requirement that acceptance of those arrangements would in future be a condition for accession to the Union. Some degree of differentiation would in any event be required between the Schengen 13 and the Common Travel Area 2. The approach now suggested, it was argued, would be a clear-cut way of providing for such differentiation (the implicit assumption being that the proposal would be accompanied by confirmation in the Treaty of the right of the United Kingdom and Ireland to maintain the Common Travel Area).

However, the proposal also gave rise to two types of potential difficulty. In the first place, it was not clear at the outset how it would work in practice. The approach of incorporating myriad existing arrangements directly "into the Treaties", rather than simply providing in the Treaties a basis for later detailed action, would be a radical departure from precedent. Many practical aspects were inevitably at that stage unclear, including how the position of the UK and Ireland (members of the Union but not Schengen) and the position of Norway and Iceland (members of Schengen but not the Union) would be accommodated. Uncertainties such as these gave rise to initial hesitations from several quarters, including not only the UK and Ireland but also a number of Schengen Member States which remained reluctant, at least well into March 1997, to envisage the straightforward incorporation of Schengen into the Union.

The other potential difficulty related to preserving coherence in the Justice and Home Affairs area at the level of the Union. While the Schengen arrangements had permitted a majority of Member States to go somewhat further on several aspects of immigration and external frontiers, the Union as a whole had also been developing significant levels of cooperation in similar areas, its decisions *in general* overlapping with Schengen provisions and *in particular*, where the precise areas of action coincided, superseding those provisions. There was a significant fear that the incorporation of Schengen could become the cuckoo in the Union's Justice and Home Affairs nest. It might displace rather than supplement existing cooperation. The fear was that the blunt approach proposed, rather than just providing the necessary differentiation within the Union, might lead to an unnecessary schism.

This potential difficulty was articulated principally by Ireland, with some sympathetic noises from the UK delegation which, to some degree, had to tread water as the British general election approached. (I am conscious of the risk of overstating the significance of positions taken by the Irish national delegation. However, this was one area in which, for various reasons, one side of the broad debate was to a large extent put by the Irish delegation – by Noel Dorr on frequent occasions at the level of IGC Representatives and, at political level, by the Minister for Foreign Affairs, Dick Spring, and the Minister of State for European Affairs, Gay Mitchell.)

There were no simple answers in the Justice and Home Affairs area. There was no "correct" solution to be looked up on the last page of a quiz book. As in other areas, the pursuit of interests dovetailed with the tentative shared exploration of a way forward which could serve the interests of the Union and at the same time address the concerns of all Member States.

For the Ministerial meeting on 24 February 1997, the Presidency produced overall proposals on the Justice and Home Affairs area which did not include incorporation of a Schengen Protocol along the lines which had been floated. These proposals appeared to go a long way in the direction of emphasizing the importance of preserving the coherence of the Union. They took as their starting point cooperation at the level of the Fifteen and offered a good basis for addressing Ireland's twin concerns that all Member States should be involved in overall policy-making, whatever about detailed implementation, and that the fullest level of practical cooperation between all Fifteen should be ensured. Ireland was among those, at the IGC Ministerial on 24 February, to welcome the approach. We argued that adequate flexibility for the Schengen 13 could be ensured within that overall framework. We took the view that, for example, something akin to the constructive abstention mechanism being considered in relation to the Common Foreign and Security Policy might be developed in this context also.

However, in the course of further reflection, the Presidency remained concerned that such coherence at the level of the Union might be at the expense of coherence between the Union and

Schengen. The "Addendum" (to our Outline Draft Treaty) submitted by the Netherlands Presidency to the IGC Ministerial in Rome on 25 March reintroduced its proposal that all relevant existing Schengen legislation would be incorporated into the European Union Treaties from the moment of the entry into force of the new (Amsterdam) Treaty. Discussion at that Ministerial meeting did not suggest that there was yet consensus – even among the Schengen Member States themselves – in the matter. During the month of April 1997, which saw a considerable amount of time devoted to informal discussion of the Schengen issue, the persuasive force of the Netherlands Presidency and its arguments gradually gained ground. On 5 May, it tabled a revised draft Schengen Protocol. Although a complex drafting exercise remained to be completed, it was clear by that time that the broad thrust of that Protocol – designed to incorporate the Schengen arrangements into the Union – was now the preferred approach of the 13 "Schengen" Member States. The approach had found its way through the dark forest of evolutionary competition and had now entered the sunlight of likely survival.

While, as in every area, the final decisions would fall to be taken at political level, the drafting exercise in relation to Schengen was, from then on, based firmly on the draft Schengen Protocol tabled by the Netherlands Presidency. It was a hugely difficult drafting exercise given the innovative nature of the entire approach and the variable geometry which had to be constructed within it.

The Irish and British delegations, the latter now representing a new Government in London, sought to ensure that their specific concerns would be reflected in the draft. Balancing provisions were incorporated to provide for the possibility of Ireland and/or the United Kingdom signing up to some or all of the existing Schengen arrangements (until the IGC it had been "all or nothing") as well as for the possibility of their participating, if and when they wished to do so, in the further development of those provisions. The detailed concerns of other delegations, relating to such matters as the precise method of incorporating Schengen into the Treaties and the involvement of Norway and Iceland, were also addressed.

It proved possible, through the efforts of the Presidency, in the course of a series of meetings at IGC Representative level throughout May, to bring the draft Schengen Protocol into a shape in which it could be submitted to Amsterdam with a good prospect of obtaining the necessary unanimous agreement.

In parallel with consideration of Schengen, the complex task of further refining the general provisions on Justice and Home Affairs was being carried through. One crucial political point remained to be resolved, namely whether the new Title on *free movement, asylum and immigration* would figure in the "first" (Community) pillar or the "third" (intergovernmental) pillar. It was perhaps not in itself a matter of earth-shattering importance. To a significant extent Community methods could be incorporated into the "third pillar". To an extent intergovernmental methods could alternatively be transferred to the "first pillar" for the matters in question. However, it had become for some, including the Presidency, a test against which progress towards closer integration would be judged.

The outcome on this issue hinged, to a considerable extent, on whatever deal would be struck between the Presidency and the new British Government on this and a number of other key issues. The issue of the location of the new Title in the Treaties had significant ramifications for the United Kingdom and consequently, because of the Common Travel Area, indirectly for Ireland. If, as seemed likely, the UK Government (like its predecessor) could not go along with the transfer of any "third pillar" items to the "first pillar", two scenarios were possible.

One scenario would be simply for the UK to block such transfer, unanimity being required as for every issue at the Conference. However, this would have led to a crisis, unwelcome and largely pointless for all, and also made it more difficult for the United Kingdom to obtain satisfaction on other issues of concern to it in the endgame at the IGC. Alternatively, it could allow the transfer of items to the first pillar, as strongly desired by most partners, and seek a formal opt-out from those provisions. This would strengthen its hand in seeking satisfaction on other issues including, for example, confirmation and formalization in the Treaties of its right to maintain border controls.

Following what amounted to several days of intensive shuttle diplomacy (back and forth across the Channel) between the Presidency and the United Kingdom immediately prior to Amsterdam, the latter was the option agreed between the Presidency and the British Government – namely incorporation of *free movement, asylum and immigration* into the "first pillar" with a United Kingdom opt-out.

Political asylum

The issue of political asylum, which fell under the overall heading of an "Area of Freedom, Security and Justice", was guided towards eventual agreement by the Netherlands Presidency. During the IGC, Spain had pressed strongly to have provisions included in the Treaty which would bar citizens of one Member State from seeking political asylum in another. It was argued that the commitments involved in common membership of the Union as well as the guarantees under the Treaties of rights and freedoms in Member States made the serious entertainment by one Member State of an application for asylum from the citizen of another Member State inappropriate. However, the issue was a sensitive one as the wider implications, including the need to respect existing obligations under the under the 1951 Convention on the Status of Refugees and the 1967 Protocol (which require every application for asylum to be considered individually and on its merits), had to be taken into account and were strongly emphasized by several delegations.

A draft Protocol, designed to address the issue, was circulated on 17 April 1997 annexed to a short Presidency Note. The Presidency indicated that it was able to recommend the version of the proposal which had been tabled by Spain following contacts with the Presidency. After careful negotiations through several meetings, a Treaty Protocol was agreed at Amsterdam which sets out the conditions under which a political asylum application by a citizen of a Member State may be considered by any other Member State. It will not affect the legal obligation on Member States to consider each asylum application individually. An agreed Declaration attached to the Treaty of Amsterdam confirms that the Protocol does not prejudice the right of each Member State to take the organizational measures which it deems necessary to fulfil that obligation.

Amsterdam: the final touches

The Dutch Masters put the final important touches to their tableau on Justice and Home Affairs for consideration by the European Council in Amsterdam on the very morning of 16 June, the first day of the meeting. These refinements reflected extensive contacts and redrafting involving the most concerned delegations during the final days and hours. Indeed, meetings and contacts had continued into the small hours on the eve of the meeting. Thus the overall Draft Treaty circulated by the Presidency to delegations some days before Amsterdam was supplemented on the morning of 16 June by the fruit of its last-minute contacts and dealings on *free movement, asylum and immigration.*

The Netherlands Presidency remained aware of and sensitive to the particular concerns of the Irish delegation in this area. It had kept us informed of developments and emerging drafts. The then Chairman of the IGC Representatives Group, Michiel Patijn, and a few of his colleagues, including his deputy Tom de Bruijn and Mathias van Bonzel, had met with Noel Dorr and myself in Amsterdam on the evening of 15 June, the eve of battle. That meeting offered us an essential basis for fine-tuning overnight the best way of reflecting our particular national position in the evolving compromise to be tabled by the Presidency the following morning. (I took the occasion to gave Michiel Patijn a T-shirt inscribed with the words "Dutch Courage". It was a slogan he had every right to wear. I understand that, having been assured by me that it was a comment on his determination rather than his sobriety, he had every intention of wearing it.)

The package submitted to Amsterdam contained the following principal elements, apart from the substantially strengthened provisions (still in the "third pillar") on the fight against crime:

• a new Title, to be incorporated in the "first pillar", containing detailed provisions on *free movement, asylum and immigration*

• a Protocol exempting Ireland and the UK from those provisions, but at the same time making provision for either or both of them to participate in the adoption and application, or in the subsequent acceptance of, any of those measures;

and for Ireland at any stage, should it so wish, to be no longer bound by the Protocol

- a Protocol covering the particular position of Denmark

- a Protocol recognizing the right of the United Kingdom and, in the context of the Common Travel Area, Ireland, to maintain border controls (as well as the right of other Member States to exercise equivalent controls *vis-à-vis* travellers from those two countries)

- a Protocol ("the Schengen Protocol") providing for the incorporation into the European Union Treaties of the large body of Schengen arrangements and decisions (negotiated outside the Treaties by 13 Member States in conjunction with two non-Member States, in areas largely overlapping with those referred to in the new Title above) as well as for the further development of those provisions. The Protocol also makes provision for Ireland and/or the United Kingdom to participate in some or all of the Schengen arrangements now being incorporated in the Treaties and in some or all aspects of its further development.

All in all, the provisions concerning an Area of Freedom, Security and Justice represent in many respects a step forward for the European Union. They will equip it to respond more effectively to the aspirations and concerns of citizens.

The procedures agreed, as far as *free movement, asylum and immigration* are concerned, are probably unprecedented in their complexity. Unlike most other areas at the Conference, I am not sure that a re-run of the negotiations would lead to precisely the same result or degree of complexity. The outcome may to an extent reflect the rhythm and vagaries of the negotiating process. If coalitions of interest had come together in a different timeframe, the provisions might, in my view, have turned out somewhat differently. If all the delegations which had, at one stage or another of the Conference, tended against a full transfer of these issues to the first pillar done so at the same time the result might well have been a beefing up of the third pillar. The decision of the Netherlands Presidency to press for a "big bang" incorporation of

Schengen was decisive as far as the outcome in that regard is concerned.

With their patchwork of opt-ins within opt-outs, the provisions will offer a rich seam for postgraduate doctoral theses. They are, however, not to be derided for their complexity, which reflects to a considerable extent the complexity of the interests and issues involved. Only time will judge their effectiveness.

Since other solutions proved impossible, the solution agreed at Amsterdam, however improbable, must in its own way have been the right one.

Despite the seeming complexity of the Amsterdam Treaty provisions on *free movement, asylum and immigration*, I have come across an explanation which neatly captures how they will function. It is one 15-year-old's description of the game of cricket:

"You have two sides, one out in the field and one in. Each man that's in the side that's in, goes out and when he's out he comes in, and the next man goes in until he's out. When they are all out, the side that's out comes in and the side that's been in goes out and tries to get those coming in out. When both sides have been in and out, including the not outs, that's the end of the game."

Chapter 16

Dutch Auction: the Amsterdam European Council

> There is a dark
> Invisible workmanship that reconciles
> Discordant elements, and makes them move
> In one society.
>
> (William Wordsworth, *The Prelude*)

The British general election on 1 May 1997 moved the IGC across the Rubicon. The Netherlands Presidency shifted into its second phase. Amsterdam beckoned.

The first European Union meeting attended by a ministerial level representative of the new British Government was the meeting of IGC Representatives in Brussels on 5 and 6 May. The opening presentation by the new British Minister for Europe, Doug Henderson, was the first presentation in Brussels of the new British Government's approach to Europe since it had taken office. It marked, in its way, a significant moment not just for the IGC but for Europe and for Britain's role in Europe. Doug Henderson spoke of the new Government's wish to make a fresh start to Britain's relations with Europe. The new Government saw Europe not as a threat but as an opportunity and they wished to work as colleagues in a shared enterprise. Tone and approach can be every bit as important in Europe as specifics. The return to the fold was low-key, but the fatted calf was looking nervous.

As far as the IGC was concerned, Doug Henderson's intervention on 5 May contained no great surprises. The Labour Party had already made its broad intentions clear while in opposition. Nevertheless, the statement did in many respects prefigure the broad lines of what would be agreed at Amsterdam. Until that point at the Conference, the British delegation had taken a somewhat distinctive position on a broad swathe of issues. While rarely entirely alone in its views, the extent to which whatever British Government was in power would be prepared to move towards an otherwise emerging consensus would play a determining role in relation to many issues at the Conference.

After Doug Henderson's opening presentation on 5 May, it was increasingly clear, for example, that there would be *some* extension of co-decision with the European Parliament and *some* further extension of qualified majority voting for normal Community business under the first pillar, that a coherent basis for social policy would be re-established with the incorporation of the Social Agreement into the main body of the treaty, and that new non-discrimination provisions would be agreed. It was equally clear, however, that firm opposition would be maintained to any lifting of Britain's border controls as well as to any merger of the European Union with the Western European Union. The British approach to flexibility also appeared to have become even more sceptical.

Overall there was a growing sense that a deal at Amsterdam was now on. While doubts about the prospects for concluding at Amsterdam lingered, these now related to the volume and complexity of the work still to be completed rather than to the possibility of a political deal being struck.

Several key political issues remained unresolved. A significant drafting exercise on a number of key topics, including flexibility and Justice and Home Affairs, was still required before Amsterdam. Texts in many other areas needed to be fine-tuned. (By way of illustration of the pressure of work, the agenda for the IGC Representatives meeting in the last week of May contained the following agenda items on which all 16 delegations would, as always, be offering views: the size of the Commission and Council voting weights; Schengen; political asylum; external economic relations; social issues and employment; flexibility; subsidiarity; public service broadcasting; simplification and codification of the Treaties; and a review of the whole Section of the Treaty dealing with the Union and the Citizen.)

The organization of the work programme for the final six weeks of the Conference became of crucial importance. The Netherlands Presidency took a number of important decisions.

First, it confirmed its decision to convene an informal meeting of the European Council on 23 May at the Huis ter Duin Grand Hotel along the vast sweeping beach at Noordwijk. Prime Minister Kok, in his letter to colleagues indicating how he intended to handle the meeting, listed for discussion in very general terms all five main Sections of the work of the Conference. This reflected precisely the political judgement which our own Presidency had made in relation to the informal meeting of the European Council in Dublin in October 1996 (Dublin 1), namely that there was no alternative to respecting the global nature of the negotiations. As is appropriate for an informal meeting, there were no formal conclusions.

The meeting, however, proved to be particularly important as a get-to-know-you (and get-to-know-your-point-of-view) session with Tony Blair in advance of Amsterdam itself. The "novelty" of having a new British Government could be disposed of. The "return of the prodigal" headlines could be got out of the system. The Noordwijk European Council also helped Heads of Government to familiarize themselves further with the issues and the sensitivities in advance of what was to be their marathon session at Amsterdam. The political feel of the most senior European politicians at Noordwijk also served to take much of the sting out of the institutional discussions: after Noordwijk any notion of the IGC deciding to discontinue the right of every Member State to nominate at least one full Member of the Commission, although not dead, was in terminal decline.

Second, the Presidency decided that in the final hectic weeks of the Conference, the IGC Representatives Group would remain the core forum in which shape would be given to the emerging package. An informal meeting of Representatives was held at Houthem in the Netherlands on 16/17 May. This offered an opportunity for the Presidency, in addition to scheduling discussion of a number of specific agenda items, to make available to delegations a set of documents setting out the Presidency's view of the state of play as it then stood on virtually all of the package (other than the sensitive institutional questions) – its first comprehensive drawing together of the strands.

The Netherlands Presidency faced the same dilemma which we had faced six months earlier, namely to judge the appropriate moment at which to table an overall draft. On the one hand, it was essential that delegations should have a sense of the emerging overall package. On the other hand, a precipitate presentation of an overall Draft Treaty would have left it vulnerable to "the jackal pack waiting to tear it apart the moment it faltered in its stride". The Presidency shrewdly emphasized that the documents which it tabled on 16 May at Houthem, taken together, did *not* constitute a draft of the Treaty which it would be submitting to Amsterdam. However, what else, in a sense, could they be? There was a certain creative ambiguity about their status.

Third, the Presidency convened a special Conclave of Foreign Ministers, under whose authority all the negotiations were proceeding, for 20 May in The Hague. This, apart from being Robin Cook's first IGC Ministerial Meeting, offered an opportunity for stock to be taken at political level of the emerging package in advance of the informal European Council meeting at Noordwijk three days later. Ministers also had a detailed further discussion of the draft Common Foreign and Security Policy provisions.

A final IGC Ministerial meeting on 2/3 June helped the Presidency to refine further the compromises which it would eventually table in some of the most important areas, including again the CFSP. Ministers also re-examined on that occasion, without new proposals having been submitted, the stubborn triangle of institutional questions on which the Presidency was trying to make progress in the only way possible, namely through the slow, painful grinding together of sensitivities at the political level. (No new papers on institutional questions had been tabled since April. Solutions did not depend on drafting.) Some outstanding points in relation to employment and the environment were also examined by Ministers.

Fourth, in order to cope with the volume of tidying-up required, the Presidency decided to set up a "Friends of the Presidency" group. This group, chaired by the Presidency (Jaap de Zwaan) and with representatives of each delegation, met under the authority of the IGC Representatives Group and in parallel with it. It met for the first time in the last week of May and on a few subsequent occasions before Amsterdam. Its remit was to refine texts in a number of important but less sensitive areas which were assigned to it. The results of its meetings were presented to the IGC Representatives Group for its consideration and for the resolution of any outstanding difficulties. (The parallel meetings of the Friends of the Presidency group added a further dimension to the already complicated work at IGC Representatives level, since urgent and sometimes contradictory reports now began to come in of skirmishes on a part of the battlefield just out of view.)

Finally, as regards the tabling of the crucial Draft Treaty which would be submitted as the basis for negotiation at Amsterdam, the Netherlands Presidency (bearing in mind, as the Irish Presidency had done, that time for digestion is also time for unravelling) decided that the appropriate balance would be to complete the dance of the seven veils on 12 June. The holding back of its Draft Treaty until 12 June also enabled the Presidency to take maximum account of Prime Minister Kok's pre-European Council tour of capitals.

One side-effect of the enormous pressure of work and time was that paradoxically it appeared, in the last few weeks of the Conference, to become easier rather than more difficult for minor new points to find their way into the package, in the form either of minor treaty amendments or declarations for inclusion in the Final Act of the Conference. It had been acknowledged for much of the Conference that it would be preferable, from the point of view of the coherence and focus of the package, to avoid the accretion of too much flotsam and jetsam. By common consent a "Christmas Tree" approach was to be avoided. There appeared, however, to be an unexpected degree of willingness to entertain the addition to the tree of last-minute decorations which, although some may have been helpful in one way or another, would have received short shrift at an earlier stage of the Conference.

The eve of battle

The hosts began to mass in Amsterdam on Sunday 15 June. The wagon-trains of the 15 national delegations and of the Commission rolled, in dribs and drabs, into their allocated hotels, bivouacked in random groups for the next morning's encounter. Each sprawling delegation comprising its generals, its footsoldiers and its camp-followers. Briefcases full of battle-plans and ammunition; the Presidency's Draft Treaty – its chosen terrain – always somewhere near at hand. Useful bartering of last minute titbits of information in hotel lobbies. Arrival times of Prime Ministers to be pinned down. Delegation meetings and press briefings to be arranged. Hotel bars turning a reasonable profit.

Serious work had already started for some on Sunday. The Presidency was finalizing its proposals in the Justice and Home Affairs area in consultation with the delegations most directly concerned (see Chapter 15) and putting the final touches to its battle plan. For the Presidency and others, late-night drafting lay ahead.

The order of battle

The Presidency, in the traditional pre-European Council letter from Prime Minister Kok to his colleagues, had prescribed the order of battle.

The two days of 16 and 17 June would be devoted almost entirely to the IGC, the aim being agreement on a "consolidated text for a new Treaty". As far as possible, the decks had been cleared. Exceptionally, no meeting had been programmed with the Heads of State or Government from the applicant countries to join the Union. The European Council conclusions would, as always, deal with a range of issues, but work was programmed so as to require as little as possible of the time of the European Council itself to be devoted to issues other than the IGC. Foreign Ministers would deal with a number of topical foreign policy questions at their working dinner on 16 June. Finance Ministers would work in parallel with the European Council on the morning of 16 June to try to finalize agreement on some important and tricky issues relating to Economic and Monetary Union. Broad agreement existed in advance on a number of other non-IGC issues. In the event it proved possible for the European Council to devote virtually all its attention to the task of finalizing the Treaty.

Heads of State or Government were to have available for their IGC discussions virtually the whole day of Monday 16 June (including their working dinner that evening, but excluding a formal lunch with Queen Beatrix) as well as the whole of the following day, Tuesday 17 June (including a working lunch with Foreign Ministers). The Presidency's stated aim was to complete proceedings "after luncheon" on 17 June. While, in the event, this estimate proved optimistic, there is always an advantage in trying to create some time pressure for the completion of business. If the meeting had been "scheduled" to continue until the early hours of 18 June, God knows when it would have ended.

Prime Minister Kok had indicated, in his pre-European Council letter to colleagues, his intention of starting business on Monday, after the usual meeting with the President of the European Parliament, with a discussion of the main issues still open at the IGC – commencing with Section II (the Union and the Citizen) and then dealing with the other Sections in numerical order. The decision to start with Section II was, I imagine, designed to obtain the small tactical advantage of opening with a harmonious discussion in an area which was already very largely agreed.

Although Prime Minister Kok acknowledged in his letter that much of the new Treaty had been agreed, the Presidency faced a formidable challenge. Some of the most sensitive issues remained to be resolved, including, notably, the following.

1. As far as the area of Justice and Home Affairs was concerned, the extent to which the unanimity requirement would be retained as the decision-making mechanism in the new Title on Free Movement of Persons, Asylum and Immigration, as well as the complex provisions which would be required in that area to provide for the necessary degree of flexibility to accommodate the objectively different situations of Member States.

2. As regards external policy, the question of the relationship between the European Union and the Western European Union, as well as the issue of extending the Union's ability to act in the area of external economic relations.

3. The triangle of sensitive institutional questions (composition of the Commission, weighting of votes in the Council and extension of qualified majority voting to additional aspects of normal Community business under the first pillar). The scope of the extension of the co-decision procedure also had to be settled.

4. As regards flexibility, a final balance still had to be struck in the new provisions. This hinged in particular on whether unanimity would be required for their use.

However, in a way the most formidable aspect of the challenge facing the Presidency was that, while the thrust of the vast bulk of its Draft Treaty could be said to reflect an emerging consensus, a very large number of points, in addition to the sensitive ones referred to above, remained to be finally settled. The European Council, in the limited time available to it, would have to revisit every significant area of the work of the Conference. Moreover, since nothing would be agreed until everything was agreed, there was nothing to prevent points which appeared to have been settled from being re-opened.

Let the battle commence

On 16 June, the Members of the European Council started arriving at the Conference Centre (the impressive Central Bank of the Netherlands) from 8.30 a.m. to be met, as protocol dictates, by Prime Minister Kok. A friendly handshake in front of a barrage of clattering cameras. The private and the public elide. A few important fresh faces. Tony Blair's comparative youth is striking. A whiff of Camelot. The new French Prime Minister, Lionel Jospin, fresh from his election victory. Two flavours of socialism.

By 9 a.m. the Members of the European Council, i.e. two politicians per delegation, make their way towards the restricted "red" area (so-called after the colour of the badge necessary for access): a large gathering area or floorspace, off which on one side is the small "Antici" room and on the other side the large meeting room for the European Council itself. The "Antici" room, provided at every European Council, is the room in which the Council Secretariat briefs national delegations – the so-called "Antici Group" – on a continuous basis on what is happening at the European Council. Each member of the "Antici Group" in turn keeps the bulk of his or her delegation – huddled like a group of anxious relatives in the overcrowded waiting room of a maternity hospital – informed of developments.

The Heads of Government, accompanied by the few members of their delegation wielding "red" badges, pass across the large floorspace into the meeting room. A large table, in the shape of a grinning mouth, stretches away from the entrance. Behind the Presidency, which occupies the centre of the nearer length of the table, are seats for the only officials allowed to be present for the meeting – from the Presidency, the Council Secretariat and the Commission. A stampede of cameramen enters, does its business and is hustled out. Last-minute riding instructions are whispered.

Those without seats withdraw like children who have lost an elaborate game of musical chairs. The door closes.

Outside temporary silence on the radar screen.

The joining of forces

In the course of its first day the European Council, in addition to a brief discussion of the non-IGC aspects of its agenda, managed to carry out a first reading of all Sections of the Draft Treaty. Sensitive institutional questions and flexibility, as well as external economic relations, were discussed by Heads of State or Government over their dinner that evening.

Clarity was growing on some of the key points. It seemed clear, for example, that the decision-making mechanism for triggering use of the flexibility provisions would be akin to the new procedure under the Common Foreign and Security Policy, combining qualified majority voting with the possibility of exercising a veto.

The complex construction of the proposed provisions tabled that day to accommodate flexibility in relation to *free movement, asylum and immigration* appeared likely to be accepted subject to refinement.

Many of the smaller points were also gradually falling into place.

At the beginning of the meeting on the second day, the Presidency tabled a working document which constituted an addendum, in the light of the first day's discussions, to certain aspects of the Draft Treaty. This working document, which covered several areas, including notably Justice and Home Affairs and the security aspects of the CFSP, now constituted, along with the Draft Treaty, the basis for the second day's discussion. During the course of the second day, the European Council, having made its way through the new working document, returned to points in the Draft Treaty which, although not covered in the working document, remained outstanding.

Lunchtime discussion on Tuesday was devoted to the relationship between the European Union and the Western European Union. The Political Committee, composed of the "Political Directors" from each Member State (senior officials dealing with the CFSP), was requested by the Heads of State or Government to meet separately in the afternoon to refine the text on the security aspects of the CFSP.

As the European Council moved into the evening of 17 June, some of the core points remained to be resolved.

The afternoon work of Political Directors provided a basis for the European Council to move fairly rapidly towards final agreement on the security aspects of the CFSP. A key element in that regard was that references to the possibility of a common defence or of the integration of the WEU into the Union would be qualified by the phrase "should the European Council so decide". The European Council, of course, acts unanimously. It was also to be specified that, in such an event, the European Council shall "recommend to the Member States the adoption of such a decision in accordance with their respective constitutional requirements".

On external economic relations, despite strong pleas from several members of the European Council, including John Bruton, it only proved possible to reach agreement on a Treaty amendment which would make it possible at a later date, without recourse to further treaty change, to take the necessary decisions to strengthen the Union's ability to act in the areas of trade in services and intellectual property.

On institutional questions, the final decision reached late at night on the extension of qualified majority voting to further aspects of normal Community business was, in the view of many, disappointing. The fact that the United Kingdom was not the delegation holding out in the end was an important sign of the times. The extent of the provision for moving to qualified majority voting in the new Title on Free Movement, Asylum and Immigration also fell short of the Presidency's proposal. For many key elements in that Title, any move to qualified majority voting will require a further *unanimous* decision of the Council.

The extension of the co-decision procedure, however, went further than many expected and will increase the role of the Parliament in a significant number of areas.

The two issues which took up most time late into Tuesday night and Wednesday morning were the composition of the Commission and the weighting of votes in the Council. They were inextricably linked, as they always had been. It had clearly emerged that the larger Member States could agree to give up their second Member of the Commission, but the nature of the necessary quid pro quo as regards the Council remained unsettled. Most delegations had a preference for the introduction of a dual majority system in the Council (to ensure that a qualified majority of votes in the Council would require also the support of Governments representing a specified percentage of the Union's population). A significant minority, however, preferred an actual reweighing of votes. Some on either side of this particular argument indicated that they were unable to compromise.

According to one view, which I share, a settlement there and then on these sensitive institutional questions was not beyond the reach of the Conference. With a rejigging of the detail of the proposal for a change in voting weights and one further push, a deal could possibly have been done once and for all. There is, of course, another entirely plausible view that, if there was to be agreement on a Treaty at Amsterdam, there was no alternative to postponing a decision on the most sensitive institutional questions. We will never know.

The outcome on the two issues in question, however, is not by any means negligible. The bones of the necessary institutional trade-off, elements of which had been rejected out of hand in the course of the Conference, have now been clearly set out in a Protocol to the Treaty, although that trade-off remains to be translated into practice. The Protocol specifies that at the date of entry into force of the first enlargement of the Union "the Commission shall comprise one national of each of the Member States provided that, by that date, the weighting of votes in the Council has been modified, whether by reweighing of votes or by a dual majority, in a manner acceptable to all Member States...". In my view, if that deal, sketched out in the Treaty Protocol, could have been definitively done at Amsterdam, it would have been a very good night's work for Europe. Others considered that there were advantages in postponement.

The Protocol, which was subject to last-minute haggling (sketched in the opening vignette in the introduction to this book), provides also for a comprehensive review of the composition and functioning of the institutions "at least one year before the membership of the Union exceeds twenty".

The European Council concluded at 3.35 a.m. on 18 June 1997.

The European Council, according to its conclusions, "successfully concluded the IGC with full agreement on a draft treaty".

The aftermath

Notwithstanding the agreement reached at Amsterdam, due largely to the outstanding efforts of the Netherlands Presidency, there remained a considerable amount of wreckage on the battlefield.

An extensive and difficult task still lay ahead for the Netherlands Presidency and indeed for the Luxembourg Presidency which was due to begin on 1 July 1997. The text of the Treaty had to be tidied up as regards minor drafting points which it had not been possible to agree before or at Amsterdam. Moreover, some of the amendments agreed in Amsterdam required consequential amendments elsewhere in the Treaty. Most importantly, on several points there was even the delicate (and occasionally acrimonious) task of reaching subsequent agreement on what the European Council had actually agreed. The substance of what had been agreed at Amsterdam also had to be cast in the definitive overall legal form of a treaty.

The post-Amsterdam "wreckage" arose from the nature of the negotiations at the European Council. My account in this chapter has tried to provide a coherent summary of the overall development of the two days of discussion. It focuses on the salient aspects of the key issues. In reality, the nature of the negotiation at Amsterdam was much more complex and at times confusing. It consisted of many hundreds of interventions by 32 politicians (often with other things on their mind) from 16 delegations in eleven languages on evolving texts in legal language covering a vast array of complex issues, much of whose detail they were coming to grips with for the first time. Issues overlapped with each other and were frequently revisited. A degree of confusion was inevitable.

The tidying-up work was carried out over many weeks by the Friends of the Presidency group, which had been established in the weeks before Amsterdam. After Amsterdam, the group worked under the authority of the Committee of Permanent Representatives in Brussels. It had a difficult job principally because in some cases there were genuinely held differences of interpretation of what had been agreed at Amsterdam. This applied, for example, to the precise scope of the extension of the co-decision procedure and to the precise mechanisms allowing Ireland and the UK to participate in aspects of Schengen cooperation. Establishing what had "happened" at Amsterdam did not always prove to be an exact and objective science. However, there was one powerful driving force towards eventual agreement, namely the reluctance of all delegations to dig any holes from which a further meeting of the European Council itself – which nobody wanted – would constitute the only means of escape.

Finally, the text of the Treaty had to be aligned in all its language versions down to the last detail. This linguistic refinement was carried out, as is the custom, with the assistance of a jurists/linguists group.

The Treaty was eventually signed in Amsterdam on 2 October 1997 by the Foreign Ministers of the 15 Member States of the European Union. The Dutch Masters had finished their work (with a little assistance from the Luxembourg Presidency). The picture was complete. The verdict on it was now in the hands of the art experts and the general public.

PART IV

TAKING STOCK

Chapter 17

Amber Lights in Amsterdam:
Europe Proceeds with Caution

Eppur si muove (Yet it moves)
(Galileo Galilei, attrib.)

It seems appropriate to attempt to draw some summary conclusions about the Treaty of Amsterdam and about how it was negotiated. Since this book as a whole tries to explain the IGC's cocktail of process and content, and constitutes in a sense my assessment of both ingredients, what follows can be relatively brief.

The Treaty of Amsterdam now has a life of its own. Its signature in Amsterdam on 2 October 1997 marked the cutting of the Treaty's umbilical cord with its own process of gestation. Its provisions, set out in black and white, now fall to be parsed and analysed for what they say rather than for what they might have said – the "what" rather than the "why". That is both understandable and appropriate.

However, there is another type of assessment, to which this book tries to make a modest contribution, which will also remain essential – an evaluation of the Conference which takes account of its context, its complexity and its constraints. Any wishing away of that reality – whether with a view to sound bites, to the creation of non-existent demons or to the conjuring up of unattainable visions – cannot serve the interests of the European Union or its citizens.

The content of the Treaty of Amsterdam

The emerging content of the Treaty has been photographed in various stages of undress in the course of this book. I do not propose, in this chapter, to rehearse in detail the "Full Monty" but only to sketch out some broad, tentative and personal conclusions.

Let me emphasize, before I go any further, that there will be many different assessments of the Treaty. It would be peculiar if that were not the case. The negotiations involved 15 Member States, as well as the Commission and the European Parliament. Each delegation will have its own perception. Indeed, within each Member State and institution a variety of views will be taken of the Treaty.

The Treaty of Amsterdam is a significant political act in the process of European integration. Differences of view about it are as natural and healthy as differences of view within any democratic process. Europe needs vision so that our sights are kept on the mountaintop. It needs caution so that our feet are kept on the ground. It needs pragmatism to keep us moving forward up the mountain over difficult terrain.

But the starting point for all views must be reality – the reality of the challenges and opportunities which the European Union faces; the reality of the achievements, potential and limits of European integration; the reality of the pursuit of national interests; the reality of the ethos of understanding and accommodation; the reality of the complexity and the constraints.

I nailed my personal colours clearly to the mast in the introduction to this book – I am a committed and pragmatic European. In the context of healthy public debate, I am not concerned so much at opposition to European integration as at the notion that there is any *simple* alternative. I am worried not by the pursuit of a European "city upon a hill" but by any suggestion that there are *easy* short cuts to getting there.

Disappointments and imperfections

Whatever views are taken of the Treaty of Amsterdam, only a fool could suggest that it is perfect. It is complex, at times opaque, and – whatever angle you are coming from – in some respects disappointing.

In my own view, for example, the very limited progress in relation to strengthening the Community's hand in relation to the defence of its external economic interests is disappointing. Despite the time and energy devoted to this issue at the Conference, a real breakthrough proved impossible. As in every area there were significant sensitivities as well as conflicting perceptions of national interest. In this area, however, the potential for addressing those sensitivities and reconciling those perceptions was probably not exploited to the full.

The unwillingness to copperfasten at Amsterdam, once and for all, the institutional deal foreshadowed in the Amsterdam Treaty Protocol on the institutions was regrettable. If, shortly before dawn at Amsterdam, that important trade-off had been not only identified, as it was, but also definitively agreed it would have represented a particularly good night's work for Europe.

Another reason for some concern is that the Treaty provisions on free movement, asylum and immigration are very complex – perhaps unnecessarily so. They represent a basis for progress but their implementation in practice will not be easy.

The further move away from the unanimity requirement for normal Community ("first pillar") business should have been more adventurous. Indeed, until the very last hours of the Conference it appeared that it would be.

The final form and presentation of the Treaty, much of it decided in the tidying-up exercise after Amsterdam, is also no great cause for celebration. With its complexity and its cross-referencing, it remains – in its undigested form – disappointingly impenetrable to the casual but interested reader. The Irish Presidency had attached very particular importance to presenting its Outline Draft Treaty in an easily readable form. However, in that exercise we had much greater flexibility than was available in the task of finalizing the text of the actual Treaty in definitive legal form. It could well be that the eventual complexity and impenetrability of the Treaty of Amsterdam were to a considerable extent inevitable, that in the end there was no other way. Nevertheless they are a cause for concern and for reflection in the context of future IGCs. The clarity and readability of a treaty *actually negotiated* at an IGC is, in my view, more important than the question – to which much time was devoted at the IGC – of the extent to which the already *existing treaties* can be simplified.

These are just some examples of areas in which, in my view, the IGC could perhaps have gone further. Others would no doubt list their own areas of disappointment. It is a fundamental and important truth that one delegation's areas of dissatisfaction are – not by chance but almost by definition – areas of satisfaction for another. A negotiation, by its very nature, is a process which cannot fully satisfy any participant.

As to why the outcome of the Conference was in some respects disappointing, there is no simple answer. Ambition and vision are precious but at the same time subtle commodities. They must always remain a priority, but merely appealing to them is, in practical terms, largely meaningless.

The answer to the imperfections of the Treaty lies, to a considerable extent, precisely in the profound difference of view between delegations as to which aspects of the Treaty should be the focus of celebration or disappointment. The catch-22 is that, if the delegations could all have agreed that a particular element in the Treaty was disappointing, they would not have agreed it in the form they did.

The answer also lies somewhere, scattered around this book, in the intricacies of the negotiations and in the human judgements which we made, individually and collectively. A complex negotiation of this sort, which involves its disappointments as well as its achievements, cannot aim for the potential perfect score of the gymnast. It should rather be judged like a football match which, whatever its quality, inevitably has its missed passes and tackles and opportunities.

The answer may also lie in the IGC's methods, on which I make some suggestions in the final chapter of this book. No serious radical alternative to IGCs has, however, been identified or proposed.

Above all, the imperfection of the outcome reflects the nature of the challenges and constraints which the IGC faced and which are set out in Chapter 1.

Overall assessment

In the context of the challenges and constraints, the overall assessment of the Treaty of Amsterdam should, in my view, be a positive one.

The Treaty will allow the Union to address more effectively the most *direct concerns of citizens* in areas such as employment, public health, the environment, social exclusion, consumer protection, social policy, equality between men and women and non-discrimination. It provides that the Union and its institutions should function more transparently. In each of these individual areas, the Treaty provides a basis for practical progress in addressing the concerns of citizens. More importantly, these new provisions *cumulatively* represent – in their intention, potential effect, and foreshadowing of future IGCs – a significant redirection of the priorities of the European Union.

In the area of *Justice and Home Affairs*, the Treaty provides first and foremost a basis for more effective action at the level of the Union in the fight against organized crime (itself an issue of very direct concern to citizens), including drug trafficking, terrorism and offences against children. It also establishes provisions for closer cooperation on the issues of free movement, asylum and immigration. The provisions in the latter areas reflect and provide reassurance for the different situations of Member States and are therefore necessarily somewhat complex, although probably more so than was strictly necessary.

The Treaty equips the Union to play a more effective role in *international relations*. It establishes, for example, improved decision-making procedures for the Common Foreign Security Policy (CFSP), while retaining the essentially intergovernmental nature of that policy. It improves also the preparation and implementation mechanisms of the CFSP. The security dimension of the CFSP is developed in a way which notably will enable the Union, availing itself of the Western European Union, to participate effectively in Petersberg tasks (in effect the essence of the current security challenges in Europe, including peacekeeping and crisis management). The Petersberg tasks have been incorporated into the Treaty.

A small improvement, although disappointing, has also been made in relation to external economic relations. At a future date substantive improvements in this area can, as a result of the Treaty, be agreed without recourse to further treaty change.

The new institutional treaty provisions should first of all make the *institutions* more responsive to *public concerns*. Apart from the provision that all the institutions should function more transparently, the role of the European Parliament has been significantly strengthened in a number of ways, notably by a wide-ranging extension of the co-decision procedure for the adoption of legislation and by enhancement of the role of the Parliament within that procedure. The Treaty also contains provisions which will facilitate the role that national parliaments play in relation to Union business. The formalization in the Treaty of the arrangements for the implementation of the subsidiarity principle, together with the making explicit of the understanding that European citizenship does not affect national citizenship, provides further reassurance where it is needed.

The Treaty will, moreover, *streamline the functioning of the institutions* in a number of ways. The number of legislative procedures is to be reduced. The co-decision procedure will be simplified. The extension of qualified majority voting to further areas of normal Community business, while many would have wished it to go further, is at least a step in the right direction. Qualified majority voting will not only *replace the unanimity requirement* in a small number of additional areas, notably the important research area. It will also apply to many of the areas being brought into the Treaties *for the first time*, such as social exclusion and the adoption of guidelines and incentive measures in the employment area.

In some ways the most important aspect of the institutional provisions of the Treaty is what they do *not* change. *The broad balance between and within the institutions has been preserved.* For some this is undoubtedly a disappointment.

Proposals floated at an early stage of the Conference which were designed to curtail the role of the European Commission – a role that remains crucial to the continued effective functioning of the Union – sank into oblivion.

More significantly, proposals which would have had the effect of shifting significantly the balance within the institutions in favour of the larger Member States were pressed vigorously until a very late stage at the Conference. Despite this, the deal sketched out eventually in the Protocol on the institutions – the larger Member States giving up their right to nominate a second Member of the Commission in return for an increase in the weighting of their votes in the Council – is both sensible and balanced. Although derided by some, the very identification of this trade-off (while it would have been preferable not to have postponed a decision on its detailed translation into practice) represents very important progress for Europe. It should not be forgotten that, in the course of the Conference, some had rejected out of hand the principle – now in practice accepted subject to future review – of one Commissioner per Member State.

Apart from the new provisions on Justice and Home Affairs, the Treaty significantly increases in other ways the *flexibility* available to the Union, while at the same time preserving its coherence. As regards foreign policy, significant scope for flexibility in relation to individual decisions will be provided both by the new "constructive abstention" mechanism and by the provision for decisions to be taken by qualified majority vote within general strategies which have been agreed unanimously by the European Council – subject ultimately, however, to the possibility of veto. At the same time, the Conference avoided the pitfall of providing for an excessive degree of flexibility in relation to external policy which would have damaged, perhaps irretrievably, the external coherence of the Union and the perception of that coherence.

The Conference has also agreed important but necessarily circumscribed provisions for flexibility under the "first pillar". These provisions represent a cautiously creative attempt to equip the Union to steer its way forward in the not fully charted waters that lie ahead.

The process of the Intergovernmental Conference

The process leading to the Treaty of Amsterdam, as should be clear from this book, was riddled with imperfections. It was a management consultant's worst nightmare.

However, it should not be imagined that there is an easy way of doing things. The substance of an IGC will always be about interests. The process will always be about compromise. Anyone who thinks there is a simple formula should table at the next IGC a proposal to change either human nature or the world in which we live, or ideally both.

Practical and carefully thought-out improvements in the functioning of IGCs should be a priority. In the final chapter, I set out some personal reflections in this regard with a view to future IGCs. Merely decrying the IGC process, however, serves no purpose. Shooting the pianist, against the strictures of Oscar Wilde, is easy and may even give a sense of self-satisfaction, but it will not cause the tune to be played any more effectively.

The Presidency

My experience was that each succeeding *Presidency* played, as it must play, a central role at the Intergovernmental Conference. Unlike normal Community business, in relation to which the Commission exercises the sole right of initiative, at an IGC it is only the Presidency that can serve as the motor for advancing the work and ensure the coherence of the negotiations. It is the Presidency which first establishes and then adapts the overall work programme. It is responsible for the strategic preparation and conduct of every meeting and controls the agenda.

Above all, unlike normal Community business, it is the Presidency which prepares and tables the papers for discussion. Throughout the process there was no shortage of proposals and papers from national delegations, sometimes tabled by several delegations together, which descended on the table like "grouse from a highland sky". These papers represented an important signalling of positions. Sometimes they represented a useful mine from which the Presidency could quarry ideas. Occasionally, the existence of national proposals significantly shaped the nature of the papers tabled by the Presidency. Only very rarely, however, did national proposals actually form the basis for discussion at a meeting. (This did happen occasionally, as for example when the range of so-called "other issues" were scheduled for discussion, i.e. proposals brought forward by individual delegations in areas falling outside the main subjects for discussion and in relation to which it was not yet clear whether a level of support would develop which would justify the tabling of proposals by the Presidency.)

A Presidency is not exercised in a vacuum. There is no shortage of advice from delegations, and a Presidency must be sensitive to that advice. While the advice is often not disinterested, our experience as Presidency was that – when it came to the procedural handling of the work of the Conference – there was a significant commonality of interest, reflected in much objective, experienced and professional – albeit sometimes conflicting – advice. Arm-twisting of a Presidency also occurs. That is a different matter. Even a small Presidency can, however, resist it. Indeed, in the interests of the Union, it must do so.

A Presidency should above all be seen to be fair. It should neither pursue its own narrow national interests nor be unduly susceptible to pressure from other quarters. That commitment to fairness – not always comfortable – is in itself correct and requires no further justification. However, it can also strengthen the hand of a Presidency in the conduct of its work. Moreover, it enhances the office of Presidency and is ultimately in the interests of the Union as a whole. It may indeed stand to the long-term credit and credibility of the Member State in question.

The crucial role played by the permanent Council Secretariat in support of the transient six-monthly Presidencies has been emphasized at several points in this book. An appropriate balance needs to be struck. It would be folly for a Presidency to do anything other than to work closely and in full harmony with the Council Secretariat, drawing on its irreplaceable experience, knowledge, legal advice and drafting skills. It would at the same time be inappropriate for a Presidency to submit to the Conference, in its own name, whatever first drafts may be produced by the Council Secretariat. It is the Presidency which must accept political responsibility. It must therefore exercise its own judgement in steering the work of the Conference. It must develop its own strategy and adapt each draft paper as appropriate. A Presidency must place its own stamp on the work. The Council Secretariat itself would not wish things any other way.

A close working relationship between succeeding Presidencies is also crucial. We were deeply appreciative of the support of both the Italian Presidency which preceded us and the Netherlands Presidency which followed us. We did our best to reciprocate. The relationship between Presidencies is, at the same time, a delicate one. The preparatory work of a Presidency overlaps with the conduct of the one which precedes it. The decisions reached during a Presidency shape significantly the work of that which follows. The necessary continuity must allow sufficient space for each Presidency to exercise its energies, its judgement and its political responsibilities. Any notion of a collective Presidency for an IGC (say a "troika" of succeeding Presidencies) would lead to nothing but confusion.

The unicity of the negotiations

The importance of what was referred to as the "unicity" of the negotiations should be emphasized. Unicity is the principle whereby there was only one negotiation, conducted at several levels (Foreign Ministers, IGC Representatives and briefly, at a late stage, a Friends of the Presidency Group – all ultimately under the authority of the European Council). Given that the nature of the IGC negotiation involved the preparation of a single package, it was essential that the work of the Conference should take place within a single structure. Discussion should not be allowed to go off in a series of tangents at other fora.

This meant, in particular, avoiding negotiations opening up among any Ministers other than Foreign Ministers. If, for example, Finance or Environment or Justice Ministers had become collectively involved in aspects of the negotiations of particular interest to them, the outcome in the areas concerned would have been quite different and the preparation of a single package would have become unmanageable. Accordingly, where it was felt necessary to respond to pressure for discussion in Ministerial fora outside the Conference as such, this was organized on an informal basis, usually over lunch, without conclusions. What mattered in the IGC negotiations was not what, say, Environment Ministers said to each other, but rather how each Environment Minister influenced the position taken by his own delegation within the negotiations themselves. Unicity had to be ensured below Ministerial level also. The preservation of unicity was an important responsibility of each Presidency. It was one which it proved possible to exercise satisfactorily because all delegations recognized unicity as being so evidently in the interests of the negotiations as a whole.

Similarly, regular caucus meetings of representatives of Governments reflecting a particular political philosophy – notably Christian Democrat or Socialist – did not constitute part of the IGC negotiations and any influence they may have had was similarly indirect.

The European Commission

The European Commission is an important participant at an Intergovernmental Conference. On every aspect it helps to identify the European interest among the national positions. On many issues, it has the expertise to judge precisely what is required and how to achieve it. The principal problem which it faces at an IGC is that its role is not its accustomed one of sole initiator. The balance that it needs to strike at every IGC is how far it can go in driving the work of the Conference in certain areas while not at the same time either over-interpreting its role or exceeding the bounds of what is realistically achievable. If it goes too far it will simply be marginalized.

In the negotiations leading to the Maastricht Treaty, the Commission tabled a number of ambitious proposals which, although in some ways admirable and inherently logical, were essentially ignored. At the more recent IGC, the Commission chose a more pragmatic approach.

As Presidency, we recognized in advance the particular importance of developing close informal practical cooperation with the Commission in relation to the Conference (in addition to the contribution the Commission would be making at the negotiations themselves). The Commission itself saw the value in such close cooperation with the Presidency – which had not always been the case at previous IGCs – and readily agreed to it. Our cooperation with the Commission, which remained informal, did not, of course, cut across in the slightest degree the role of the Council Secretariat, which remained the Presidency's principal support.

The Presidency and the Commission had a shared interest in advancing the work of the Conference and maintaining its level of ambition. We found the Commission's support and advice particularly useful both at the level of detail and in the formulation of our strategy at key points during our Presidency.

No Member State is more strongly supportive than Ireland of the role of the Commission, and we have always worked comfortably with it, as proved to be the case at the IGC.

The European Parliament

The role assigned to the European Parliament in relation to the IGC (described in Chapter 5) meant that, although it was not a participant at the Conference itself, it was closely associated at every twist and turn of the negotiations. Every political level IGC meeting was preceded by an exchange of views with the President of the European Parliament. Twice a month the Parliament's IGC Representatives met with the IGC Representatives Group (which itself was meeting weekly). This latter arrangement – which represented the maximum frequency of contact with Parliament at Representative level that the Member States had been able to agree unanimously – was in practice somewhat clumsy. It meant that what the Parliament's IGC Representatives had to say was sometimes "out of sync" with the negotiations because some of the issues addressed by them had inevitably been addressed by the IGC Representatives Group the previous week. Successive Presidencies tried to plug the holes by meeting bilaterally also every week with the Parliament's IGC Representatives.

The Parliament's contribution was always constructive and helped significantly to maintain the ambition of the Conference at the highest attainable level. This was due to the personal quality and commitment of Parliament's IGC Representatives, as well as to the political balance, realism and sensitivity of the Parliament's overall approach.

The European Council

The European Council, as it was expected to do, made the fundamental choices in relation to the direction of the IGC. This was true especially of its formal end-of- Presidency meetings, from the Madrid European Council in December 1994 through to the final deal at Amsterdam in June 1997. The more informal meetings of Heads of State or Government also fulfilled an important function in the evolutionary process.

The European Council at Amsterdam, as can be seen from the previous chapter, was of a somewhat different nature to the other meetings at that level. As well as agreeing the key political trade-offs, it involved detailed textual negotiations with a view to finalization of the Treaty.

The process of lengthy and ultimately late-night discussions at Amsterdam involving the working and reworking of a multitude of diverse texts, leaving in some cases the considerable task of divining subsequently what had actually been agreed, is open to two evaluations. It may, on the one hand, be the only way for the Union to do business. It may be that the political leaders have to be allowed to cut a political deal in the absence of the officials (other than from the Presidency, Council Secretariat and Commission) who are familiar with every nuance of every disputed provision. On the other hand, one could take the view that it is an unnecessarily sloppy way of doing business in relation to important matters which will ultimately become law throughout the Union, a process which could – according to that view – be improved by providing more time (perhaps an extra day) for all the texts to be revised, reviewed and definitively approved by Heads of State or Government.

The functioning of the European Council as an institution is in many ways remarkable. Such a body, in which a large number of Heads of State or Government meet regularly actually to negotiate matters of great political and economic significance, as distinct from merely approving pre-cooked conclusions, is certainly without direct parallel. If its functioning is imperfect, it has nevertheless stood the test of time. If it ain't broke, we should be slow to call the repair man. The work methods at Amsterdam mirrored the denouement of previous IGCs and may well be inevitable. The question, however, merits further reflection.

The media

The role of the media is crucial in relation to an Intergovernmental Conference, as indeed with regard to Union business more generally. Addressing the concerns of citizens is deprived of much of its value to the extent that those citizens remain unaware of what is being done in their name. Informing the public, through the media, about the IGC was a priority of every Presidency – press conferences were given after every meeting at Ministerial and Representative level – as well as of national delegations.

Overall the media coverage, while often of high quality, was not always as extensive as the importance of the issues justified and the volume of briefing made possible. The media coverage was hamstrung by the very nature of the negotiations. A gradual evolutionary process represents in a sense the enemy of sound bites. "Big bang" makes a better headline than "New sub-species evolves over 1 million years". The lack of headline material was at times interpreted by some in the media as a lack of progress. When, at Amsterdam, the media eventually had what they like to handle, a few days of wheeler-dealing, there was a tendency to over-interpret a few last-minute developments.

The gulf of comprehension between the Union and the man or woman in the street, although the IGC may have made some progress, remains perhaps the principal challenge facing the Union.

The sky remains in place

The prophecies of doom, as usual, are not in short supply. We are warned, on the one hand, that the Treaty of Amsterdam will lead inexorably to the dreaded "European Superstate". We are told, on the other, that the IGC has failed the integration process and that Europe has lost its way.

What we must ask ourselves in relation to every prophet of doom is whether we are dealing with a Cassandra or a Chicken Licken. The tragedy of Cassandra, whom none would believe, was that she spoke the truth. Chicken Licken was a comic figure because he interpreted the landing of an acorn on his head as a portent that the sky was falling down.

Our knowledge of Cassandra must lead us to treat Chicken Lickens with a degree of respect. Maybe there is some element of truth in the prophecies. The Treaty of Amsterdam *does* mark one further significant step in the process of European integration feared by some. It does *not* constitute the great leap forward seen as necessary by others.

I have to say, speaking personally, that I do not have the impression that the sky is falling down.

The Treaty of Amsterdam marks a limited but important step forward for the European Union. It does not contain a Protocol on the abolition of original sin. It will not in itself change the face of Europe.

It has, however, kept the remarkable European show on the road. The Treaty's contents will make our complex Union somewhat more effective, internally and externally, as well as more responsive to the concerns of citizens.

The Treaty's conclusion, to the necessary satisfaction of all, has provided one of the necessary bases for the Union to move ahead to shoulder its growing responsibilities as a source of prosperity and stability for its own people as well as for the wider European continent and beyond. The enlargement process has opened. The establishment of a single currency is on course. The Union can look forward to the new millennium with controlled confidence.

The earth still moves around the sun. If we could be forced by an Inquisition to recant on our belief that the continued process of European integration is both possible and on course, we might, I think, be tempted, like Galileo, to mutter:

"Eppur si muove (yet it moves)!".

Chapter 18

A Few Modest Proposals

So two cheers for democracy. . . there is no occasion to give three.

(E.M. Forster)

The IGC process is easy to criticize. Suggesting how it might be improved for the future is just a little trickier. It nevertheless seems opportune to make a few modest proposals in that regard. The next IGC is always somewhere down the pipeline.

There are no simple answers. Perhaps it could be said with some truth of IGCs, as Churchill once said of democracy, that it "is the worst form of government except all those other forms that have been tried from time to time". Maybe the IGC process deserves the "two cheers" that E.M. Forster was prepared to accord to democracy.

Others, more experienced than me and as well placed, will undoubtedly have valuable ideas on the conduct of future IGCs which will not coincide with my own. Nevertheless, on a tentative and personal basis, I offer my ha'pence worth, under eight headings.

1. The timing of an IGC

The first important thing about an IGC is to get the timing right. This applies both to the date on which it is to open and to the target date for its conclusion. Problems arose in relation to both aspects of timing at the IGC which negotiated the Treaty of Amsterdam.

The Maastricht Treaty, signed in 1992, had provided that there should be an IGC in 1996. This created a degree of artificiality about its opening. The IGC would have been necessary to address a number of objective challenges, but its precise timing was somewhat arbitrary. The Reflection Group which met during the second half of 1995, although it fulfilled a useful function, was necessary – at least in part – to address the dilemma of establishing, according to a slightly artificial timeframe, an agenda for what for a long time was known as the "1996 IGC". That title was gradually made redundant by events.

Equally, the decision early on at the IGC that it should conclude at Amsterdam in June 1997, although it later operated as a target to speed up work, had the effect for a long time of restraining progress at the Conference. The early decision to conclude at Amsterdam, principally because of the wish to avoid concluding negotiations before the British general election, was in the circumstances probably correct. However, the net effect was that a Conference that had opened somewhat earlier than strictly necessary was doomed to conclude somewhat later than a natural pace in the negotiations would have dictated as optimal. While I think it is true to say that no *stage* of the negotiating process could have been bypassed, I think it is equally true that, in different circumstances, something between six and twelve months could have been knocked off the 24 that it took to get from the opening of the Reflection Group to the Treaty of Amsterdam.

The next IGC, whenever it takes place, has thus far been spared the first of these problems. Unlike the Maastricht Treaty, the Treaty of Amsterdam (although this was confirmed only at Amsterdam itself) does not specify a particular date for the next IGC. There will, of course, be further IGCs. However, the precise timing, of the next major IGC at least, can grow reasonably naturally – undoubtedly in the context of the further enlargement of the Union – from the pressure of events and conflicting interests.

The possibility of the second problem recurring, namely that political events in one or more Member States could delay the conclusion of a future IGC, can neither be accurately predicted nor fully avoided. Nothing, of course, would do more to facilitate the Union's decision-making process than a harmonization of the timing of national elections. However, that is pie in the sky; and, as long as it remains so, we will have to use political judgement, foresight and sensitivity as our imprecise compass for charting the Union's course through the choppy waters of domestic politics.

2. The process of reflection

It was, I think, useful that the IGC itself was preceded by a process of reflection. The task of undertaking that reflection was assigned to the Reflection Group.

The question which arises is whether, in advance of a future IGC, a similar Group – consisting of a representative of each Member State as well as of the Commission and Parliament – should be established; or rather whether the process of reflection should be more divorced from the positions of individual delegations by the appointment of a number of "wise persons", considerably smaller than the number of Member States, to undertake the process of reflection.

On the face of it, there could be certain attractions in the appointment of a small number of distinguished, genuinely independent individuals to undertake the task of sketching a way forward from a European perspective. However, it is necessary to enter two caveats. First, the value of what emerged from such a process of reflection would be almost entirely dependent on its acceptability as a basis for discussion by every Member State. It might be possible to put the accommodation of interests on a back burner, but it would not be possible ultimately to bypass it. Second, the worst of all worlds would be if a group of "wise persons" were chosen and appointed to pursue an unbalanced agenda, a temptation which some Member States would find difficult to resist, or if the "wise persons" themselves chose to pursue such an agenda. The composition of a group of "wise persons" would have to represent an appropriate balance of perceptions. Otherwise the exercise would serve no useful purpose.

If, on the other hand, the Reflection Group formula – one representative from each Member State – were to be repeated, its composition would need careful consideration. One question is whether the type of participant should be specified or whether, as in the case of the 1995 Reflection Group, Member States should be entirely free to decide whether their Representative should be a politician, an official or a somewhat more independent spirit. Probably the Member States should be allowed latitude in that respect. A second question is whether, as in the case of the Dooge Committee which blazed the trail for the Single European Act negotiations in 1985, the members of the Group should be representatives of Heads of State or Government or, as in the 1995 Reflection Group, of Foreign Ministers. While the issue certainly merits consideration, the quality and authority of the individuals is probably, in the end, more important than whom they are stated to represent.

3. The process of negotiation

The negotiating process, involving meeting after meeting at official and political level to refine ideas and later texts into a package which could be acceptable to every Member State, is certainly lengthy and in some ways unwieldy. Apart from the fact that the process could in the right circumstances (as explained above) be telescoped in time, the question arises as to whether it could be otherwise improved. Could one, for example, reduce significantly the number of multilateral meetings and envisage the appointment of a facilitator, or a group of facilitators, to advance the negotiations through a process of bilateral meetings with every delegation?

I am not convinced that the basic structure of the negotiations, including the role of the Presidency, should or could be substantially changed. The quest for the right answer for Europe will remain inextricably bound up with the development of a package acceptable to all delegations under the guidance of successive Presidencies. I cannot see an alternative to an intensive and painstaking schedule of multilateral meetings, at both ministerial and official level, through which texts are gradually refined by delegations *together* in a way which will gradually make them acceptable to *all*. While positions taken at bilateral meetings can be more frank, they lack the added value of being able to influence and sensitize all 16 delegations simultaneously, and cannot be immediately tested on the anvil of compromise.

However, while preserving the basic multilateral structure of negotiation, a Presidency already makes use of bilateral contacts and the possibility of expanding these might be considered. The traditional pre-European Council tour of capitals already offers a Presidency some opportunity to tease out key issues with individual partners. As Presidency we also held two rounds of bilateral "confessionals" with each delegation at IGC

Representative level in Brussels. While these "confessionals" offered us a useful opportunity to outline some of our broad intentions and to make an assessment of what mattered most to each delegation, they were relatively brief and did not allow scope to address in detail outstanding points of difference at the Conference.

Consideration might be given by Presidencies of future IGCs to developing a more systematic and central role for such bilateral discussions. Instead of allocating a few days for such "confessionals", a Presidency might find it useful to build into its Presidency programme, from the outset, two or three weeks to allow for substantive bilateral meetings with each delegation at the key strategic moment. Each Presidency would clearly have to evaluate this option and reach its judgement in the circumstances prevailing at the time. (Presidencies would, I think, find it useful to invite the Secretary General of the Commission to participate with a small Presidency/Council Secretariat team in such a round of bilaterals.)

4. The role of the European Parliament

The precise manner for associating the Parliament with the work of future IGCs will have to be considered in due course. The experience of its association with this IGC was very positive, due to a considerable extent to the quality and judgement of the individuals involved. The only complication arose from the somewhat clumsy arrangements agreed by the Member States for the Parliament's involvement.

The Parliament cannot perhaps be a full and equal participant at an inter*governmental* Conference. However, the limitation on participation by its Representatives to two meetings a month with the IGC Representatives Group, one formal and one informal, served no useful purpose, introduced a dislocation into the work of the Conference and imposed a significant extra burden on successive Presidencies.

If it were considered necessary to preserve the *intergovernmental* nature of an IGC at political level by providing systematically for meetings between Ministers (or Heads of State or Government) and the President of the Parliament to take place *prior* to the actual

IGC negotiating sessions, at least at the level below that the Parliament's Representatives should be allowed to attend meetings and to participate on a systematic basis.

5. Deadline for the submission of proposals

It is probably impossible for a Presidency to establish any hard-and-fast deadline for the submission of national proposals to an IGC. There is no legal deadline and the only effective barrier to the late tabling of proposals is whether other delegations are prepared to entertain them. While a large majority of the substantive elements in the Treaty of Amsterdam can trace their roots to an early stage of the Conference or even to the Reflection Group, a few useful proposals – such as that on public health late in our Presidency – got off the ground at a relatively late stage.

However, it is of some concern that a large number of disparate and relatively unimportant proposals found their way at a very late stage into the Treaty of Amsterdam or the Final Act of the Conference, often in the form of non-legally binding declarations. The pressure of work at the Conference reached a point where it perhaps became easier to say "yes" than "no" to such insubstantial proposals. While each of these "decorations" is innocuous in itself, taken together they create what has been called a "Christmas tree" effect and add neither to the coherence nor to the readability of the Treaty.

It might be possible to agree an embargo on the consideration of such last-minute proposals, without at the same time imposing any artificial deadline on the substantive work of the Conference.

6. Conduct of the decisive European Council

Clearly the conduct of the endgame of an IGC at the decisive European Council will always be of the greatest importance. The Amsterdam European Council was handled with skill and great determination by the Netherlands Presidency. Someone more closely involved than me with the conduct of that meeting would be better placed to suggest for the future any substantive adaptations to the method used.

It would be wonderful if ways could be found of rationalising the negotiating process at a European Council, to avoid a conclusion at 3.35 a.m., to avoid subsequent confusion as to what has been agreed, to enable the systematic approval of final treaty texts to take place at the meeting itself. However, that may be wishful thinking. There are certainly no easy answers.

Consideration might be given to whether it would be possible to submit to the decisive European Council the actual draft of the final Treaty rather than, or perhaps preferably in addition to, an amalgam of all the substantive provisions under discussion. The *substance* of the Treaty of Amsterdam was agreed at Amsterdam but the *presentation* of the Treaty, as a Treaty, was finalized subsequently. The Draft Treaty submitted to Amsterdam, as amended at that meeting, constituted therefore the *substance* of the Treaty of Amsterdam but certainly *did not, in presentational terms, look like it*. The point is not perhaps as significant as some might suggest. Nevertheless, if the actual draft Treaty had been available at Amsterdam, it might have helped to focus efforts on making it more reader-friendly as well as avoiding some of the difficulties of the subsequent tidying-up process.

Ideally, there should perhaps also be a process whereby the final text, at least of the substantive Treaty provisions, is approved at the European Council itself. The arrangement that leaves it to a Presidency to circulate subsequently its interpretation of what has been agreed, theoretically allows different interpretations to be discussed and reconciled. However, that process is not so much an objective exercise in piecing together what happened as a pragmatic exercise involving competing interests, without any serious possibility of reconvening the European Council to resolve outstanding differences. I refer to this as an "ideal" aim, however, because it would be extremely difficult to envisage a scenario requiring the Heads of State or Government to stay for an extra day to endorse a tidying-up exercise. If they did not stay for such an exercise, it would represent no improvement over present arrangements.

One specific problem which arose at the Amsterdam European Council related to the initial media reading of the outcome. At around 4 a.m. on 18 June 1997, exhausted Heads of State or Government, who had been buried in the negotiation of complex documents over almost 48 hours and had handled the most difficult and potentially divisive issues right at the end, went – almost without time to draw breath – to give an account of themselves to an equally tired media. In the circumstances, feelings of frustration inevitably came more to the fore than would otherwise have been the case. The presentation of the outcome by members of the European Council and the questions put to them by the media tended to focus on a few, albeit important, disappointments that arose in the final hours rather than on the bulk of the Treaty, whose thrust had remained largely unaffected. The initial presentation of the outcome, as well as the initial media reading of it, led to a more negative overall appreciation that night than the events or the Treaty justified.

While the assessment in most Member States became more balanced over the following days, the unduly downbeat initial appreciation took a while to dissipate and perhaps lingers even still. Presentation to the media is not an exact science and is never easy. A few lessons can perhaps be drawn from Amsterdam.

7. Technology

Another issue, which I would like to see explored in a fundamental way with a view to future IGCs, is the use of technology. I believe that the potential of technology to facilitate the negotiating process, both at Intergovernmental Conferences and in the European Union more generally, is vast and to a considerable extent untapped. As the number of Member States continues to grow, inevitably making the negotiating process more unwieldy, innovative adaptations in the functioning of the Union must be considered. The technology now available offers one possibility for such innovation.

It would make no sense to address the question of technology exclusively in the context of the IGC. Any relevance of what I have to say would be of more general application to the work of the Union.

I have no particular expertise in relation to technology. I have no grand plan. What I would like to do is to throw out a few preliminary thoughts, to set a few balls rolling. Some of my ideas may be impractical or be considered to have little merit. It is all to the good if others have better suggestions.

There have already been some advances in the use of technology by the institutions of the European Union. For example, in the course of the IGC, the use by the Council Secretariat of e-mail, in preference to fax, for the circulation of documents increased significantly. I have in mind, however, something much more radical than that.

Signal lights

In the first place, why not consider the introduction of a system of *signal lights* for each delegation to allow some scope at meetings for the signalling of preferences in relation to the subject-matter under discussion? This could avoid recourse to time-consuming interventions or table rounds when these, as is often the case, should be unnecessary. In a Union of Fifteen, it is not unusual for a table round to last two or three hours. For the Presidency to ascertain the position of 16 delegations (including the Commission) on even the simplest of issues can take the guts of an hour. It is a problem which will be aggravated by every further enlargement of the Union.

If each delegation had on the table in front of it a set of signal lights, it would be possible, at the simultaneous flick of switches, to go a long way towards ascertaining the positions of all delegations. At its simplest, each delegation could have a choice of four lights: green to signal agreement, red to signal opposition, amber to signal a neutral or nuanced position, white to request the floor. Each delegation would also have in front of it a scoreboard summarizing at a glance the responses of delegations on a particular question put by the Presidency.

Of course, it is quite clear that such a system of signal lights could not *replace* individual interventions or table rounds, which would remain at the core of the negotiating process. It is often the *reason for* and *strength of* opposition, rather than merely the fact of it, that matters. Positions on many issues cannot be boiled down to a simple "yes" or "no". Negotiation cannot be done by numbers. Great care would be needed in the use of a system of signal lights to avoid any unhelpful pigeon-holing of positions. However, there is little doubt that, used correctly, it could eliminate many unnecessary interventions. If it could eliminate even one intervention in ten, and I am sure it has the potential to do much more than that, it would surely be worth pursuing.

Distribution of documents

The use of *information technology for the distribution of documents* should become much more systematic. The volume of documentation which needs to be processed in Brussels is staggering. It is not a meaningless paper-mountain, as the tabloids would have it, but the lifeblood of the Union – a constant barrage of complex proposals and compromises, in an ever-widening range of areas, on which the positions of each delegation have to be coordinated and formulated, usually in a compressed timeframe.

The question of the distribution of documents should be looked at in as radical a way as possible. Consideration should be given, for example, to an even more systematic distribution of documents by e-mail to an optimal range of addressees – in Permanent Representations in Brussels and in national capitals. Some documents could perhaps also be e-mailed as appropriate to all national delegation rooms, whether in the Council buildings in Brussels and Luxembourg or at a European Council. At political level meetings especially, where time can be of the essence, the simultaneous making available in delegation rooms of documents distributed at the meeting could on occasion help the process.

Information technology for delegations at meetings

The making available of a range of *information technology for each delegation attending a meeting* should also be considered. At present, the only technology of any sort on the table in front of each delegation at a European Union meeting is a microphone. The scope for greater use of technology in this context is almost endless.

At its most basic, each delegation should be able to call up all relevant documentation on a screen in front of it. If, for example, reference is made to an earlier proposal in relation to a matter under discussion, it should not lead to an anxious and often fruitless rummaging through 16 (or 32, or more) briefcases. It should not be necessary for delegates to act as mobile libraries or ambulant filing systems – bringing with them every paper under the sun except the one that's needed. It does not help discussion when reference to an obscure treaty article, a frequent occurrence, leads to "an ecstasy of fumbling" and a looking-over of shoulders. It should be possible to call up the treaty article or document referred to at the press of a button. It is also comfortably within the scope of modern technology to make it possible for each delegation to print out, necessarily silently, for itself any relevant pages.

Consideration should also be given to making it possible for each delegation to communicate from meeting rooms with the outside world. The systematic use of telephones within meeting rooms would have an obvious downside. The introduction of new technology should not be pursued if its cumulative impact would be to create a disruptive racket. What I would suggest is that consideration be given to making available, for each delegation attending a meeting, the technology to make it possible to receive and to send messages by e-mail. (Indeed, the availability of an e-mail link might make it possible to impose a stricter ban on the use of mobile phones.)

At present a meeting room witnesses, in the nature of things, a constant to-ing and fro-ing of messages. Messages *from* the delegation in the meeting room relaying some significant development, reporting on a lunchtime discussion, seeking a view, communicating an important procedural indication which will influence the preparation of briefs in its capital or affect a Minister's travel plans. Messages *to* the delegation requesting information, suggesting a response to a recently tabled paper, asking for a return call. Messages, indeed, which may have nothing to do with the particular meeting in question – it would be as much a fallacy to think that it is possible in Brussels to do one thing at a time as to accept the "TV detective" fallacy that there is at any one time only one case for the police station to deal with.

The technology available to each delegation could, however, go much further. I would like to see explored the contribution which information technology could make to the actual drafting process at meetings. In the current system, all inputs at meetings are made orally, accompanied very occasionally by the circulation of floating pieces of paper reflecting a drafting suggestion. It is a very time-consuming process.

Moreover, the net effect is that each delegation can only try as best it can during meetings to take notes on the evolving discussion, to record – in relation to every aspect and detail of what is often a range of complex papers – the support, the opposition and the drafting suggestions. After every meeting, each delegation prepares its own reports, detailed or otherwise. (Reporting is an essential element in the process since delegations are not independent republics but part of national policy formulation processes which need to be kept fully informed.)

The system, as it operates at present, means not only that the meetings are unnecessarily drawn out, but that at the end of each meeting each delegation has its own picture of what has happened – pictures which necessarily do not coincide, which are at best not fully complete and at worst inaccurate. The report writing after every meeting is also hugely time-consuming.

Could technology not be made available in meeting rooms for each delegation making it possible for it to record its positions and, where appropriate, its drafting suggestions, directly in writing in a way immediately available to all delegations? Could one not envisage that in front of each delegation there would be a screen on which the document under discussion could be called up, with a blank page opposite every page of text? Each delegation would have the option, according to detailed rules to be established, to record its position in relation to a text on the blank page opposite it. In most cases the positions recorded would consist simply of a delegation listing itself as broadly supportive or opposed to a particular provision. Specific drafting suggestions could also be recorded. Lengthy explanations in writing of national positions would have to be avoided; these would continue to be set out orally as at present.

Not only would a clear summary picture of positions emerge at meetings, but this would be recorded directly in writing. Every delegation would, moreover, end up with the same picture. The record of meetings would be more complete, more accurate and less subject to dispute. Significant time could saved at meetings. Report writing would also become a vastly simpler exercise; in some cases a simple print-out of the document with facing commentary would suffice. (If the suggestions regarding e-mail above were pursued, the summary report could also be in national capitals at the touch of a button.)

Video-conferencing

Thought should be given to the potential of video-conferencing. I am absolutely convinced that long-distance communication could never replace the face-to-face negotiating process. It emphasizes separateness rather than what is shared. It favours comprehension rather than understanding. At the same time, there are occasions when video-conferencing could be a useful adjunct to the negotiating process. For example, it would be useful on occasions when a Presidency may wish to make a first presentation of a significant document to partners, without partners being required to respond in a detailed substantive way.

Chess-clocks?

More whimsically, I have sometimes wondered, in the course of seemingly interminable interventions, whether something could not also be said for a system akin to "chess-clocks" applying to each delegation. The aim would not be to limit real debate in any way but to counter the human foible of longwindedness, for which the price to be paid – not insignificant in relation to the Union's effectiveness – increases the larger the Union becomes. It would clearly be out of the question to limit the length of individual interventions or the amount of time available to a delegation for the sum total of its interventions at a single meeting – the point at issue at a particular meeting may require one or more delegations to intervene at particular length. It would be more tempting to limit the time available to each delegation over a longer period of time (the chess game principle). After its allocated time was exhausted the delegation in question would have to limit itself to simple statements of support or opposition.

I realize that this last suggestion, although in its way deeply attractive, will rightly be seen as somewhat frivolous. It could not be in the Union's interests to establish a hard and fast limit on any delegation's right to intervene. It could indeed be used by a delegation as an excuse for intransigence. Maybe simply keeping an informal but available record over a period of time of the total length of the interventions of each delegation within a particular forum could exercise a mild and acceptable form of pressure.

Conclusion on technology

My suggestions in relation to the use of technology are no more than the elements of what is known in Brussels as a *projet martyr* (a first draft offered in a spirit of martyrdom), something to be shot down in the hope of provoking a debate on an issue which remains important and, as far as I am aware, to an extent unaddressed. If my ideas were considered to contain any sense, they would have to be translated into detailed coherent form by experts before being thrashed out towards agreement. If any of them were pursued further, they should be tried out first, not at an IGC, but over time on a pilot basis in a few relatively routine working groups in Brussels. Perhaps one or two meeting rooms in the Council building could be used as a laboratory?

Whatever new technology is introduced will, of course, remain only an instrument at the service of people. The process will still be about the patient and subtle reconciliation and accommodation of interests. The human factor will always remain at the heart of the process of negotiation in the European Union.

I would emphasize, in conclusion, that budgetary constraints cannot be the starting point for reflection about the introduction of new technology. If the introduction of expensive new technology could improve, even in a small way, the functioning of the European Union, it would be money well spent. Priorities should not be allowed to get out of proportion. Costs should be measured not against the yardstick of last year's budget but in comparison with, say, the price of a few fighter bombers. There is every reason why the Union should have available to it, even at great expense, the most sophisticated and innovative technology available anywhere in the modern world.

8. Sensitive institutional questions

I will conclude with a comment on one of my favourite themes. Nothing, of course, would do more to lighten the agenda of any future IGC and to improve its atmosphere than to settle at a very early stage issues relating to the balance between large and smaller Member States – nothing, that is, other than preventing such issues from arising in the first place. My experience of the 1996/1997 IGC was that the existence of such issues created unproductive tensions and quite unnecessarily sapped political energies.

In the end, when the collective political judgement of Heads of State or Government was brought to bear, after two years of discussions at the IGC, the balance was preserved. The deal sketched out at the end could, with political will, have been struck at the beginning.

My firm view is that the balance on which the Union is constructed will always be preserved. The sooner that could be recognized, at or preferably before the next IGC, the better. I regret, however, that on this and many other issues the Brave New World is likely to witness a few more late nights.

Annex 1

Members of the IGC Reflection Group

The following were appointed to be the personal representatives of each Foreign Minister and of the President of the European Commission on the IGC Reflection Group which met between June and December 1995. All members of the Reflection Group had equal status within the Group. They are categorized under the headings below for illustrative purposes only.

Ministers of State

Werner Hoyer (Germany)
Carlos Westendorp (Chairman, Spain)
Michel Barnier (France)
Gay Mitchell (Ireland)
Michiel Patijn (Netherlands)
Gunnar Lund (Sweden)
David Davis (United Kingdom)

Member of EU Commission

Marcelino Oreja Aguirre (European Commission)

Senior and retired officials and others

Franklin Dehousse (Belgium), Professor
Niels Ersboell (Denmark), Former Secretary General of the Council
Stephanos Statathos (Greece), Retired Ambassador
Silvio Fagiolo (Italy), Senior Foreign Ministry Official
Joseph Weyland (Luxembourg), Ambassador
Manfred Scheich (Austria), Permanent Representative to the EU
Andre Goncalves Pereira (Portugal), Professor
Ingvar S. Melin (Finland), Former Minister

The European Parliament

The European Parliament also appointed two Members of the Reflection Group:

Elmar Brok MEP
Elisabeth Guigou MEP

Annex 2

Members of the IGC Representatives Group

The following were appointed as the representatives of each Foreign Minister and of the President of the European Commission to the working party, envisaged by the Madrid European Council in December 1995, which came to be known as the IGC Representatives Group. The Group, which met on an almost weekly basis from April 1996 to June 1997, largely shaped the Treaty of Amsterdam, refining the options for decision where necessary at Ministerial and European Council level. As in the case of the Reflection Group (see Annex 1), all members of the Group had equal status and are categorized below for illustrative purposes only.

Ministers of State

Werner Hoyer (Germany)
Michel Barnier* (France)
Michiel Patijn (Chairman, January to June 1997; Netherlands)
Fransisco Seixas da Costa (Portugal)
Gunnar Lund (Sweden)

Member of the European Commission

Marcelino Oreja Aguirre

Permanent Representatives

Philippe de Schouteete de Tervarent (Belgium)
Javier Elorza Cavengt (Spain)
Jean-Jacques Kasel (Luxembourg)
Manfred Scheich (Austria)
Antti Satuli (Finland)
Stephen Wall** (United Kingdom)

---

*Later replaced by the French Permanent Representative, Pierre de Boisieu.
**Minister of State, Doug Henderson, was IGC Representative for a brief period after the UK general election in May 1997.

Others

Niels Ersboell (Denmark)
Yannis Kranidiotis MEP* (Greece)
Noel Dorr (Chairman, July to December 1996; Ireland)
Silvio Fagiolo (Chairman, March to June 1996; Italy)

The European Parliament reappointed its two IGC Reflection Group Representatives, Elisabeth Guigou MEP and Elmar Brok MEP. These were not members of the IGC Representatives Group as such, but met regularly with it.

---

*Later replaced by Stelios Perrakis, Secretary General for European Affairs at the Greek Foreign Ministry.

THE INSTITUTE OF EUROPEAN AFFAIRS (IEA)

Patron: Mary Mac Aleese, President of Ireland

Comite d'Honneur: An Taoiseach Bertie Ahern; John Bruton; Albert Reynolds; Padraig Flynn; Patrick Hillery; Garret FitzGerald; Charles J. Haughey; Jack Lynch; Richard Burke; Ray MacSharry; Michael O'Kennedy; Peter Sutherland.

The Institute of European Affairs is an independent self-governing body which promotes the advancement and spread of knowledge on the process of European integration and, in particular, on the role and contribution of Ireland within Europe.

The Institute provides a permanent forum for the identification and development of Irish strategic policy responses to the continuing process of European integration and to the wider international issues which impact on Europe. The main aim is to provide objective analysis of the key political, economic, social and cultural issues for those charged with representing Irish views within the European policy-making structures. This is done by facilitating policy discussion with inputs from all relevant sectors, assembling information on key topics and disseminating research results.

As an independent forum, the Institute does not express opinions of its own. The views expressed in publications are solely the responsibility of the author.

The legal form of the Institute is that of a company limited by guarantee and not having share capital. It is funded by annual membership subscriptions, from companies, organisations, institutions and individuals. A number of founding sponsors enable the Institute to operate on a financially secure basis.

IEA FOUNDATION MEMBERS

The Institute is particularly indebted to its *Foundation Members* which enable it to operate independently on a financially secure basis.

Aer Lingus
Aer Rianta
AIB Bank plc
An Bord Tráchtála
An Post
Arthur Andersen
Avonmore Foods plc
Bank of Ireland
Bord Gáis
Bord na Móna
Bristol-Myers Squibb Co.
Cityjet
CRH plc
Deloitte & Touche
Electricity Supply Board
FBD Insurances plc/ *Irish Farmers Journal* /IFA
First National Building Society
FitzPatrick Hotel Group
Forbairt
FORFÁS

Glen Dimplex
Guinness Ireland Ltd.
IBEC
IDA Ireland Ltd
Independent Newspapers plc
Irish Dairy Board
Irish Distillers
Irish Life
Irish Permanent plc
National Irish Bank
National Treasury Management Agency
New Ireland Assurance Company plc
RTÉ
Siemens Ltd
SIPTU
Smurfit (Ireland) Ltd
Telecom Éireann
The Irish Times
Ulster Bank
Waterford Crystal plc

IEA CORPORATE MEMBERS

Agriculture and Food, Department of • All Party Oireachtas Committee on the Constitution • Arthur Cox • Arts, Heritage, Gaeltacht and the Islands, Department of • ASTI • Attorney General/Chief State Solicitors Office, Office of the • Bizquip • British Embassy • Central Bank • Centre for International Co-operation • Church of Ireland Working Group on Europe • Citibank • Committee on European Affairs of the Irish Episcopal Conference • Construction Industry Federation • Co. Tipperary (North Riding) VEC • Defence, Department of • Defence Forces Library • Department of History UCC • Director of Public Prosecutions, Office of the • Dublin City University • Dublin Corporation • Education, Department of • Embassy of Greece • Employment Equality Agency • Enterprise and Employment, Department of • Environment and Local Government, Department of the • European Commission Library Service • European Foundation for the Improvement of Living & Working Conditions • FÁS • Finance, Department of • Foreign Affairs, Department of • Fyffes • Government of Quebec, London Office • Gypsum Industries plc • Health and Children, Department of • Higher Education Authority • Howmedica International Inc. • ICOS • ICTU • IMPACT • INTO • Irish Bankers Federation • Irish Ferries • Irish Intercontinental Bank • Irish Management Institute • Justice, Equality and Law Reform, Department of • Lansdowne Market Research Ltd • Léargas • Marine and Natural Resources, Department of the • McCann FitzGerald • Moore Europe Research Services • NCB Group • NESC • Northern Ireland Public Sector Enterprises • Ombudsman, Office of the • Revenue Commissioners, Office of the • Royal Danish Embassy • Royal Norwegian Embassy • Ryan Hotels plc • Social, Community and Family Affairs, Department of • Taoiseach, Department of the • Public Enterprise, Department of • TSB Bank • UCC • UCD • Údarás na Gaeltachta • University of Dublin, Trinity College • Wavin Ireland Ltd • Zeneca Ireland Limited

INSTITUTE OF EUROPEAN AFFAIRS PUBLICATIONS

Studies in European Union
Political Union
Editor: Patrick Keatinge
ISBN 1 874109 00 1, 200 pages, IR£12.95, 1991
Economic and Monetary Union
Editor: Rory O'Donnell
ISBN 1 874109 01 X, 148 pages, IR£12.95, 1991
Maastricht and Ireland: What the Treaty Means
Editor: Patrick Keatinge
ISBN 1 874109 03 6, 180 pages, IR£10.00, 1992
Social Europe: EC Social Policy and Ireland
Editor: Seamus Ó Cinnéide
ISBN 1 874109 06 0, 176 pages, IR£15.00, 1993
Constitution-building in the European Union
Editor: Brigid Laffan
ISBN 1 874109 21 4, 256 pages, IR£15.00, 1996
Britain's European Question: the Issues for Ireland
Editor: Paul Gillespie
ISBN 1 874109 22 2, 224 pages, IR£15.00, 1996
European Security: Ireland's Choices
Patrick Keatinge
ISBN 1 874109 24 9, 224 pages, IR£15.00, 1996
Justice Co-operation in the European Union
Editor: Gavin Barrett
ISBN 1 874109 33 8, 256 pages, IR£15.00, 1997
Amsterdam: What the Treaty Means
Editor: Ben Tonra
ISBN 1 874109 35 4, 224 pages, IR£15.00, 1997

Implications for Ireland
Political Union
Paul Gillespie and Rodney Rice
ISBN 1 874109 02 8, 60 pages, IR£5.00, 1991
EMU and Irish Fiscal Policy
Donal de Buitléir and Don Thornhill
ISBN 1 874109 05 2, 74 pages, IR£7.50, 1993
Ireland and the IGC
Dermot Scott
ISBN 1 874109 19 2, 64 pages, IR£3.95, 1996

Understanding Europe
Eastern Exchanges
Interchange of Education, Training and Professional Formation between Ireland and Czechoslovakia, Hungary and Poland.
Miriam Hederman O'Brien
ISBN 1 874109 04 4, 48 pages, IR£5.00, 1992
Managing the Finances of the EU: the Role of the European Court of Auditors
Barry Desmond
ISBN 1 874109 35 7, 80 pages, IR£5.00, 1996

Occasional Papers
No. 1 **Irish Public Opinion on Neutrality and European Union**
Michael Marsh IR£4.00, 1992
No. 2 **The Economic Consequences of Maastricht**
Paul Tansey IR£5.00, 1992
No. 3 **Subsidiarity: Its Application in Practice**
Ciaran F. Walker IR£5.00, 1993
No. 4 **Ireland's Contribution to the European Union**
Dermot Scott ISBN 1-874109-08-7, 48 pages, IR£7.50, 1994
No. 5 **Knowledge of the European Union in Irish Public Opinion: Sources and Implications**
Richard Sinnott ISBN 1-874109-09-5, 48 pages, IR£7.50, 1995
No. 6 **Citizenship of the European Union**
Niamh Hyland, Claire Loftus, Anthony Whelan
ISBN 1-874109-13-3, 64 pages, IR£7.50, 1995
No. 7 **The Role of the Commission and Qualified Majority Voting**
John Temple Lang and Eamonn Gallagher
ISBN 1-874109-14-1, 48 pages, IR£7.50, 1995

Final Reports
Maastricht: Crisis of Confidence
Paul Gillespie • Brendan Halligan • Philip Halpin • Patrick Keatinge • Brigid Laffan, IR£4.00, 1992
What Price CAP? Issues and Challenges Facing Agricultural and Rural Policy in the European Union
Editor: Brendan Kearney ISBN 1 874109 15 X, IR£30.00, 1995
The 1996 Intergovernmental Conference: Issues, Options, Implications
IEA Bureau ISBN 1-874109-18-4, 288 pages, IR£30.00, 1995
IGC Conference Report
Edited by Ben Tonra ISBN 1-87109-32-X, 80 pages, IR£5.00, 1997

Interim Reports
Europe – Community and Continent: the enlargement of the European Union and its relationships with its continental neighbours
Tony Brown, 250 pages, IR£12.50, 1994
Towards a Safer Europe – Small State Security Policies and the European Union: Implications for Ireland
Editor: Patrick Keatinge ISBN 1-874109-10-9, 160 pages, IR£30.00, 1995

Summary of Interim Reports
Europe — Community and Continent
Tony Brown ISBN 1-874109-10-9, 48 pages, IR£4.00, 1995
Towards a Safer Europe
Editor: Patrick Keatinge ISBN 1-874109-11-7, 56 pages, IR£7.50, 1995

Research Papers
A European Cultural Identity: Myth, Reality or Aspiration
Ben Tonra and Denise Dunne, ISBN 1-874109-27-3, 32 pages, IR£5.00, 1997
Social Policy and the IGC
Joe Larragy, ISBN 1-874109-28-1, 32 pages, IR£5.00, 1997
EMU – The Third Stage (Treaty & Non-Treaty Basis of EMU)
Gavin Barrett, ISBN 1-874109-31-1, 104 pages, IR£15.00, 1997
Hungary, Ireland and the European Union,
Editor: Martin O'Donoghue ISBN 1-874109, 32 pages IR£5,00, 1997

Seminar Papers
Recent Changes in Multilateral Security
Foreword: Patrick Keatinge
Facsimile pages, IR£10.00, 1995
Britain's European Question: the Issues for Ireland – Seminar Papers
Editor: Paul Gillespie, ISBN 1-874109-23-0, 176 pages, IR£20.00, 1996
EMU Prospects and Problems
Seminar 9 July 1997. ISBN 1-874109-36-2. IR£15
EMU: Final Preparations Conference
18 November 1997. ISBN 1-874109-37-0. IR£18
Legal and Constitutional Implications of the Amsterdam Treaty
ISBN 1-874109-38-9. IR£15

Working Papers
The Third Stage of EMU: Procedures and Timetable
Brendan Halligan ISBN 1-874109-34-6, 16 pages, IR£5.00, 1997

Seminar Reports
Austria our New Partner
Tony Brown (Rapporteur) ISBN 1-874109-15-X, 44 pages, IR£7.50, 1995
Sweden in the European Union
Tony Brown (Rapporteur) ISBN 1-874109-17-6, 48 pages, IR£7.50, 1995
Finland in the European Union
Tony Brown (Rapporteur) ISBN 1-874109-16-8, 48 pages, IR£7.50, 1995
Norway and the European Union
Tony Brown (Rapporteur) ISBN 1-874109-20-6, 48 pages, IR£7.50, 1996
Report on the Netherlands Presidency of the Council of Ministers
Ben Tonra (Rapporteur) ISBN 1-874109-29-X, 16 pages, IR£5.00, 1997

Published on behalf of the European Commission Representation in Ireland
European Social Policy – Options for the Union
David Gardner (Rapporteur): Free distribution

Periodicals
European Document Series
Contemporary/Historic Documents Archive
Editor: Tony Brown ISSN 0791-8097, c. 64 pages an issue, 297 x 210 mm
Annual subscription (4 issues) IR£40.00
Annual subscription to members IR£25.00, Individual issues IR£15.00
Back issues available – No. 1 spring 1993 to No. 17 winter 1997
German Commentary
Editor: Jill Donoghue, ISBN 1-874109-30-3, 32 pages, IR£5.00, current issue No. 2, 1997
IEA NEWS – *Newsletter for Members*
Editor: Dermot Scott
Quarterly: Current issue No. 17, Autumn 1997

Index